WOMEN'S SOCIOECONOMIC STATUS AND RELIGIOUS LEADERSHIP IN ASIA MINOR

WOMEN'S SOCIOECONOMIC STATUS AND RELIGIOUS LEADERSHIP IN ASIA MINOR

IN THE FIRST TWO CENTURIES C.E.

KATHERINE BAIN

Fortress Press
Minneapolis

WOMEN'S SOCIOECONOMIC STATUS AND RELIGIOUS LEADERSHIP IN ASIA MINOR

In the First Two Centuries C.E.

Cover design: Alisha Lofgren

Library of Congress Cataloging-in-Publication Data

Print ISBN: 978-1-4514-6992-9

eBook ISBN: 978-1-4514-7983-6

The paper used in this publication meets the minimum requirements of American National Standard for Information Sciences — Permanence of Paper for Printed Library Materials, ANSI Z329.48-1984.

Manufactured in the U.S.A.

This book was produced using PressBooks.com, and PDF rendering was done by PrinceXML.

For Will, Kate, Elizabeth, and Liam

CONTENTS

Acknowledgements

Thanks, first and foremost, to Elisabeth Schüssler Fiorenza, for her incisive intellectual guidance and encouragement. I am also indebted to Laura Nasrallah, David Mitten, Ellen Aitken, Karen King, and the members of the dissertation seminar in New Testament and Early Christianity at Harvard University for their insights and questions. Participants in the Religion, Gender, and Culture seminar proved invaluable for their critiques and support. I also received helpful criticism and encouragement from audiences who heard parts of this work in progress at meetings of the Society of Biblical Literature, the North American Patristics Society, and the American Academy of Religion. I have benefited particularly from conversations with Kitty Murphy, Steven Friesen, John Lanci, Betsy Robinson, Helmut Koester, and other contributors to the study of archaeology in the ancient Mediterranean.

This publication would not been possible without access to the collections and the generous help of experts at Harvard University's Fine Arts Library, Mary Clare Altenhofen and Joanne Bloom, and most especially, András Riedlmayer, who offered a treasure trove of information and assistance. Dr. Scott Redford, the staff at the Research Center for Anatolian Civilizations in Istanbul, and Şeyda Çetin of Koç University were invaluable for communicating with the Istanbul Archaeological Museum and the Bursa Museum. For permission to reproduce images, I am grateful to Istanbul Archaeology Museums Director Zeynep Kiziltan and to Bursa Museum Director Koncagül Hançer. The Art Resource in New York facilitated the granting of permission to use images of objects in the collections of the Museé du Louvre in Paris and the Staatliche Museen in Berlin. I am also indebted to Beacon Press for the use of the diagram of kyriarchy. Dr. Rudolph Habelt Press of Bonn also granted permission for the use of essential images.

I am grateful to Paine College for institutional research support and for warm support from the entire campus community.

The *Journal of Feminist Studies in Religion* has graciously allowed the reproduction of material in the Introduction and Chapter Two.

I am grateful for the kind guidance and reliable expertise from Neil Elliott, Esther Diley, Michael Moore, and Lisa Gruenisen at Fortress Press.

Illustrations

Abbreviations of Inscriptional Sources

All abbreviations for inscriptional sources are standards as seen in B. H. McLean, "Abbreviations of Epigraphical and Related Classical Productions," in *An Introduction to Greek Epigraphy of the Hellenistic and Roman Periods from Alexander the Great down to the Reign of Constantine (232 B.C.–A.D. 337)* (Ann Arbor, MI: University of Michigan Press, 2002), 387–4100.

AÉ	L'Année Épigraphique
BÉ	Bulletin Épigraphique
CIG	Corpus Inscriptionum Graecarum
CIJ	Corpus Inscriptionum Iudaicarum
CIL	Corpus Inscriptionum Latinarum
CIRB	Corpus Inscriptionum Regni Bosporani
CPJ	Corpus Papyrorum Judaicarum
FD	Fouilles de Delphes
IG	Inscriptiones graecae
IK	Inschriften griechischer Städte aus Kleinasien
IEph	Die Inschriften von Ephesus
IEry	Die Inschriften von Erythrai
IHistria	Die Inschriften von Histria
IMT	Inschriften Mysia & Troas
MAMA	Monumenta Asiae Minoris Antiqua
Merkelbach	*Steinepigramme aus dem griechischen Östen,* ed. Reinhold Merkelbach and Josef Stauber. Stuttgart: B.G. Teubner, 1998–2002.
OGI	Orientis graeci inscriptiones selectae
P. Yadin	Yadin Papyri
SEG	Supplementum Epigraphicum Graecum
TAM	Tituli Asiae Minoris

Introduction

Oppression of lower-status persons in the form of socioeconomic deprivation is widespread. The political struggle against oppression unites everyone interested in liberation and justice. Around the globe, women experience socioeconomic gender discrimination multiplied by race, class, age, religion, sexual preference, and ethnicity discrimination.[1] My scholarship constitutes an effort to intervene in this discrimination through comparison of different historical understandings of women. I aim to contribute to emancipatory knowledge of gender as it appears in frameworks of socioeconomic analysis. In this book, I investigate the socioeconomic situation and religious status of women in the first two centuries of the common era. In writing history, we contribute to the knowledge that articulates and legitimizes our worlds of meaning since we rely on contemporary frameworks to understand the past. Telling the history of women draws from and constructs contemporary understandings of women. I hope that this study of religious history contributes to knowledge about women's socioeconomic status and about how understandings of women have been inflected by wealth, race, ethnicity, religion, and legal status.

In the following sections, I describe the parameters of the study, then I introduce the texts and my analytical approach to them. I have selected texts on the basis of their significance in scholarship on women's religious status[2] and scholarship on women in socioeconomic institutions. Investigation of these texts requires a critical framework that integrates material relations, ideology, and the production of difference. I draw on materialist feminist theory as well as socioeconomic and feminist histories of the Roman Empire. After introducing this analytical framework, I turn to a brief overview of the rest of the study.

---

1. Martha Chen, Joann Vanek, et al., *Progress of the World's Women 2005 Overview: Women, Work & Poverty* (New York: United Nations Development Fund for Women, 2005). *Women and Children: The Double Dividend of Gender Equality* (The State of the World's Children 2007; New York: United Nations Children's Fund, 2006).

2. By "religious status," I refer to women's status in religious groups; I analyze religious groups as an integral component of social relations.

1

Parameters of the Study

The subjects of this historical study are texts about religious women in western Turkey (Asia Minor) in the first two centuries of the common era. I eschew the labels "Jewish, Christian, Pagan" since all are anachronistic for the first century. These texts about women are analyzed as part of the political, historical, social situation of the eastern Roman Empire. I focus on sources that originated in western Asia Minor in the first two centuries of the common era. In the first century, the earliest documents of the movement that would become Christianity appeared. These documents are particularly interesting because few literary sources survive from this period that directly address non-elite persons in religious groups. The end of the second century is a practical approximation to close the period, since the grant of universal citizenship in 212 c.e. marks an era easily recognizable in epigraphic sources.[3]

The types of sources used in this study include inscriptions and iconography in addition to literary texts. The sources all represent the same social historical context, although a few vary from the target date or geography. For each item, I note the date and geographical provenance. Most of the sources are from western Asia Minor, while a few belong to the wider cultural context around the Aegean Sea during the late Hellenistic and early Roman era. I proceed on the assumption that images and inscriptions from within or near western Asia Minor in the first two centuries of the common era belong to the same cultural context as the literary sources from religious groups of the same era and locale.[4] For example, the iconography of women on funerary monuments represents the symbolic world of a specific historical cultural context, which was shared by artists, viewers, authors, readers, and hearers of the region in that era.

Even though I seem to imply a cultural unity by demarcating geographic and temporal parameters, I have not sought to unify the sources to establish one metanarrative of women's status. The themes of diversity and struggle characterize my models of economic and religious history.[5] Rather than

3. On dating inscriptions, A. Geoffrey Woodhead, *The Study of Greek Inscriptions* (Norman and London: University of Oklahoma Press, 1992), 52–66.

4. On property ownership by funerary inscribers, see Elizabeth A. Meyer, "Explaining the Epigraphic Habit in the Roman Empire: The Evidence of Epitaphs," *Journal of Roman Studies* 80 (1990): 74–96. Also see Greg Woolf, "Monumental Writing and the Expansion of Roman Society in the Early Empire," *Journal of Roman Studies* 86 (1996): 22–39.

5. See Elisabeth Schüssler Fiorenza, *But She Said: Feminist Practices of Biblical Interpretation* (Boston: Beacon, 1992), 94–96.

reconstructing a narrative of decline or progress for women's status over time, I posit an ongoing negotiation of diversity among religious groups.

Sources

Scholarship on women continues to debate wealthy women's access to leadership in the ancient world.[6] Scholarly interpretations of women's religious status have rested on views of women's (subordinate) social status. However, the frameworks used to analyze social status have not included a thorough economic analysis.[7] This economic aspect is crucial because these texts depict women with reference to institutions of particular socioeconomic significance: the household, patronage, and slavery. Thus I focus on texts about women's religious status and their socioeconomic status in households, patronage, and slavery.

In order to study the status of freeborn wealthy women in households, I examine the two letters of Ignatius to religious groups in Smyrna.[8] Scholarship on these texts has discussed the status of both unmarried women in households without men as well as wives in their husbands' households.[9] I inform my interpretation of these texts by drawing on scholarship about iconographic and epigraphic representations of wealthy married and widowed women.[10] Studies of these representations are based on funerary monuments and legal inscriptions. I analyze representations that originate in the same historical

6. I cite prominent studies in the following discussion.

7. See Steve Friesen's critique of the category of social status and his suggestion that scholarship attend more closely to economic categories. Steven J. Friesen, "Poverty in Pauline Studies: Beyond the So-called New Consensus," *Journal for the Study of the New Testament* 26, no. 3 (2004): 323–61.

8. These are Ignatius' *To the Smyrnaeans* and *To Polycarp*.

9. While 1 Timothy is another text that discusses both wives and widows, the household situation of the widows in this text is somewhat less clear than it is in the two letters of Ignatius to Smyrna. However, it is possible that one could make an argument for that text very similar to the one I make for the letters to Smyrna.

10. Ernst Pfuhl and Hans Möbius, *Die ostgriechischen Grabreliefs*, 2 vols. (Mainz am Rhein: Von Zabern, 1977–79). Marielouise Cremer, *Hellenistisch-römische Grabstelen im nordwestlichen Kleinasien*, vol. 1 Mysien (Asia Minor Studien Band 4.1; Bonn: GMBH, 1991). Johanna Fabricius, *Die hellenistischen Totenmahlreliefs: Grabrepräsentation und Wertvorstellungen in ostgriechischen Städten* (Studien zur antiken Stadt 3; München: Friedrich Pfeil, 1999). Miltiade B. Hatzopoulos, *Revue des Études Grecs* 115, no. 254 (2002): 672. G. Petzl, *Die Beichtinschriften Westkleinasiens* (Epigraphica Anatolica 22; Bonn: Habelt, 1994). H. W. Pleket, *Epigraphica II: Texts on the Social History of the Greek World* (Leiden: Brill, 1969). Paul Zanker, "Bürgerliche Selbstdarstellung am Grab im römischen Kaiserreich," in *Die Römische Stadt im 2. Jahrhundert nach Christ* (Köln: Rheinland, 1992).

context as the Ignatian texts in order to understand wealthy women's status in households in Smyrna.

Studies on the leadership status of women have ventured beyond consideration of women's household status to explore their involvement in patronage. Texts that mention the status of wealthy widows in religious groups have received scholarly attention, but the relationship between women's religious status and social status remains unclear. Scholarship on women's patronage of religious groups has focused especially on female figures in several texts and an inscription: Phoebe in Paul's Letter to the Romans, Tryphaena in the *Acts of Thecla*, and Rufina in an inscription from Smyrna.[11] Social historical studies have presented epigraphic and legal sources that feature wealthy women.[12] I analyze the material that depicts wealthy women's socioeconomic relationships with regard to patronage, especially patronage of religious associations. This analysis provides historical context for interpretation of the texts about wealthy widows' religious status.

In addition to households and patronage, slavery and freedom determined women's status and access to wealth. The third category of texts I examine highlights the status of slave women. Understanding slaves' religious status is critical for study of texts about slave manumissions.[13] The texts relevant to Asia

11. Respectively, these are Rom. 16:1-2, the *Acts of Paul and Thecla*, *CIJ* 2.741. Phoebe was from Cenchreae, near Corinth, rather than Asia Minor. However, Paul, our informant in this case, traveled throughout the eastern Mediterranean. The land areas around the Aegean in both Greece and Asia Minor were on the major route between Rome and its eastern provinces. Scholarship usually discusses the area around the Aegean Sea as a single cultural unit. I discuss Phoebe in terms of patronage, an institution that operated in a similar way throughout the eastern Mediterranean.

12. See the sources cited in note 9 above. Riet van Bremen, *The Limits of Participation: Women and Civic Life in the Greek East in the Hellenistic and Roman Periods* (Amsterdam: J. C. Gieben, 1996). Bernadette J. Brooten, *Women Leaders in the Ancient Synagogue: Inscriptional Evidence and Background Issues* (Chico, CA: Scholars, 1982). T. Rajak, "Benefactors in the Greco-Jewish Diaspora," in *Geschichte—Tradition—Reflexion*, vol. 1, *Judentum*, ed. Peter Schafer (Tübingen: J. C. B. Mohr, 1996). Elisabeth Schüssler Fiorenza, *In Memory of Her: A Feminist Theological Reconstruction of Christian Origins* (New York: Crossroad, 1982). M. Misset-van de Weg, "A Wealthy Woman Named Tryphaena: Patroness of Thecla of Iconium," in *The Apocryphal Acts of Paul and Thecla*, ed. Jan N. Bremmer (Kampen: Kok Pharos, 1996), 16–35. M. R. Lefkowitz and M. B. Fant, *Women's Lives in Greece and Rome* (Baltimore: Johns Hopkins University Press, 1992). Ross Kraemer, *Maenads, Martyrs, Matrons, Monastics: A Sourcebook on Women's Religions in the Greco-Roman World* (Philadelphia: Fortress Press, 1988). Onno M. van Nijf, *The Civic World of Professional Associations in the Roman East* (Amsterdam: Gieben, 1997).

13. J. Albert Harrill, "Ignatius, Ad Polycarp. 4.3 and the Corporate Manumission of Christian Slaves," *Journal of Early Christian Studies* 1, no. 2 (1993): 107–42. E. Leigh Gibson, *The Jewish Manumission Inscriptions of the Bosporus Kingdom* (Tübingen: Mohr Siebeck, 1999). Carolyn Osiek, "Ransom of Captives: Evolution of a Tradition," *Harvard Theological Review* 74, no. 4 (Oct. 1981): 365–86. G. H. R.

Minor include inscriptions and a letter: Bosporan synagogue manumissions and the Letter of Ignatius to Polycarp.[14] The Bosporus region was north of Asia Minor, on the north shore of the Black Sea. This region sustained connections to cities around the Aegean throughout antiquity by way of commercial ties, political relations, and Greek immigration. Jewish communities in the Bosporus shared cultural forms with synagogues in Asia Minor; thus I analyze the Bosporan synagogue inscriptions as part of the study of slaves' religious status in Asia Minor. My study of these texts seeks first to understand slavery and slave women's socioeconomic status by analyzing inscriptional and iconographic sources on slave women that scholarship has identified in Asia Minor.[15] This socioeconomic analysis of slave women's status enables a more thorough understanding of their religious status than reliance on social analysis alone. The socioeconomic analysis informs my interpretation of the texts about slaves' status in manumission and religious groups.

Investigation of these texts about religious status and socioeconomic status requires a critical framework that analyzes gender, race, ethnicity, marriage, slavery, and colonialization as well as religion and access to wealth. In the following section, I propose a method of historical material inquiry.

Horsley and S. R. Llewelyn, eds., *New Documents Illustrating Early Christianity* (Grand Rapids: Eerdmans, 1981). Jennifer Glancy, *Slavery in Early Christianity* (Oxford: Oxford University Press, 2002). J. Albert Harrill, *Slaves in the New Testament: Literary, Social and Moral Dimensions* (Minneapolis: Fortress Press, 2006); Allen Dwight Callahan, Richard A. Horsley, and Abraham Smith, eds., *Slavery in Text and Interpretation* (Semeia 83/84; Atlanta: SBL, 1998); J. Albert Harrill, *The Manumission of Slaves in Early Christianity* (Tübingen: J. C. B. Mohr, 1995); and Dale Martin, "Slavery and the Ancient Jewish Family," in *The Jewish Family in Antiquity*, ed. Shaye Cohen (Atlanta: Scholars, 1993), 113–29.

14. J. Albert Harrill, "Ignatius, Ad Polycarp. 4.3," 107–42. E. Leigh Gibson, *Jewish Manumission Inscriptions of the Bosporus Kingdom*.

15. Ernst Pfuhl and Hans Möbius, *Die ostgriechischen Grabreliefs*, 2 vols. (Mainz am Rhein: Von Zabern, 1977–79). Dale B. Martin, "The Construction of the Ancient Family: Methodological Considerations," *Journal of Roman Studies* 86 (1996): 42. Martin P. Nilsson, *Timbres Amphoriques de Lindos*, Exploration Archéologique de Rhodes 5 (Copenhagen: Imprimerie Bianco Luno, 1909), 101–3. Jean-Jacques Aubert, *Business Managers in Ancient Rome: A Social and Economic Study of Institores, 200 B.C.–A.D. 250* (Leiden: Brill, 1994); G. H. R. Horsley and S. R. Llewelyn, eds., *New Documents Illustrating Early Christianity* (Grand Rapids: Eerdmans, 1981). Reinhold Merkelbach and Josef Stauber, eds., *Steinepigramme aus dem griechischen Osten* (Stuttgart: B. G. Teubner, 1998–2002).

METHOD AND MODEL

HISTORICAL MATERIALIST FEMINISM

My approach to this investigation relies on methods of gathering evidence and analyzing sources that prevail in historical studies. I work with the assumption that historiographic quality depends on attention to the particularity of the contexts in which evidence originated. I defined temporal and geographic parameters for the sources in the preceding discussion in the interests of historical accuracy and completeness. Within these limits, I have drawn on different types of sources, since feminist historians have established a connection between critical analysis and the use of different genres.[16] Historical work requires a self-reflexivity necessary to analyze the contexts and interests of scholarship. Since texts and interpreters all have particular interests, the relationship between source and history requires theoretical attention.

This historical inquiry draws on the theory of materialist feminism, particularly the thought of Rosemary Hennessy. The challenge has been to develop a framework to study simultaneously socioeconomic structures and texts about religious women. Hennessy links discourse to social structures through her explanation of "the materiality of language."[17] She analyzes discourse as ideology that produces material structures and relations even as this materiality shapes ideology.

> As the medium of social action and the mechanism through which subjects are constructed, ideology produces what can be seen, heard, spoken, thought, believed, valued––in other words, what counts as socially made "reality." . . . The discourses that constitute the *material*

16. For example, Natalie Kampen, *Image and Status: Roman Working Women in Ostia* (Berlin: Mann, 1981). I return to this point in the following discussion.

17. Study of the materiality of language is particularly significant to the study of religion because material relations and structures in religion have not received enough attention from scholars. David Chidester has called for intervention aimed at developing theory in the study of religious materiality, possibly by "reconstructing the genealogy of dematerialized religion." Chidester, "Material Terms for the Study of Religion," *Journal of the American Academy of Religion* 68, no 2 (June 2000): 367–80. The article reviews Mark C. Taylor, ed., *Critical Terms for Religious Studies* (Chicago: University of Chicago Press, 1998). "Under the impact of European colonialism, as Sam Gill suggests, colonized people have undergone a dematerialization—or deterritorialization—'in the terms that have satisfied Western territorial needs, whether colonial, conceptual, or observational' (312). In support of a variety of colonizing projects, the colonial fantasy of a disembodied 'primitive mentality,' and its conceptual descendants, substantially contributed to the production of a dematerialized religion" (376).

structures through which ideology works are shaped by the *material relations* which comprise economic and political practices.[18]

As ideology, discourse takes specific historical forms. However, ideology is not monolithic in any historical configuration, but negotiated and contested. "The dominating ideology never dominates without contradiction."[19] Economic and political practices involve steady articulation and reproduction of the dominant social relations. Competing ideologies and material relations become visible in critical analysis of the elaboration of social relations.

The dominating ideology and material relations smooth over contradictions and ambiguities. In Hennessy's terms, this work of concealment occurs through the naturalizing operation of the discursive "preconstructed"—that which "everyone knows" and which "serves as an anchor in the symbolic order for the articulation of subjectivities across race, class, gender, and other salient differences." Feminist analysis intervenes in this preconstructed through analysis of contradictions and ambiguities in political and economic terms. For instance, Maria Mies's analysis of the constructions of gender, race, and class underpins her study of colonialization and family formation in the eighteenth and nineteenth centuries by highlighting contradictions in the process of "'naturalization' of colonized women."[20] As a feminist study, Mies's history displaces gender, race, and class from their positions as naturalized knowledge so that a different knowledge of women's history becomes available.

Feminist economics places women and non-elite men in the foreground by exposing the preconstructed in economic categories. For instance, it has been "natural" to conceive of a mother's place in the household as necessary and nonarbitrary. Mies has evaluated this conception of the role of women as biological determinism.

18. Rosemary Hennessy, *Materialist Feminism and the Politics of Discourse* (New York: Routledge, 1993), 75. Italics in original.

19. For the following discussion, see Hennessy, *Materialist Feminism*, 76–79.

20. Maria Mies, "Colonization and Housewifization," in *Materialist Feminism: A Reader in Class, Difference, and Women's Lives*, ed. Rosemary Hennessy and Chrys Ingraham (New York: Routledge, 1997), 179. A closely related branch of scholarship uses "intersectional analysis" to study the operations of gender, race, and class as multiplicative factors in oppression. See Bonnie Thornton Dill and Ruth Enid Zambrana, eds., *Emerging Intersections: Race, Class and Gender in Theory, Policy, and Practice* (New Brunswick, NJ: Rutgers University Press, 2009).

> Too often this concept [biological determinism] has been used to explain social inequalities or exploitative relations as inborn, and hence, beyond the scope of social change. Women should be particularly suspicious when this term is used to explain their status in society. Their share in the production and reproduction of life is usually defined as a function of their biology or "nature." Thus, women's household and child-care work are seen as an extension of their physiology. . . . All the labour that goes into the production of life, including the labour of giving birth to a child, is not seen as the conscious interaction of a human being with nature, that is, a truly human activity, but rather as an activity of nature.[21]

In contrast with birth and childcare, a male worker's use of his bodily strength, for instance, to dig a foundation, has not been seen as a fact of nature, but as paid labor. A biological conception of the natural role of women emerges in economic assumptions because gender operates as a preconstructed given already embedded in material structures. Economic and political systems maintain reproduction, and child and elderly care as "private" work, unskilled, and unpaid or poorly paid. These material structures lower women's economic status (as a social group) even as the political system proclaims the equality of men and women in democratic processes. Material feminist analysis seeks to displace the ascriptions of difference (such as gender) that function in discrimination and exploitation.

Feminist economists have investigated economic models for factors at work in the omission or marginalization of the situation of women and lower-status men.[22] In a study of agrarian societies, B. Lynne Milgram concludes:

> Marginalization of the "domestic" sphere by neoclassical economists has overlooked how such activities for women in Southeast Asia encompass economic and commercial value beyond the normal consumptive needs of the family and household . . . women's labor

21. Maria Mies, *Patriarchy and Accumulation on a World Scale: Women in the International Division of Labour* (London: Zed Books, 1986).

22. "Feminist economics argues that gender inequality stems from a system of gendered power relations that permeate the whole economy and underpin norms for male and female roles and responsibilities." Diane Elson, Caren Grown, and Irene van Staveren, "Why a Feminist Economics of Trade?" in *The Feminist Economics of Trade*, ed. Irene van Staveren, Diane Elson, Caren Grown, and Nilufer Çagatay (New York: Routledge, 2007), quotation p. 1.

thus makes a significant contribution to the well-being and economic productivity of their household and plays a fundamental role in maintaining the peasant economy and reproducing cultural capital.[23]

Also, within the United States, there are "hundreds of thousands" of "women, who, because they are immigrant and/or undocumented, remain doubly marginalized, voiceless, and invisible."[24] Subsistence workers and "hidden" labor must be made visible in our analyses of economy in order to reconstruct the history of women's socioeconomic and religious status.

Economic distinctions that reinscribe gender overlap with categories of class (or strata), colonial status, race, and ethnicity.[25] Economic analysis has strongly devalued some kinds of work and workers.

> The legacies of the positivist IR/IPE [international relations/ international political economy] inquiry persist in the tendency to view power as a tangible entity or resource, and to seek out power-wielding people as the subjects of research. Work is thus equated with monetized economic activity and workers are conceptualized as a commodity, so those whose working practices are unprotected or subordinate receive little or no recognition in IR/IPE research. In a sense it is assumed that those who do not possess power as a resource are not significant to our understanding of the global political economy.[26]

While this is a statement about our current situation, exclusionary economic analysis persists also in historical economic studies. Our thinking

23. B. Lynne Milgram, "Women, Modernity, and the Global Economy: Negotiating Gender and Economic Difference in Ifuago, Upland Philippines," in *Gender at Work in Economic Life*, ed. Gracia Clark (Walnut Creek, CA: AltaMira, 2003), 98–99.

24. Daisy L. Machado, "Response to 'Solidarity and the Accountability of Academic Feminists and Church Activists to Typical (World Majority) Women,'" *Journal of Feminist Studies in Religion* 20, no. 2 (2004): 152.

25. Kwok Pui-lan notes that economic analysis must include the ways gender has featured in relationships between colonizers and colonized. Kwok Pui-lan, "Mercy Amba Oduyoye and African Women's Theology," *Journal of Feminist Studies in Religion* 20, no. 1 (2004): 8.

26. Louise Amoore, "Invisible Subject(s): Work and Workers in the Global Political Economy," in *Poverty and the Production of World Politics: Unprotected Workers in the Global Political Economy*, ed. Matt Davies and Magnus Ryner (New York: Palgrave Macmillan, 2006), 21.

about the ancient economy depends on contemporary economic theory, and women and lower-status men remain in the margins even in analyses of contemporary economic systems.

The omission of gender, race, class, and colonialism as categories of analysis has significant consequences for economic models since these distinctions are embedded in notions of wages, productivity, family, household, and the sexual division of labor. A number of studies have argued the gendered, racialized, and class-bound character of concepts of skill, wages, labor, and productivity.[27] For instance, Yildiz Ecevit's modern study of work done by Turkish women suggests that the skills that women acquired in the home, such as dexterity and accuracy, are attributed to women's nature instead of to their training and education.[28] Such findings of feminist economists challenge us to interrogate critically the frameworks we use to write histories of ancient economies.[29] A model of the Roman economy, for instance, would be inadequate if it classified the work of wives or slaves as unskilled and dismissed them from economic analysis.

The insights of feminist economists are helpful for investigating the correlation between modern economic systems and historiography. In a global perspective, the consumer capitalist economies of "overdeveloped" countries are intertwined with the subsistence economies of "underdeveloped" countries. Maria Mies argues that "this general production of life, or subsistence production—mainly performed through the non-wage labour of women and other non-wage labourers as slaves, contract workers and peasants in the colonies—constitutes the perennial basis upon which 'capitalist productive labour' can be built up and exploited."[30] From a global perspective, most scholars enjoy the positions of elites in the world system. Steven Friesen theorizes the lack of attention to poverty in studies of Pauline communities in terms of the economic assumptions and contexts of biblical interpreters.[31]

27. Ava Baron, *Work Engendered: Toward a New History of American Labor* (Ithaca, NY: Cornell University Press, 1991). Elizabeth Higginbotham and Mary Romero, eds., *Women and Work: Exploring Race, Ethnicity, and Class* (London: Sage, 1997).

28. Yildiz Ecevit, "Shopfloor Control: The Ideological Construction of Turkish Women Factory Workers," in *Working Women: International Perspectives on Labour and Gender Ideology*, ed. Nanneke Redclift and M. Thea Sinclair (London: Routledge, 1991), 56–78.

29. However, two recent publications on methodology in the study of ancient economies omit women, gender, and feminist scholarship. Peter F. Bang, Mamoru Ikeguchi, and Hartmut G. Ziche, eds., *Ancient Economies, Modern Methodologies: Archaeology, Comparative History, Models and Institutions* (Bari, Italy: Edipuglia, 2006). J. G. Manning and Ian Morris, *Ancient Economy: Evidence and Models* (Stanford: Stanford University Press, 2005).

30. Mies, *Patriarchy*, 48.

The privileges of elites influence our perspective and add to the difficulty of modeling the ancient agrarian subsistence economy.[32] A view from the top obscures the lower strata that support positions of privilege.

The study of economics relies on critical feminist analysis to investigate economic distinctions and models for embedded ascriptions of difference in terms such as gender, race, class, and colonialism. Feminist economists have complicated the use of dualisms in feminine/masculine roles, domestic/public, house/market, skilled/unskilled, paid/unpaid, and the status of work and workers associated with these distinctions. Hennessy's materialist feminism theorizes these studies as interventions to displace the prevailing constructions of gender, race, class, and colonialism that produce (and are produced by) dominant social relations in political and economic systems. Hennessy and others have shown that this can be done by focusing on contradictions and ambiguities that indicate the presence of less prominent and submerged ideologies. For instance, a contradiction emerges between the view that "domestic" work is hidden unpaid labor and that "domestic work" is essential subsistence labor. Such contradictions highlight assumptions of gender, race, class, and colonialism in "domestic" work. A materialist feminist approach allows the emergence of new understandings of work and the status of workers, understandings essential to the transformation of political and economic systems.

In sum, this study incorporates three principal modes of inquiry—historical, materialist, and feminist—which structure my approach to sources and writing history. Since each historical artifact about women is analyzed in terms of dominant ideologies and material relations, I turn first to describe a model of dominant relations with respect to political power, imperial ideologies, and the production of socioeconomic status.

MODELING THE ROMAN EMPIRE

Ideally, a socioeconomic model presents not only the production and exchange of goods and services, but also the production of socioeconomic inequality, or differential access to resources. The model explains the reproduction of groups with various socioeconomic interests. It shows relationships between

31. Friesen, "Poverty in Pauline Studies."

32. See Richard Saller, "Framing the Debate over the Growth in the Ancient Economy," in *The Ancient Economy*, ed. Manning and Morris, 223–38; Stephen Mitchell and Constantina Katsari, "Introduction: The Economy of Asia Minor," in *Patterns in the Economy of Asia Minor*, ed. Mitchell and Katsari (Swansea: Classical Press of Wales, 2005), xiii–xxxii.

such groups and how those relationships might change. It explains the production and maintenance of categories of access to socioeconomic resources. The model shows how socioeconomic forces vary with social location, and it allows for integration between socioeconomic structures and other social relations, such as politics and religion.

Narrative socioeconomic models are better suited to the available data for the ancient world than are mathematical models.[33] Networks, change, horizontal distinctions, and relationships are difficult to diagram, and require narrative. Diagrams and visual models supplement narrative reconstructions. Geza Alföldy has constructed a model of the society of the Roman Empire as a pyramid ranging from emperor at the apex to masses living at and below subsistence level at the base.[34] This model emphasizes differences between men based on legal definitions and economic status. However, it does not articulate either women as distinct groups or gender as a determinant of status. With minor variations, this model of ancient society has been widely accepted and qualified.[35]

Ekkehard Stegemann and Wolfgang Stegemann have built on Alföldy's model of stratification by adopting an emphasis on property as a criterion for determination of stratum.[36] (See Figure 1.[37]) "The material possession of personal and real property conveys, on the one hand, a form of power (namely, influence), but is, on the other hand, an (essential) part of the *privileges* that members of the upper stratum enjoy." The other important source of power belonged to those who held political office; it was not available to women, male slaves, and freedmen, who were excluded from high political or military office. The Stegemanns refer to "women and family members" as influential because of their possessions, but as distinct from "the ruling class."[38] This distinction between the ruling class and others in the same household is obscured where the

33. Neville Morley, "Narrative Economy," in *Ancient Economies, Modern Methodologies: Archaeology, Comparative History, Models and Institutions*, ed. Peter F. Bang, Mamoru Ikeguchi, and Hartmut G. Ziche (Bari, Italy: Edipuglia, 2006).

34. Geza Alföldy, *The Social History of Rome* (London: Croom Helm, 1985), 94–156, esp. 146, Fig. 1.

35. Walter Scheidel and Steven J. Friesen, "The Size of the Economy and the Distribution of Income in the Roman Empire," *Journal of Roman Studies* 99 (2009): 61–91; Glenn R. Storey, "Cui Bono? An Economic Cost-Benefit Analysis of Statuses in the Roman Empire," in *Hierarchies in Action: Cui Bono?*, ed. Michael W. Diehl (Carbondale: Southern Illinois University Press, 2000), 340–74.

36. For the following discussion, Ekkehard W. Stegemann and Wolfgang Stegemann, *The Jesus Movement: A Social History of Its First Century*, trans. O. C. Dean (Minneapolis: Fortress Press, 1999), 61–65.

37. Ibid., 72.

38. Ibid., 64.

socioeconomic model is based on the ranks of free men (as in Alföldy's model). While the Stegemanns discuss the difficulties in representing women on the pyramid of stratification, their model remains based on the socioeconomic position of men.

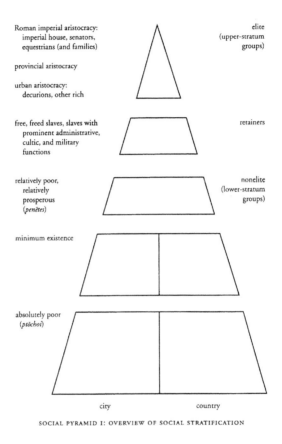

SOCIAL PYRAMID I: OVERVIEW OF SOCIAL STRATIFICATION

Figure 1. Diagram of the Stegemann's Pyramid.[39]

Feminist historian and theorist Elisabeth Schüssler Fiorenza has developed a sociostructural model of the comprehensive structure of domination and

39. Ekkehard W. Stegemann and Wolfgang Stegemann, The Jesus Movement: A Social History of Its First Century, trans. O. C. Dean (Fortress Press, 1999), p. 72.

stratification in the Roman Empire, that is, kyriarchy. (See Figure 2.[40]) Kyriarchy, a neologism introduced by Schüssler Fiorenza, refers to "the domination of the lord, slave master, husband, the elite freeborn educated and propertied man over all wo/men and subaltern men."[41] In this model, gender overlaps with other status-producing distinctions and systems of domination. Since the various systems for producing differences overlap, interact, and multiply oppressions, none can be thoroughly analyzed in isolation from its effects on the whole.[42] Kyriarchy has operated in discrete social institutions as well as in the symbolic realm where, as kyriocentrism, it has "the ideological function of naturalizing and legitimating not just gender but all forms of domination."[43] Kyriocentrism produces preconstructed "commonsense" understandings of kyriarchal religious, political, and socioeconomic institutions.[44]

40. Schüssler Fiorenza, *But She Said*, 117.

41. Elisabeth Schüssler Fiorenza, *Jesus and the Politics of Interpretation* (New York: Continuum, 2000), 95.

42. According to Schüssler Fiorenza, classical ideal forms of Greek and Roman kyriarchy have been the prevailing forms in the Western history of patriarchal democracy, and they provide the model for modern capitalist democracy. *But She Said*, 114–26.

43. Schüssler Fiorenza, *Jesus*, 95. This differs somewhat from the use of kyriocentrism by Schottroff, who defines it as "society's orientation in terms of the class of ruling men." Luise Schottroff, *Lydia's Impatient Sisters: A Feminist Social History of Early Christianity*, trans. Barbara and Martin Rumscheidt (Louisville: Westminster John Knox, 1995), 231, n. 115; 34–36.

44. Schüssler Fiorenza, *Jesus*, 97.

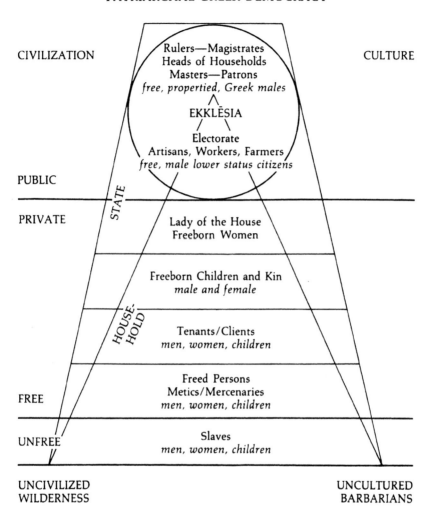

Figure 2. From "But She Said" by Elizabeth Schüssler Fiorenza.[45]

45. *But She Said: Feminist Practices of Biblical Interpretation.* Copyright © 1992 by Elizabeth Schüssler Fiorenza. Reprinted by permission of Beacon Press, Boston

As an analytical framework, kyriarchy provides a perspective and implies a series of questions. Historical analysis proceeds by inquiring about a source's relationship to kyriarchal structures and kyriocentric ideology. Setting texts in this framework improves previous methods by highlighting how the operation of gender works with the structures and ideologies associated with households, slavery, patronage, access to wealth, ethnicity, and legal and colonial status, and how all of these intertwine and overlap. If the goal of critical feminist theory is to help us move toward a more just society, its tools must center on political systems and networks. Since kyriarchy focuses on oppression, it adopts a perspective "from below" in order to illuminate systems of domination.

Socioeconomic analysis has received scant attention from feminist thinkers, and publications on the economy of the Roman Empire have been less than attentive to feminist concerns. The problem with this omission is that gender and socioeconomic status are interlocking systems of domination. For example, wealthy free women enjoyed a position of privilege that was not available to women who lived at or near subsistence level (90 percent of the population). Socioeconomic distinctions that reinscribe gender overlap with categories of class (or strata), colonial status, race, and ethnicity.[46] To fully appreciate ancient understandings of gender, and the position of women, we must undergird feminist analysis with socioeconomic analysis. A feminist position of political advocacy further requires naming socioeconomic deprivation as oppression and recognizing the system that sustains it as exploitative. Feminist materialist analysis involves investigation of all the systems that produce and are reproduced by socioeconomic oppression and exploitation. Feminist materialist analysis seeks to displace the ascriptions of difference (such as gender) that function in discrimination and exploitation.

Before elaborating further, I note the limits of the model: its shortcomings, and how its use could mislead. The pyramids of Alföldy, the Stegemanns, and Schüssler Fiorenza show stratifications or levels. This visual depiction should not obscure analysis of the dynamism of the relationships between different positions and the multiplicity of systems in operation. Furthermore, repeated references to a single model may give an impression of homogeneity that elides geographical difference, tensions between kyriocentric ideologies, and struggles within kyriarchal systems. The model is an intellectual tool designed to help us improve quality in analysis and understanding. Analysis of texts of

---

46. Kwok Pui-lan notes that socioeconomic analysis must include the ways gender has featured in relationships between colonizers and colonized. Kwok Pui-lan, "Mercy Amba Oduyoye and African Women's Theology," 8.

early Christianity would be enriched with attention to materialist dimensions, and kyriarchy is a useful framework for doing materialist analysis.

The pyramid model of kyriarchy of the Roman Empire depicts the hierarchy of socioeconomic benefits, that is, access to the basic means of livelihood. Pictorial depictions of the pyramid do not accurately reflect the quantitative dimensions of kyriarchy because the difference was so great between the top levels and the bottom.

Glenn Storey has conducted a quantitative analysis for different levels of socioeconomic status on the pyramid.[47] Based on figures derived from the situation in Italy, his evaluation of costs and benefits illustrates the degree to which elites derived their income from exploitation of laborers and farmers, free and slave. Freeborn Italian farmers and laborers in the city of Rome were dependent on state-sponsored handouts to obtain a subsistence-level food supply.[48] Slaves, whether manumitted or lifetime, produced enormous benefits for their owners.[49] In terms of cash value, a senator such as Pliny the Younger earned nearly 2,000 times as much as the average individual. Inequalities in the ownership of land, both agricultural and urban, were primarily responsible for the differentials. Storey's analysis is based on Alföldy's single-axis model and numbers drawn from sources in Italy, both rural and urban.

Steven Friesen has also contributed significantly to socioeconomic analysis of the eastern Mediterranean and to the refining of Alföldy's model. He proposes a model that he names a "poverty scale" to analyze access to wealth for inhabitants of cities.[50] This scale depicts seven degrees of access to economic goods ranging from imperial elites to beggars. Socioeconomic status was patterned in a sharply hierarchical structure, with about 90 percent of the population living at or near subsistence. The superwealthy elite comprised the top 3 percent, while another 7 percent (approximately) were successful merchants, or owners of small properties, which allowed them to have income from rents, or owners of skilled slaves who increased the profitability of owners' workshops. These merchants, landlords, and workshop owners belonged to the middle strata where subsistence was not an issue. Friesen's demarcations represent an improvement in precision from a two-tiered scale.[51] Gradations in extreme wealth and poverty are more readily apparent in this model. Further,

47. Glenn R. Storey, "Cui Bono? An Economic Cost-Benefit Analysis of Statuses in the Roman Empire," in *Hierarchies in Action: Cui Bono?*, ed. Michael W. Diehl (Carbondale, IL: Southern Illinois University Press, 2000), 340–74.

48. Ibid., 356–59.

49. Ibid., Table 17–11, p. 360.

50. Friesen, "Poverty in Pauline Studies."

the appearance of the middle group with some disposable property fits more precisely with evidence concerning small-scale traders and property owners.[52]

Quantitative models of socioeconomic status by Storey and Friesen are especially significant for this study.[53] The range in wealth from top to bottom of the scale was enormous. The middle group that did have access to property were far removed from imperial elites yet they were still much wealthier than the majority 90 percent who hovered near subsistence level. With their relative wealth, members of the middle group could act as patrons for persons from the lower groups.

The hierarchy of socioeconomic stratification was sustained and reproduced by institutions and customs such as legal and property systems, the patron-client system, the occupational system, the institutions of slavery and marriage, and a variety of practices and ideologies of legitimization.[54] At least three main interrelated themes recur in kyriocentric ideologies and institutions legitimating imperial hierarchical rule: prosperity, paternalism, and peace or concord. The peace engendered by Roman military domination was praised as the basis for commerce and thus prosperity. Benevolent paternalism on the part of emperor and elite patrons ensured continuity and benefit for all. This decree by the "assembly of Greeks in Asia" in 9 B.C.E. praises imperial rule.

Whereas the providence which divinely ordered our lives created with zeal and munificence the most perfect good for our lives by

51. Several studies depend on a model with just two socioeconomic levels, rich and poor: Justin J. Meggitt, *Paul, Poverty and Survival* (Edinburgh: T. & T. Clark, 1998); Ivoni Richter Reimar and Linda M. Maloney, *Women in the Acts of the Apostles: A Feminist Liberation Perspective* (Minneapolis: Fortress Press, 1995).

52. Jeremy Paterson, "Trade and Traders in the Roman World: Scale, Structure, and Organisation," in *Trade, Traders and the Ancient City*, ed. Helen Parkins and Christopher Smith (London: Routledge, 1998), 149–67. Glenn R. Storey, "Roman Economies: A Paradigm of Their Own," in *Archaeological Perspectives on Political Economies*, ed. Gary M. Feinman and Linda M. Nicholas (Salt Lake City: University of Utah Press, 2004), 105–28.

53. See also Walter Scheidel and Steven J. Friesen, "The Size of the Economy and the Distribution of Income in the Roman Empire," *Journal of Roman Studies* 99 (2009): 61–91.

54. Peter Garnsey and Richard Saller, *The Roman Empire: Economy, Society and Culture* (Berkeley: University of California Press, 1987), 109–11. Hannelore Schröder, "The Economic Impoverishment of Mothers Is the Enrichment of Fathers," in *Women, Work and Poverty*, ed. Elisabeth Schüssler Fiorenza and Anne Carr (*Concilium*; Edinburgh: T. & T. Clark, 1987), 14. Schröder argues that feminist economists' "analysis has to start with the domestic economy and the domestic dominance fixed by marriage-, family-, and inheritance laws. The historical process is indispensable, for economy begins in the home (oikos)" (13).

producing Augustus and filling him with virtue for the benefaction of humanity, sending us and those after us a savior who put an end to war and established all things; and whereas Caesar when he appeared exceeded the hopes of all who had anticipated good tidings, not only by surpassing the benefactors born before him, but not even leaving those to come any hope of surpassing him; and whereas the birthday of the god marked for the world the beginning of good tidings through his coming.[55]

In this inscription, benevolent paternalism appears in the person of "Providence." It acts through Caesar Augustus who has brought peace and an end to the wars that had plagued Asia Minor and the eastern Mediterranean. The associated benefactions are good news for everyone. The cosmic significance of Caesar's rule receives emphasis by universalizing space and time: "the Greeks in Asia," "humanity," "all things," "surpassing all," "the world," and reorientation of the calendar to Augustus' birthday. Similar sentiments were echoed in Rabbinic and Christian literature.[56] The logic of the inscription expresses the interdependence of representations of paternalism, peace, and prosperity in the empire. The rapid appearance of imperial ideology in Asia Minor suggests the ready adaptation of Roman societal structures in the eastern provinces.[57] The extravagance of the vocabulary highlights the geographical and temporal extension of imperial rule.

An essential support for the emperor's legitimization of his right to rule rested in visually apparent elements of material prosperity. Some modern historians follow Aristides and Tertullian in praising Roman accomplishments

55. *OGI* 458. The decree recalibrates the calendar around the birthday of Caesar Augustus. Translation from S. R. F. Price, *Rituals and Power: The Roman Imperial Cult in Asia Minor* (Cambridge: Cambridge University Press, 1984), 54. (ἔδοξεν τοῖς ἐπὶ τῆς Ἀσίας Ἕλλησιν . . .) ἐπε[ιδὴ ἡ θείως] διατάξασα τὸν βίον ἡμῶν πρόνοια σπουδὴν εἰσεν[ενκαμ]ένη καὶ φιλοτιμίαν τὸ τεληότατον τῶι βίωι διεκόσμη[σεν ἀγαθὸν] ἐνενκαμένη τὸν Σεβαστόν, ὃν εἰς εὐεργεσίαν ἀνθρώ[πων] ἐπλήρωσεν ἀρετῆς, <ὥ>σπερ ἡμεῖν καὶ τοῖς μεθ' ἡ[μᾶς σωτῆρα χαρισαμένη] τὸν παύσαντα μὲν πόλεμον, κοσμήσοντα [δὲ εἰρήνην, ἐπιφανεὶς δὲ] ὁ Καῖσαρ τὰς ἐλπίδας τῶν προλαβόντων [εὐανγέλια πάντων ὑπερ]έθηκεν, οὐ μόνον τοὺς πρὸ αὐτοῦ γεγονότ[ας εὐεργέτας ὑπερβαλόμενος, ἀλλ' οὐδ' ἐν τοῖς ἐσομένοις ἐλπίδ[α ὑπολιπὼν ὑπερβολῆς,] ἦρξεν δὲ τῶι κόσμωι τῶν δι' αὐτὸν εὐανγελί[ων ἡ γενέθλιος ἡμέ]ρα τοῦ θεοῦ

56. Clifford Ando, *Imperial Ideology and Provincial Loyalty in the Roman Empire* (Berkeley: University of California Press, 2000), 55–57.

57. The monuments attributed to Plancia Magna of Perge, the reliefs in the Sebasteion at Aphrodisias, the competition among the cities for a temple of the imperial cult, and the popularity of the epigraphic habit itself all indicate the strength and popularity of the presence of Roman imperial culture in Asia Minor.

in engineering and urban construction.[58] If such praise is not balanced with an account of the rhetorical functions of the prosperity discourse, our histories risk leaving invisible the vast majority of the population who lived near subsistence.[59]

Contrary to the ideology of prosperity, Jongman and Kleijwegt have argued that periods of growth corresponded to increases in social inequalities as rents and labor supplies both increased while available land decreased.[60] All of these factors resulted in a lower standard of living for the masses during periods of expansion.[61] Thus the portrayal of the imperial era as a time of prosperity requires critical nuance for persons at different positions in kyriarchal socioeconomic structures.

A critical approach to ancient socioeconomic history, exemplified by Rostovtzeff and De Ste. Croix, theorizes that the generation of wealth for an elite few was based on the exploitation of semi-free laborers and slaves.[62] Storey's cost-benefit analysis (in the preceding discussion) supports this reconstruction by quantifying the degree of exploitation by the upper strata of elites. The short violent lives typical of millions who lived at or below subsistence level in high-density unsanitary cities has been detailed by Alex Scobie.[63]

Wealthy elites imitated Augustus in providing benefaction and propagating the ideology of paternalism. The Res Gestae detailed the accomplishments and good deeds of Augustus; it was reproduced and displayed all over the empire. Elite benefactions recorded by inscriptions reinforced socioeconomic inequality even as they portrayed social responsibility. Ostensibly, various laws restrained the rich and protected the poor.[64] For instance, a first-century (C.E.) inscription from Pisidian Antioch calls it unjust

---

58. See Ando, *Imperial Ideology*, 14, 66–67, 50–51.

59. This "view from the top" also tends to minimize the possibilities for conflict in historical reconstruction. See Bruce Winter, *Seek the Welfare of the City: Christians as Benefactors and Citizens: First-Century Christians in the Graeco-Roman World* (Grand Rapids: Eerdmans, 1994).

60. Willem Jongman and Marc Kleijwegt, "H. W. Pleket, Epigraphist and Comparative Historian," in *After the Past*, ed. Jongman and Kleijwegt (Mnemosyne 233; Leiden: Brill, 2002), xxi.

61. The Antonine plague may have temporarily reversed these trends; a smaller population led to reduced labor supply, lower rents, and more land at lower prices. Thus it is perhaps more accurate to think of the imperial era as a time of economic expansion and contraction. Ibid., xxi.

62. Michael Rostovtzeff, *The Social and Economic History of the Roman Empire*, 2 vols. (Oxford: Clarendon, 1957). G. E. M. de Ste. Croix (Ithaca, NY: Cornell University Press, 1981). De Ste. Croix discussed men and women as belonging to different classes based on differing relationships to modes of (re)production; this perspective does not consider women's activities besides that of sexual reproduction.

63. Alex Scobie, "Slums, Sanitation and Mortality in the Roman World," *Klio* 68 (1986): 399–433.

to make a profit on hunger by increasing the price of grain during a famine.[65] However, no practical imperial protection or enforcement existed.[66]

Land-owning elites minimized their socioeconomic risks through tenant farmers and through slave or freed rent collectors and commercial agents. In times of food-shortages when riots threatened them, elites increased benefaction so that basic socioeconomic structures were maintained. Rulers actively discouraged tendencies toward horizontal grouping, which may have resulted in solidarity among non-elites.[67] The vertical networks engendered by patronage reproduced kyriarchy and regulated the integration of newcomers to privileged and elite orders.[68] The verbal and visual repetition of the generosity of wealthy women and men diverted attention from the gains they derived from ownership and public service.

This discussion of imperial rule and patronage shows how they were intertwined with ideologies of prosperity, concord, and paternalism. Kyriarchal households, marriage, and slavery also worked together with these ideologies.

> Augustus and his contemporaries began to understand his authority and caretakership of the state as that of a Roman father to his family. Important stages in the redefinition of public and private in the context of imperial family include: the dedication of the Altar of Peace in 9 B.C.E., on which images of peace and security come in the individually depicted forms of Augustus and his relatives; the institution of a series of state, neighborhood and private cults honoring Augustus and his relatives on the model of private family cult; and the dedication of a shrine to the goddess of political and

---

64. Luuk de Ligt, "Restraining the Rich, Protecting the Poor: Symbolic Aspects of Roman Legislation," in *After the Past*, ed. Jongman and Kleijwegt, 1–45.

65. AÉ 1925 no. 126. See Robert K. Sherk, ed. and trans, *The Roman Empire: Augustus to Hadrian* (Cambridge: Cambridge University Press, 1988), no. 107.

66. De Ligt, "Restraining the Rich," 22.

67. Glenn R. Storey, "Cui Bono? An Economic Cost-Benefit Analysis of Statuses in the Roman Empire," in *Hierarchies in Action: Cui Bono?*, ed. Michael W. Diehl (Carbondale, IL: Southern Illinois University Press, 2000), 364–66.

68. Alföldy, *Social History*, 153–56. Garnsey and Saller, *The Roman Empire: Economy, Society and Culture*, 125. "It cannot be sufficiently emphasized that the relative 'success' of the Roman Empire, by comparison with other much more violently extractive, and unstable, preindustrial empires, lay largely in the extension of the euergetic system of unequal exchange very widely through the Empire." Richard Gordon, "The Veil of Power," in *Pagan Priests: Religion and Power in the Ancient World*, ed. Mary Beard and John North (Ithaca, NY: Cornell University Press, 1990), 224.

familial accord by Augustus' wife Livia in 7 B.C.E. Moreover, in a practical sense, Augustus came to manage the city and the empire as republican men managed their households: Augustus' slaves and freedmen managed state finances, his wife hosted foreign ambassadors, his sons and stepsons commanded the Roman armies, and he raised the children of allied kings in his own home.[69]

The kyriarchal household provided a model for imperial governance, ideology, and authority; at the same time, Augustus took on the title and role of the father who brought military peace, and Livia associated herself with Concordia, domestic harmony. In this way, imperial ideology was used to inculcate in subordinate wives the role of manager of accord and unity. Slaves and freed persons functioned as imperial agents and managers because they stood for the person of Augustus, the wealthiest person in the Empire. The household ideal of good kyriarchal management provided the ethos guiding the investment of inherited wealth.[70] The pairing of household and state was thus further associated with the ideal of prosperity.

Speaking of imperial ideology, Clifford Ando writes, "we should not forget that most of the work of iterating and reiterating the state ideology took place not at the level of explicit state publication but in the day-to-day lives of the population, both in their contact with branches of the imperial administration and most particularly in their encounters with those private institutions that had a stake in the status quo."[71] The hierarchies of empire, patronage, and household combine repetition, coercion, and ideological legitimization.

This depiction of the Roman system highlights conflicts of interest, stratification, and some of the mechanisms that maintained inequality. Kyriocentrism was so effective that the emperors had no need to station armies around the Aegean Sea to maintain order in the colonized provinces of Greece and Turkey. Kyriarchy models the ways in which dominant ideologies and political and economic relations interacted and multiplied in producing the socioeconomic status of women in households, patronage, and slavery. Roman kyriarchy featured exploitation of the lower strata by the elite. Institutions and the ideologies that justified them sustained this exploitative system. Peace or

---

69. Beth Severy, *Augustus and the Family at the Birth of the Roman Empire* (New York: Routledge, 2003), 5. See also Paul Zanker, *The Power of Images in the Age of Augustus*, trans. Alan Shapiro (Ann Arbor: University of Michigan Press, 1988).

70. Storey, "Roman Economies: A Paradigm of Their Own."

71. Ando, *Imperial Ideology*, 41.

concord, paternalism, and prosperity were crucial ideologies supporting the imperial system. Households, patronage, and slavery all figure prominently in the institutions and ideologies that maintained Roman kyriarchy. Thus sources about women in antiquity must be analyzed in terms of the ideologies and material relations modeled in kyriarchy.

READING THE SOURCES

Researchers investigating the activities of women have developed sophisticated principles of interpretation since the sources for writing history were inscribed in contexts marked by kyriocentrism. According to Suzanne Dixon, "The tendency to regard women as an afterthought and special 'marked' category in most discourse and the tendency to re-formulate female activities to suit notions of the feminine colours representations of women's economic activity in all genres, literary and non-literary."[72] We could expand Dixon's "notions of the feminine" to include ethnicity, wealth, and servility.

Studies that critically examine representations of less privileged members of society have documented the myriad ways in which such representations often correspond to the interests of ruling elites.[73] Portrayals of elites, free citizens, and men (or all three) are more common than those of slaves, women, and people living at subsistence level. So, if more perspectives favorable to elite landowners appear in surviving sources than those favorable to peasants, it is better to ascribe this phenomenon to the prevalence of kyriocentric genres supportive of the

---

72. Suzanne Dixon, *Reading Roman Women* (London: Duckworth, 2001), 100.

73. For example, for the Roman era, see Keith Bradley, *Slaves and Masters in the Roman Empire: A Study in Social Control* (New York: Oxford University Press, 1987). Bradley, *Slavery and Rebellion in the Roman World* (Bloomington: Indiana University Press, 1989). Suzanne Dixon, *Reading Roman Women: Sources, Genres and Real Life* (Bath, UK: Duckworth, 2001). Jennifer Glancy, *Slavery in Early Christianity* (Oxford: Oxford University Press, 2002). Richard A. Horsley, ed., *Paul and Politics: Ekklesia, Israel, Imperium, Interpretation* (Harrisburg, PA: Trinity Press International, 2000). Horsley, *Paul and Empire: Religion and Power in Roman Imperial Society* (Harrisburg, PA: Trinity Press International, 1997). Tal Ilan, *Integrating Women into Second Temple History* (Tübingen: Mohr, 1999). Anne Jensen, *God's Self-Confident Daughters: Early Christianity and the Liberation of Women* (Louisville: Westminster John Knox, 1996). Sandra R. Joshel and Sheila Murnaghan, eds., *Women and Slaves in Greco-Roman Culture: Differential Equations* (London and New York: Routledge, 1998). Nancy Sorkin Rabinowitz and Amy Richlin, eds., *Feminist Theory and the Classics* (New York: Routledge, 1993). Luise Schottroff, *Lydia's Impatient Sisters: A Feminist Social History of Early Christianity*, trans. Barbara and Martin Rumscheidt (Louisville: Westminster John Knox, 1995). Elisabeth Schüssler Fiorenza, *But She Said: Feminist Practices of Biblical Interpretation* (Boston: Beacon, 1992). Antoinette Clark Wire, *Corinthian Women Prophets: A Reconstruction through Paul's Rhetoric* (Minneapolis: Fortress Press, 1990).

status quo rather than to majority opinion. Surviving materials do not often provide the density of data needed for reliable statistical analysis. Sociological metrics dependent on inscriptions remain tentative while problems inherent in studying demography of ancient societies quantitatively continue to challenge scholars.[74]

Elite men appear either as authors or subjects of almost all surviving texts. Women, free and slave, are underrepresented in historical sources and the degree to which this occurs is unknown; therefore persuasive reconstructions must assume the presence of many more women and lower-status men than actually appear in extant texts. For example, many surviving sources depict urban settings although the Roman economy depended primarily on agriculture, and as much as 90 percent of the population engaged in farm work. Cross-cultural studies of agricultural labor indicate that women have been vital to food production in subsistence economies, but women's agricultural work remains almost invisible in archaeological sources from ancient Asia Minor.

Personal names present translation issues in the interpretation of literary, legal, and inscriptional sources. Ancient Greek names reveal few conclusive markers to identify slave women.[75] Onomastic compilations indicate the willingness of Greek speakers to borrow names from a wide range of sources with overlap between men and women, slave and free. Parents named both boys and girls after male or female gods.[76] Slaves, lower-status people, and elites alike used the matronymic (mother's name).[77] Similar overlaps occurred with gender and grammatical cases as well.[78] Male names that appear without the patronymic (the father's name in the genitive case) are often assumed to belong to slaves. Female names, however, might appear with their husband's name in the genitive case, so that the presence or absence of her father cannot be determined. Both slave and free women can appear with their husbands'

74. See detailed discussions in Walter Scheidel, ed., *Debating Roman Demography* (Leiden and Boston: Brill, 2001.)

75. Olivier Masson, *Onomastica Graeca Selecta*, 2 vols. (Paris: Université de Paris, 1990). Heikki Solin, *Die stadtrömischen Sklavennamen: Ein Namenbuch* (Stuttgart: Franz Steiner, 1996). Ladislav Zgusta, *Kleinasiatische Personennamen* (Prague: Tschechoslowaksichen Akademie der Wissenschaften, 1964). Heikki Solin, *Die griechische Personennamen in Rom: Ein Namenbuch*, CIL, Auctarium, 3 vols. (Berlin: W. de Gruyter, 1982).

76. B. H. McLean, *An Introduction to Greek Epigraphy of the Hellenistic and Roman Periods from Alexander the Great down to the Reign of Constantine (323 B.C.-A.D. 337)* (Ann Arbor: University of Michigan Press, 2002), 77.

77. Ibid., 94.

78. One class of female names ended in –ης, gen –ηδος. Another group ended in –ιον.

names.[79] The patronymic is a much less reliable indicator of status for women than for men.

Susan Treggiari has noted limitations for historians' use of epigraphy. For example, while a number of women are known from literary and legal sources to have been sex workers, very few of these are portrayed in epigraphs; some occupations are nearly invisible in inscriptions because of their reputation, and others because such workers lacked the resources for stone markers.[80] An extensive survey of Roman inscriptions completed by Sandra Joshel found women absent from certain occupational titles in which men appear, such as building, banking, and transportation, and quite rare in sales or administration.[81] Occupational inscriptions rarely depict women engaged in production work or as managing large businesses, yet many women's names appear on brick stamps as managers and owners. Language itself presents problems for interpretation: women workers were not infrequently referred to with a masculine singular occupational title.[82] And since masculine plurals in Greek and Latin, and many masculine nouns, can include or refer to women, the referents have to be questioned in each occurrence.

As a general principle, representations of women that remain to us depict some aspects of their existence while muting others. This principle holds across such genres as letters, burial inscriptions, ceramics, iconography, and legal texts. The various genres of sources, literary, legal, inscriptional, and visual have their own conventions of representation and present different challenges.[83] Many inscriptions record honorable accomplishments while few describe less savory deeds. Even simple funerary epitaphs—that a name is given in one form and not another, or whether age, occupation, genealogy, or spouse appear—evince the arbitrary character of sources.

---

79. Slaves could not legally marry under Roman law, but neither could noncitizens. Clearly, the legal situation, however, did not mirror social practice. See Dale Martin, "Slavery and the Ancient Jewish Family," in *The Jewish Family in Antiquity*, ed. Shaye Cohen (Atlanta: Scholars, 1993), 113–29.

80. Susan Treggiari, "Lower Class Women in the Roman Economy," *Florilegium* 1 (1979): 69, 73. Sandra R. Joshel, *Work, Identity and Social Status at Rome: A Study of the Occupational Inscriptions at Rome* (Norman: University of Oklahoma Press, 1992), 71ff.

81. Joshel, *Work, Identity and Social Status*, 69.

82. Suzanne Dixon, "Exemplary Housewife or Luxurious Slut? Cultural Representations of Women in the Roman Economy," in *Women's Influence on Classical Civilization*, ed. Fiona McHardy and Eirann Marshall (London: Routledge, 2004), 64–65. Treggiari, "Lower Class Women," 72. For the Greek East, see the inscription for Magnilla in the following.

83. See also Celia E. Schultz, *Women's Religious Activity in the Roman Republic* (Chapel Hill: University of North Carolina Press, 2006), 47–49.

In epigraphic and legal materials, women owned, bought, and sold land in Asia Minor. References to agricultural products in inscriptions "suggest that women owned grain land, vineyards, olive groves and pasture land," according to Riet van Bremen.[84] She goes on to note, "Women also matched men in the straightforward financial activity of money lending, either to individuals or to cities."[85] Women in Asia Minor routinely served in official roles as magistrates and priests, although with geographic variation.[86]

The evidence from Italy is more plentiful than from Asia Minor. Legislation of Claudius mentions freedwomen who imported grain to Italy. Päivi Setälä's study of brick stamps in the second century C.E. showed that, among owners of senatorial rank, almost half were women.[87] According to Suzanne Dixon, "Legal references to women owning or managing businesses confirm that they were not viewed as an oddity. . . . They also contributed to the commercial culture of Roman towns and to the patronage networks which underpinned small businesses."[88] Participation in patronage and in large businesses required property ownership or management.

Scholarship indicates that women from Rome through the eastern empire owned and managed property. Janne Pölönen reasons that "women received at least forty percent, if not a share equal to men, of the private property by means of inheritance at Rome."[89] Ville Vuolanto's study of children's property in Roman Egypt concludes, "the mother could manage the wealth of her child freely and independently," even when legal principles prohibited women from guardianships.[90] Two wealthy Egyptian women who became Roman citizens under Hadrian appear in an inscription as shipowners and merchants.[91] Finally,

84. Riet Van Bremen, "Women and Wealth," in *Images of Women in Antiquity*, ed. Avril Cameron and Amélie Kuhrt (Detroit: Wayne State University Press, 1983), 228.

85. Ibid., 229. Amphora stamps indicate that Roman females such as "Calvia Crispinilla and Caedicia apparently engaged in viticulture and wine export." Dixon, "Exemplary Housewife," 62.

86. Examples of variation in: Steven Friesen, "'Highpriests of Asia and Asiarchs: Farewell to the Identification Theory," in *Steine und Wege*, ed. Peter Scherrer (Vienna: Austrian Archaeological Institute, 1999), 303–7; Sviatoslav Dmitriev, *City Government in Hellenistic and Roman Asia Minor* (Oxford: Oxford University Press, 2005).

87. Päivi Setälä, "Female Property and Power in Imperial Rome: Institutum Romanum Finlandiae," in *Aspects of Women in Antiquity: Proceedings of the First Nordic Symposium on Women's Lives in Antiquity*, ed. Lena Larsson Lovén and Agneta Strömberg (Jonsered, Sweden: P. Åstroms, 1998), 101.

88. Dixon, "Exemplary Housewife," 65. "Gender divisions were expressed in different ways, notably in the public representation of work categories and the apparent exclusion of women from guilds."

89. Janne Pölönen, "The Division of Wealth Between Men and Women in Roman Succession (ca. 50 B.C.—A.D. 250)," in *Women, Wealth and Power in the Roman Empire*, ed. Päivi Setälä et al. (Rome: Institutum Romanum Finlandiae, 2002), 178. "The primary reason for daughters' lesser shares was the need to compensate sons for the burdens of heirship and for the dowries their sisters received" (179).

Babatha, a Judean woman living in Arabia, profitably managed seven date palm groves and lent money to her husband.[92]

These representations of women's property transactions in epigraphic and legal materials contrast with representations of wealthy women in literary sources where elite women often appear as relatively passive consumers or users.

Natalie Kampen has investigated this elite passivity in visual and literary sources through her analysis of texts and relief representations, chiefly from Italy.[93] She develops a typology of the portrayals of women engaged in economic transactions, and compares types of visual images to reports in written sources. Kampen finds that inscriptions preserve and testify to a value structure different from that of the jurists and literary men. She interprets the different types of representation as serving different rhetorical functions.

Kampen concludes that male status was enhanced when women's work was represented less frequently than that of men, and when women were depicted as passive figures.[94] Women's work appears in expensive visual portrayals only as a function of the values and affection of the patron (who pays for the art). The portrayals suggest "that women performed very few jobs outside the home and did so only rarely."[95] Even within the household, Romans display a reluctance to portray elite women at work: most commonly, women are depicted in passive attitudes. Historians have noted that the symbols of a Roman wife were the distaff and spindle, in accord with the idealized tasks of women as spinners and weavers of cloth. Rarely, however, were elite women depicted actively engaged in weaving or spinning.[96]

Visual representations of non-elites are also marked by their production in a kyriarchal socioeconomic structure. Kampen has compared occupational reliefs for men and women artisans.

90. Ville Vuolanto, "Women and the Property of Fatherless Children in the Roman Empire," in *Women, Wealth and Power in the Roman Empire*, ed. Päivi Setälä, 242.

91. SEG 8.703. See Steven E. Sidebotham, *Roman Economic Policy in the Erythra Thalassa, 30 B.C.–A.D. 217* (Leiden: Brill, 1986), 86–87. These wealthy merchants "styled themselves *matronai stolatai*—terms indicating that they were women with more than three children who owned property and were free to pursue their own commercial ventures without a guardian" (87).

92. P. Yadin, 17.

93. Kampen, *Image and Status*.

94. The ideal of Roman kyriarchal rule depended on the portrayal of an elite free man's independence, contrary to the realities of his physical dependence on the labor of wives and slaves.

95. Kampen, *Image and Status*, 100.

96. This stands in contrast to the many portrayals of women's activities from classical Greece: women spin, weave, draw water, dance, perform music and gymnastics, and engage in foot-races.

Despite the fact that inscriptions report a few women metalworkers (one a smith married to a smith), as well as weavers and garland makers, and in spite of the undoubted presence of some female slaves and family members in small production shops, the visual imagery offers little evidence for the existence of these women. Although wool baskets and spindles appear on funerary reliefs from Gaul to Asia Minor, they denote women's feminine virtues rather than their moneymaking occupations.[97] By contrast, male artisans are both liberally and literally documented, not only because they were plentiful and visible, but also because they gained status within their own social stratum through their work. By contrast, the work of a woman, whether in her own shop or that of her father, husband or owner, was either not recognized as conferring status or was actually considered to lower her status.[98]

In Italy, representations of free women's activities and work were related to conventions for the presentation of male primacy and the male role as active and visually prominent. Kampen shows that we need to resist the tendency in our sources to render women invisible so that we can imagine women present in historical reconstructions. Kampen's work highlights the ways in which portrayals of women's presence and activities in the ancient world depend on the interactions of several factors: rhetorical interests of the owner, the type of source (whether inscription, literary text, or engraved motif), and the interaction of gender with socioeconomic status.

Furthermore, the image of the wealthy woman provided a handy figure for a host of ascriptions of social value. As members of the elite, wealthy women appear in more representations than do poor women and men. These representations of wealthy women served a variety of rhetorical goals. According to Ria Berg, adornment signified constructions of gender, class, ethnicity, and virtue. "In Roman rhetoric, *luxuria* is quite often connected with feminine characteristics. Women were seen as especially susceptible to

97. I prefer to speak of constructions or ideals of femininity rather than "feminine virtues." On the idealization of women, see Paul Zanker, "Bürgerliche Selbstdarstellung am Grab im römischen Kaiserreich," in *Die Römische Stadt im 2. Jahrhundert nach Christ* (Köln: Rheinland, 1992), 356–57.

98. Natalie Kampen, "Social Status and Gender in Roman Art: The Case of the Saleswoman," in *Roman Art in Context: An Anthology*, ed. Eve D'Ambria (Englewoods Cliffs, NJ: Prentice Hall, 1993), 126. One might add that such depictions would also lower the status of the men involved. Engravings of images were more expensive than simple inscriptions (129–30).

luxuria, and men accused of effeminacy were also defined as "luxurious."[99] Thus a conspicuous absence of jewelry could demonstrate a woman's virtue and lack of avarice.[100] Some imperial women were depicted without jewelry, or with male jewels only, to suggest their capability to control desires and to rule well.

However, this symbolization is complicated because "emblems of power—political, military and rank insignia—are often objects made of precious metals, not infrequently jewels."[101] Since adornment such as gold jewelry could signify Roman equestrian and senatorial ranks, these visual symbols were usurped by the wealthy of lower ranks, such as freedmen and women, to display their wealth and power in a potent idiom.[102] A decorative façade accompanied the stereotyped elite woman's passivity. As a rhetorical topos, representation of a woman's adornment through jewelry or clothing might signal discussion of socioeconomic status (rather than vanity or profligacy). This conclusion relies on analysis of gender in conjunction with wealth, ethnicity, and legal status.

In a way similar to adornment, the education of women in wealthy families signaled status. Emily Hemelrijk has studied educated women in the Roman elite. She notes the apparent conflict between the ideal of the *matrona,* associated with traditional elite female values, and the indication that some upper-class women were highly educated.[103] Hemelrijk argues that a daughter's education displayed the wealth and increased the prestige of her family. Education of women functioned as a form of conspicuous consumption. Such portrayals were popular among Pompeian sub-elites:

> Their dress, jewelry and elegance show that the pictures are (idealized) representations of young Roman women of some standing, probably the mistresses of the house, who wanted to be portrayed not only as young and prosperous, but also as well educated by means of their pencil and writing-tablets. . . . It would show their assimilation to the values and literary culture of the upper classes and the emphasis on education as a mark of status among those who lacked high birth.[104]

99. Ria Berg, "Wearing Wealth: *Mundus Muliebris* and *Ornatus* as Status Markers for Women in Imperial Rome," in *Women, Wealth and Power in the Roman Empire,* ed. Päivi Setälä et al., 25.

100. Ibid., 71–72.

101. Ibid., 41. The signet ring, worn and used by women and men, was necessary for legal actions (45).

102. Ibid., 46–50; 42. Laws regulating adornment seem not to have been enforced.

103. Emily A. Hemelrijk, *Matrona Docta: Educated Women in the Roman Elite from Cornelia to Julia Domna* (London: Routledge, 1999), 7.

Just as sub-elites imitated imperial elites, the wealthy in the colonized cities of Asia Minor could show off their education of women to enhance their social status.

Scholarship on women's status, such as the texts collected by Lefkowitz and Fant, has identified and focused on sources for women's education.[105] For example, in this slightly damaged text, Aufria, perhaps from Bithynia, receives honors for her series of talks at the Pythian games in the second century c.e.

[θε]ός. τύχαι ἀγαθᾶ[ι].
[ἔδοξ]εν τῇ πόλει
[τῶν Δε]λφίων Αὐφρίαν
[....]νὴν Δελφὴν εἶναι,
[ἐπειδ]ή, παραγενομένη
[πρὸς τ]ὸν θεόν, πᾶν τὸ
[ἦθος τῆ]ς παιδείας ἐπε-
[δείξατο], λόγους τε πολ-
[λοὺς καὶ κ]αλοὺς καὶ ἡδί-
[στους ἐν] τῇ π[υ]θικῇ συ-
[νόδῳ τῶν] Ἑλ[λήν]ων δ[ιέ]-
[θετο, ...]
(7 lines)
[. . . . . φ]ανῇ [ἐφ' . . . . .]
[. . . . .] πεποιημέν[.]
[. . . . . τ]ῷ θεῷ ἀγαθ[ὰ π]οι-
[. . . . .] ἐψηφισάμεθα.
[ἐπὶ δὲ Αἰ]λ. Πυθοδώρου ἐψηφισάμεθα
[τὰς τῶν ἀν]δριάντων ἀναστάσεις.

To God for good fortune. The city of Delphi has decreed that Aufria of ___ is a citizen of Delphi since she was present at the festival of the god, and demonstrated the entire range of her education, and delivered many excellent and enjoyable lectures at the assembly of

---

104. Ibid., 75. In this passage, Hemelrijk comments on portraits painted on the walls in Pompeii. Because women's education did stand in tension with the figure of the matron, it remained a subject of controversy.

105. Lefkowitz and Fant, eds., *Women's Lives.*

the Greeks at the Pythian games. . . . During the term of office of Ail.
of Pythodoros, we voted to erect statues.[106]

The text praises Aufria for the breadth of her education, and for her many excellent enjoyable speeches. She pleases the crowd at the Pythian games, a large festival in Delphi. The Delphians honor her with citizenship. The passage does not identify Aufria's family or marital status: these are not elements of the presentation of her honors. Her rhetorical education suggests that she was a freeborn elite woman.

Besides the literary training Aufria received, girls apparently received instruction in music and athletics.[107] A curriculum of literature, music, and athletics reflected the Hellenic ideal of physical and intellectual education.[108] An inscription from the early second century c.e. honoring youths and their singing instructors in Laodicea (on Lycus) lists six girls and six boys.[109] The Isthmian games included contests for girls and women from the year 2 b.c.e.[110]

One inscription presents so many accomplishments for a family of girls that scholars have investigated their status as professional athletes and musicians.[111]

---

106. *FD* 3.4.79. English translation in Lefkowitz and Fant, eds., *Women's Lives*, 192.

107. Painted bowls from ancient Greece (early fifth century b.c.e.) depict female youths participating in athletics. Spartan women were reputed to train for physical speed and strength. Lefkowitz and Fant, eds., *Women's Lives*, 84. A group of Attic vases show women at or after exercise. In the classical era, "Greeks sometimes painted women with strigils on pots and buried them with strigils in graves." Mark Golden, *Sport and Society in Ancient Greece* (Cambridge: Cambridge University Press, 1998), 125. The strigil, a curved wooden paddle used to clean the body by scraping off oil and dirt, represented athletes iconographically. Pausanias describes girls' foot-races that took place every four years in the stadium at Olympia (*Peri.* 5.16.2–4).

108. R. E. Wycherley, *How the Greeks Built Cities* (New York: Norton, 1962), 140.

109. *SEG* 37.961. Lines10–27: ὑμνήσας τὸν θεὸν κατὰ χρησμόν, τὰ τῶν συνυμνησάντων παίδων καὶπαρθένων ὀνόματα ἀνέθηκεν, παιδονομοῦντος Μ. Ἀκειλίου Παυλείνου τὸ ε′,παρεδρευόντων Ἀπολλωνίου καὶ Διονυσίου· . . . εἰσὶν δέ Π. Κλαύδιος Διονύσιος Αἰλιανός, Π. Κλαύδιος Ἄτταλος Φιλάδελφος, Π. Κλαύδιος Τατιανὸς Αἰλιανός, Σκύμνος β′, Καλλίνικος Σείλιος, Κλαυδιανὸς Περσικοῦ, Κλαυδία Ἀτταλὶς Σαλβίου, Ἀμμία Ἀσκληπιάδου, Ἀρίστη Ἀριστοκρίτου, Νικόπολις Νίκωνος, Τατία Νίκωνος, Ἀγελαὶς Περσικοῦ, [κ]αθηγησαμένου τὸν ὕμνον

110. Athenaeus (*Diep.* 13.566) reported seeing boys and girls wrestling in the gymnasia at Chios in the second century c.e.

111. For Konstantinos Mantas, it suggests "the existence of female athletes who pursued a career," that is, who participated in athletics "as professionals," or "quasi-professionals." Mantas, "Women and Athletics in the Roman East," in *Nikephoros* 8 (1995): 133.Ἑρμησιάναξ Διονυσίου Καισαρεὺς Τραλ[λιαν]ὸς ὁ καὶ Κο[ρίνθιος]τὰς ἑαυτοῦ θυγατέρας ἐχούσας καὶ α[ὐτ]ὰς τὰς αὐτὰς πο[λειτείας].(α) Τρυφῶσαν νεικήσασαν Πύθια ἐ-πὶ ἀγωνοθετῶν Ἀντιγόνουκαὶ Κλεομαχίδα· καὶ Ἴσθμια ἐπὶἀγωνοθέτου Ἰουβεντίου Πρό-κλου· στάδιον κατὰ τὸ ἑξῆς πρώ-τη παρθένων.Ἡδέαν

Hedea, from Asia Minor, won contests in both foot-racing and lyre playing in this inscription from Delphi in 45 C.E.[112] The text presents many achievements for the three freeborn girls. Their citizenship suggests that the family belonged among the more wealthy strata of Asia Minor. These three appear well trained in athletics and music and widely traveled. Games and contests for girls indicate the prevalence of athletic training for girls in Asia Minor and Greece in the Hellenistic and Roman eras.[113]

The three young athletes perform in some of the largest public arenas in ancient cities. This image conflicts sharply with the figure of the passive wealthy wife. Far from quiet modesty exercised in household space, the inscription represents these daughters as exerting themselves physically and competitively, and gaining recognition for their accomplishments. They appear competent and poised, trained to perform in the spotlight of public attention as Aufria did in her lectures at Delphi.

Aufria was not alone as a woman in rhetorical education. Some girls participated in the educational system of the gymnasium along with their brothers.[114] A law of the second century C.E. from Ionia that regulated the education of free children refers to boys and girls together.[115] The funerary

νεικήσασαν Ἴσθμια ἐπὶ ἀγωνο-θέτου Κορνηλίου Πούλχρου ἐνόπλι-ον ἅρματι· καὶ Νέμεα στάδιον ἐπὶ ἀγω-νοθέτου Ἀντιγόνου· καὶ ἐν Σικυῶνι ἐπιἀγωνοθέτου Μενοίτα· ἐνείκα δὲ καὶπαῖδας κιθαρωδοὺς Ἀθήνησι Σεβάστειαἐπὶ ἀγωνοθέτου Νουίου τοῦ Φιλεί-νο(υ)· πρώ[τη ἀπ' αἰῶ]νος ἐγένετο πολεῖ-[τις — —]ρώ παρθένος.Διονυσίαν νεικ[ήσασαν . . . . . .]ἐπὶ ἀγωνοθέτου Ἀν[τιγ]ό[νου]·καὶ Ἀσκλάπεια ἐν Ἐπιδαύρωτῆ ἱερᾶ ἐπὶ ἀγων[ο]θέτου Νεικο-τέλου στάδι[ον].Ἀπόλλωνι Πυθίω. Hermesianix, son of Dionysius, of Caesarea in Tralles (also from Corinth), for his daughters, who themselves have the same citizenship. (1) Tryphosa, at the Pythian games with Antigonus and Cleomachis as judges, and at the Isthmian Games, with Juventius Proclus as president, each time placed first of the girls in the single-course race. (2) Hedea, at the Isthmian games with Cornelius Pulcher as judge, won the race in armor, and the chariot race; at the Nemean games she won the single-course race with Antigonus as president and also in Sicyon with Menoites as president. She also won the children's lyre contest at the Augustan games in Athens with Nuvius son of Philinus as president. She was first in her age group . . . citizen . . . a girl. (3) Dionysia won at . . . with Antigonus as president, the single-course race at the Asclepian games at the sanctuary of Epidaurus with Nicoteles as president. To Pythian Apollo.

112. H. W. Pleket, *Epigraphica II: Texts on the Social History of the Greek World* (Leiden: Brill, 1969), 9. Translation adapted from Lefkowitz and Fant, eds., *Women's Lives*, 162.

113. Other inscriptions record the victory of Seia Spes, who won a 200-meter race in Italy circa 154 C.E., and that of Nikegora at a 400-meter in Roman Greece. Pleket, *Epigraphica II*, 17 and lost inscription (undated). See also Damodika, IK Kyme 46, from Asia Minor in the first century B.C.E.

114. *SEG* 15.667, an inscription from Magnesia, Asia Minor, dated to 197/6 B.C.E., refers to female students.

115. *SEG* 14.751. Line 10: τοὺς παῖδας καὶ τὰς παρθένους

marker for Abeita, a ten-year-old girl who died in the second century C.E., commemorates her with scrolls and stylus.[116] A poetry contest and other competition for girls at Isthmia appear in an inscription of 23 C.E.[117]

Henry Pleket published this funerary inscription about Magnilla. She lived in Mysia (northwest Asia Minor) in the second or third century C.E. The text identifies her first as a philosopher, second as a daughter, and third as a wife.

Μάγνιλλα[ν φιλό]-
σοφον Μάγν[ου]
φιλοσόφου θυ[γα]-
τέρα, Μηνίο[υ φιλο]-
σ[όφ]ου γυ[ναῖκα].

For Magnilla, philosopher, daughter of Magnos, philosopher, and wife of Meanios, philosopher.[118]

The identification as a philosopher suggests that Magnilla was educated and a teacher herself; mention of her father indicates that she was freeborn. The term *philosopher* is applied in grammatically masculine form not only to Magnilla's father and husband, but also to Magnilla herself. Feminist historians have noted this usage for the masculine nouns of occupational titles in other inscriptions, in legal sources, and in both Greek and Latin (discussed above). This suggests that readers did not distinguish between (for example) Magnilla and Meanios in their roles as philosophers. If they did, we might expect different terms to mark distinct occupations. When the same noun appears, however, we should assume that "masculine" titles refer to both women and men.

Inscriptions and tombstones portray girls who receive education and training in rhetoric, literacy, philosophy, lyre playing, and running. Thus it is possible to conclude from ancient sources that girls and women were

---

116. Pfuhl and Möbius, *Die ostgriechischen Grabreliefs*, 959. "Der Bildhauer zeigt, daß die Kleine schreibt und liest, nicht spielt, was der Hund offenbar wünscht" (245). Similarly, the memorial for Auphilia, a girl with a Roman name, depicts book rolls. This marker is from Akmonia in the province of Asia, between 135 and 175 C.E. Marc Waelkens, *Die kleinasiatischen Türsteine: Typologische und epigraphische Untersuchungen der kleinasiatischen Grabreliefs mit Scheintür* (Mainz am Rhein: P. von Zabern, 1986), 414.

117. J. H. Kent, *The Inscriptions, 1926-1950. Corinth: Results*, vol. 8, pt. 3 (Princeton: American School of Classical Studies at Athens, 1966), 70–73, no. 153.

118. Pleket, Epigraphica II, no 30.

students, achieved excellence in speaking or pursuing philosophy, and were accomplished musical and athletic competitors. Like their male counterparts, women from elite families received an education in subjects across the range of the classical gymnasium curriculum and could expect to display their achievements in the public forum and in their occupation.

Some would argue that these inscriptions represent a tiny fraction of the women who lived in antiquity. Many more men than women appear as victors of contests, displaying education, and competing in public. It may seem easy to dismiss a few examples as exceptions and to imagine that such women were quite rare. This argument is weak, however. Scholarship has shown repeatedly that our sources are not representative of the relative numbers of persons involved in activities. Ancient artists and writers were not concerned with leaving behind accurate sociological data. The portrayals that remain to us of persons of lower socioeconomic status and even high-ranking women have been projected through the dominant values and systems modeled as kyriarchy.

This discussion has highlighted some of the methodological problems inherent in analysis of the iconography, texts, and ideology of archaeological sources. Scholarship on ancient women has established principles of interpretation and identified constructions of femininity in texts on women's socioeconomic status. The sources used for historical reconstructions require critical analysis attentive to the interplay of rhetorical interests, genre, gender, wealth, ethnicity, and legal status. Progress relies on the assumption of kyriocentrism in the sources and analysis in terms of kyriarchy. Conventions that upheld the dominance of male patrons and heads of households determined depictions of women in occupations or as wives. Iconographic and literary sources portray elite women as passive and decorative even while legal sources and epigraphy depict them engaged in commercial transactions, intellectual competitions, and athletics. These findings highlight the need to investigate the range of available sources and to approach them with a critical historical framework, such as materialist feminism, that addresses the relationship between discourse and materiality.

Overview of the Study

GENDER AND STATUS

The following chapter begins by posing the question of wealthy women's religious status, then reviews scholarship on texts about women in religious groups, focusing on frameworks used to study women in ancient society. While a few scholars have proposed that elite women held positions of religious leadership in antiquity, a dominant stream maintains that women's secondary status precluded or limited such leadership. Significant differences among interpretations of the texts arise from different accounts of gender asymmetry; however, they all depend on a limited conception of social status. I also review and evaluate studies of religious status that have included economic analysis; these point to the need for a more robust model for socioeconomic analysis. The structures of patronage, marriage, and slavery are crucial in two ways: they supported and reproduced Roman kyriarchy and they determined women's socioeconomic status. Thus I argue that investigation of women's religious and socioeconomic status entails investigation of the institutions and ideologies of patronage, marriage, and slavery. This phase of the study occupies the following three chapters.

WEALTHY WOMEN AND HOUSEHOLD STATUS

The status of wealthy women in households forms the topic for this chapter. The literary texts I highlight are from the letters of Ignatius in which he addresses women in households, both wives and widows. In order to explore the significance of the household in antiquity, I analyze representations of wealthy freeborn women in households from sources identified in scholarship: funerary inscriptions, funerary iconography, confession inscriptions, and Xenophon's *Oikonomos*. I describe two types of representation of elite women: married women in their husband's households and widows in their own households. Portrayals of wealthy married women of Asia Minor resemble the figure of the Roman matron. I argue that sources depict wealthy single women, especially widows, as heads of households by displaying the same motifs that they deploy to portray male heads of households. With these depictions of women's status in households as matrons and widows, I return to the letters of Ignatius to Smyrna and discuss his advice to the bishop in Smyrna with respect to wealthy widows and wives.

WOMEN PATRONS

If wealthy women were religious leaders, they may have been involved in patronage, as wealthy men were. In this chapter, I continue the study of wealthy widows but shift from households to the institution of patronage. Studies of women's patronage of religious groups have focused on female figures in several texts and an inscription. Phoebe appears in Paul's Letter to the Romans, Rufina appears in an inscription from Smyrna, and Tryphaena plays a major role in the Acts of Thecla.[119] Scholars have discussed the significance of the two nouns that Paul applies to Phoebe: *prostatis* and *diakonos*. Investigation of these terms leads to questions about wealthy women's status as patrons and their potential for religious leadership. Interpretation of Phoebe's religious status hinges on understanding wealthy women's status in patronage.

Studies of elite women's patronage in Asia Minor have drawn primarily from honorary inscriptions. This genre of inscriptions represents the socioeconomic status of the local leaders of cities in Asia Minor under kyriarchal Roman rule. I select examples from this genre that are especially rich for investigating wealthy women's leadership and socioeconomic status as patrons. This analysis of representations of patronage contributes to my evaluation of scholarship about the inscription that presents Rufina as a wealthy widow with a title of Jewish leadership.

Scholarship on wealthy women's status as patrons of religious groups has also centered around wealthy women in the Apocryphal Acts, particularly Tryphaena in the *Acts of Paul and Thecla*. I analyze this literary portrayal of women's patronage and religious status and compare it to the portrayals presented in the epigraphic sources above.

Finally, I return to interpretation of Phoebe's status based on Paul's characterization of her activities and the representations of wealthy widows' status in the other sources I investigate.

WOMEN SLAVES

I have argued the necessity of determining women's religious status by studying their socioeconomic status in the institutions of household, patronage, and slavery. So far I have discussed wealthy unmarried women represented as heads of households and patrons of religious groups. In this chapter I take up the topic of slave women's status.

In the first section of this chapter, I focus on the socioeconomic status of women slaves in Asia Minor. I carefully examine a range of genres that promise the most material for socioeconomic analysis. The portrayals of slave women depend on their relationships with others in the representations. While some depictions, particularly visual depictions, emphasize slave women's subordination in the household, there are funerary inscriptions that highlight slave women's skills and occupational responsibilities. I analyze the

---

119. Respectively, these are Rom. 16:1-2, and *Acts of Paul and Thecla*, *CIJ* 2.741.

contradiction between these portrayals in the political economic model of kyriarchy.

With this understanding of the complex socioeconomic status of slave women, I turn to texts that portray slave women's status with respect to religious groups. A synagogue inscription presents the manumission of the woman Elpis; scholarly debate has focused on her relationship to the synagogue. Ignatius' *To Polycarp* indicates that religious groups in Smyrna financed slave manumission by using the group's common fund. Scholarly interpretation of these texts has not been informed by the study of wealthy slave women. While scholarship has emphasized the low status of slave women, some slave women worked in occupations that allowed them access to wealth and manumission. I argue that the wealth of a slave or freed woman may have enabled her access to patronage of religious groups.

SOCIOECONOMIC RELIGIOUS STATUS

In the concluding chapter I summarize this historical study focused on texts about women from Asia Minor in the first two centuries of the common era. I argue that scholarship on texts about women's religious status has been based on inadequate assessments of gender and women's status. Investigation of religious status requires investigation of the socioeconomic institutions of the household, patronage, and slavery. Careful examination of these institutions shows that women's socioeconomic status was conditioned by marital status, wealth, and occupational and legal status. The socioeconomic status determined by these factors similarly determined women's religious status.

This study relies on an approach that differs from those used in most scholarship on these texts. I rely on the model of kyriarchy developed through historical materialist feminist inquiry. I also select from a wider range of sources than that found in most scholarship in this area. This critical approach enables a more complete historical reconstruction of the worlds in which texts function. My aim is to improve understandings of women's agency by investigating how gender, marital and legal status, ethnicity, wealth, and religion are interrelated and embedded in economic and historiographic frameworks.

1

Gender and Status

In this chapter I review studies of texts about women's religious status in Asia Minor in the first two centuries of the common era. While a few scholars have proposed that wealthy women held positions of leadership in antiquity, a dominant stream in scholarship maintains that women's secondary status prevented or limited women's leadership. Important variations among interpretations of texts arise from different approaches to the analysis of women's history. My discussion is organized around these different approaches. Scholars have analyzed women's status in terms of prominent cultural values, an honor/shame paradigm, households, associations, patronage, and economics. This previous scholarship has informed the approach of my study in significant ways.

I will argue that investigation of women's religious status depends on investigation of women's status in households, slavery, and patronage. While scholarship has not ignored these socioeconomic institutions, the most widely known models have not adequately theorized gender in a framework that allows a thorough analysis of women's status. A better understanding of women's status in the ancient world requires a theory that situates the study of gender in the study of socioeconomic status. The discussions of methods and models in this chapter, along with the preceding introduction, provide necessary groundwork for investigating wealthy women's status in households and patronage.

REVIEW OF SCHOLARSHIP

A QUESTION OF STATUS

Elisabeth Schüssler Fiorenza has argued that women were leaders in ancient religious movements and suggested that "women's actual social-religious status must be determined by the degree of their economic autonomy and social roles rather than by ideological or prescriptive statements."[1] Schüssler Fiorenza addresses this point for freeborn elite women in particular, pointing to inscriptions that honor wealthy women as patrons of associations and patrons who performed leadership functions in these groups.[2] Similarly, Bernadette Brooten has examined women's titles of leadership in synagogue inscriptions.[3] She argues that women held the same status as men who held the same leadership titles. Many, if not all, of these persons were wealthy donors and patrons. According to Schüssler Fiorenza and Brooten, women's wealth mattered more than gender in determining their eligibility for leadership positions.

More recently, Joan Connelly's compelling history of priestesses in the Greek eastern Mediterranean has drawn from a wide range of sources to study women's roles.[4] Connelly links representations of women's religious leadership with an idealized image of femininity:

> Engagement in cult service was what a good woman did. As with spinning, this exercise was more than just a mark of virtue. It was a signifier of social and symbolic capital, of prestige and desirability, that came together to construct a feminine ideal. Cult service was inextricably linked to social status, family fortune, health, and wholeness, and thereby set a powerful archetype for female behavior.[5]

In Connelly's view, gender and wealth together determined "a feminine ideal." Family roles determined gender. A prestigious and desirable daughter made a marriage to ensure continuation of a family's elite status. This account leaves open the question of widowhood: once a woman's roles as daughter and wife concluded, how did wealth and gender determine her religious roles? I explore this question in this chapter and the following one. The variable of

---

1. Elisabeth Schüssler Fiorenza, *In Memory of Her: A Feminist Theological Reconstruction of Christian Origins* (New York: Crossroad, 1982), 109.

2. Ibid., 181–82, 250, 287, 290–91.

3. Bernadette J. Brooten, *Women Leaders in the Ancient Synagogue: Inscriptional Evidence and Background Issues* (Chico, CA: Scholars, 1982).

4. Joan Breton Connelly, *Portrait of a Priestess: Women and Ritual in Ancient Greece* (Princeton: Princeton University Press, 2007).

5. Ibid., 192.

fortune raises a question as well. With their focus on wealthy women, Schüssler Fiorenza, Brooten, and Connelly have left unexplored the relationship between religious status and gender ideology for non-elite women. This question becomes prominent in chapter 4, on slave women.

While most scholars seem to agree that gender limited women's religious leadership, a close look reveals that we still lack a consensus on why this might be the case. In general, studies of women's social religious status and potential for leadership have relied on an idea that women's social status was secondary to that of men of the same economic level. This secondary status has been theorized as part of various concepts, and I will address each in turn, beginning with the notion of status as integral to dominant cultural values.

CULTURAL IDEALS

There seems to be evidence in the ancient sources that cultural ideals ascribed secondary status to women. Paul Achtemeier has discussed "the general status" of women in his analysis of 1 Peter 3:1-7.

> The subordination of wives to husbands reflected in this passage must be seen against the background of the general status of women in the Hellenistic world of that time. Dominant among the elite was the notion that the woman was by nature inferior to the man. Because she lacked the capacity for reason that the male had, she was ruled rather by her emotions, and was as a result given to poor judgment, immorality, intemperance, wickedness, avarice; she was untrustworthy, contentious, and as a result, it was her place to obey. [The rest of the paragraph discusses legal status and marriage.] It is against this background that one must view the status of women reflected in the NT as a whole, and specifically in this passage in 1 Peter.[6]

Achtemeier marshals quotations from elite authors and examples from legal materials to document the subordination of women.[7] The commentary explains

---

6. Paul J. Achtemeier, *A Commentary on First Peter* (Hermeneia; Minneapolis: Fortress Press, 1996), 206–7.

7. Since the focus is on subordination and women's inferior social status in marriage, the discussion omits consideration of women's status outside of marriage. Achtemeier argues that marriage to a

how the biblical author reflects the dominant ethos of elite men. For scholars interested in women, many questions remain. What was the basis for these notions about women? How did the discourse and legal traditions operate to make women subservient? What were the effects of this subordination? What was the relationship between legal traditions and actual social practices?[8] It is not clear how the rhetoric of the letter's author represents historical situations. A focused analysis of women's status would address the relationship between rhetorical interests of the biblical author and reconstruction of the historical political socioeconomic context. Omission of this step tends to foreclose critical analysis of gender ideals, and discussions of religious criticisms of marriage, women's possibilities for separation and divorce, and practices among non-elites.

An association between women's secondary status and cultural ideals has appeared elsewhere in scholarship. John Elliott has quoted misogynist texts from a long list of authors to evince support for his assertion that "in the world of biblical antiquity, patriarchal structures and patriarchal mindsets were the order of the day."[9] This argument seems to gather weight as it lumps together "Greek, Roman, Israelite and Christian authors" and indeed "*every* known society from ancient to modern time," as marked by female subordination.[10] Nonetheless, Elliott provides evidence of a conflicting ideology when he writes, "The cult of Isis, because of its emphasis on the equality of females and males, held a particular attraction to women."[11] This caveat seems to imply that women as a group preferred gender equality, and that some people in "the Mediterranean culture" of biblical antiquity did challenge female subordination. This is an intriguing suggestion of cultural diversity. Since Elliott's account emphasizes attitudes and literary texts, questions about possible connections between different ideologies and actual socioeconomic relations remain to be explored.

Elsewhere, scholars have invoked cultural ideals to understand texts about slavery and the status of female and male slaves. In the history of interpretation of biblical texts, acceptance of dominant cultural ideals has supported acceptance

---

nonbeliever posed risks for a Christian woman, but he does not address alternatives to marriage, such as a Christian woman's separation and divorce from the nonbeliever.

8. Achtemeier, *Commentary on First Peter*, 207.

9. John H. Elliott, *A Home for the Homeless: A Sociological Exegesis of 1 Peter, Its Situation, and Strategy* (Philadelphia: Fortress Press, 1981), 591, 589.

10. Ibid., 590. The claim functions as the background environment to account for 1 Peter 3:1-7 and place it at a distance from ethical evaluation by contemporary feminists: "the Petrine author also is a child of his times" (596). Also 591.

11. Ibid., 584.

of slavery. Jerome Quinn has underlined obedience, order, and subordination in his discussion of the household code in the Letter to Titus.[12] He envisions the entire household as Christian; he seems to support the command to slaves "to be subject . . . in all matters," because he assumes that the Christian master or mistress would not command un-Christian acts.[13] Quinn focuses on the behavior of the slave and the repetition of the ideology of masters. According to Richard Horsley, elite authors did not question the system of slavery as "a fact of ancient life."[14] Nonetheless, slaves did run away and rebel, so some ancients questioned and resisted slavery for themselves.[15] Biblical commentaries have been slow to explore slave resistance and the role of discourse on slavery in exploitation. Rather than reproduce the prejudices of antiquity, a more thorough analysis would analyze their rhetorical constructions.[16]

Rhetorical constructions that reflect cultural ideals recur in biblical texts concerned with instructing wives and slaves. Achtemeier and Quinn allude to historical situations that may have triggered concern for the behavior of wives and slaves in the biblical texts. For Quinn, the culprit is characterized as "enthusiastic zeal," for "individual equality and freedom" and "unrealistic expectations."[17] For his part, Achtemeier notes, "That the Christian faith inherently meant equal status for women in the sight of God is evident from such a passage as Gal 3:28, and from the important role played by women in the early church."[18] This statement points toward interest in reconstruction of the historical situation. Up to now, commentaries have not investigated economic aspects of the cultural values of subordination of wives and of slaves.

---

12. Jerome D. Quinn, *The Letter to Titus* (Anchor Bible; New York: Doubleday, 1990), 137–50.

13. Ibid., 149. Yet, slaves are given similar instruction in 1 Tim. 6:1-2 with respect to non-Christian owners. Jennifer Glancy, in particular, has juxtaposed the sexual morals promulgated in biblical texts against the lack of moral freedom for slaves in Christian assemblies. Jennifer Glancy, *Slavery in Early Christianity* (Oxford: Oxford University Press, 2002), 49–70.

14. Richard A. Horsley, "The Slave Systems of Classical Antiquity and Their Reluctant Recognition by Modern Scholars," in *Semeia* 83/84 (1998): 59.

15. "Indeed, women, slaves, and members of other socially subordinated groups in the early Christian churches may have been less willing than Paul to leave the hierarchical social order intact during the interim before Christ's return." Sheila Briggs, "Slavery and Gender," in *On the Cutting Edge: The Study of Women in Biblical Worlds*, ed. Jane Schaberg, Alice Bach, and Esther Fuchs (New York: Continuum, 2004), 186.

16. For example, Quinn cites references to passages that name slaves as thieves, but misses the chance to discuss the phenomenon in a context of power relations between masters and slaves. Quinn, *Letter to Titus*, 149. He evinces little interest in distinguishing between women and men slaves.

17. Ibid., 138 and 148.

18. Achtemeier, *Commentary on First Peter*, 207.

Achtemeier alludes to discrepancies in women's status when he notes that women inherited, held property, and "acquired legal independence and full right to participate in business"(207). These aspects of women's socioeconomic status seem inconsistent with the idea of the women's subordinate status. And this suggests areas for investigation: How would a woman's socioeconomic status affect her household status as a wife or a single woman in this religious group?

The attribution of women's secondary status to dominant cultural ideals leaves us with questions about the move from text to historical reconstruction. We need a critical analysis of assumptions entailed in moving from text to historical reconstruction. Many commentators read biblical texts from the perspective of the master/husband/father. This viewpoint leaves ancient wives and slaves as secondary persons and marginal topics. We need a different perspective to help us understand free women and slaves as actors and agents in their own right.

A second major group of scholars have attempted to explain women's status in a specific cultural system.

HONOR/SHAME

Methods and models drawn from the social sciences have informed the anthropological construction of honor/shame in "the Mediterranean culture." A recent example is the study by Carolyn Osiek and Margaret MacDonald, *A Woman's Place*.[19] These authors have proposed to use "the cultural values of honor and shame," based on their meaning in a Mediterranean context, as one of three key assumptions of their investigation of early Christian women.[20] Osiek and Macdonald continue to use this cultural model while citing literature that questions the value of the Mediterranean model. One of the critics is Mark Golden, who concluded his review of the literature by questioning "the idea of the Mediterranean as a culture-area."[21] Other critics of the model have raised the issue of method. Mary Ann Tolbert has argued that biblical anthropological studies "tend to invert the social science method; rather than making the theory the conjectural topic of investigation, and the social data the arena of proof,

19. Carolyn Osiek and Margaret MacDonald with Janet Tulloch, *A Woman's Place: House Churches in Earliest Christianity* (Minneapolis: Fortress Press, 2006), 233.

20. Ibid., 7–9. The authors associate honor/shame with patriarchy and with a different set of standards for females.

21. Mark Golden, "The Uses of Cross-Cultural Comparison in Ancient Social History," *Echos du Monde Classique* 36, no. 11 (1992): 331.

New Testament explorations have often made the textual data the topic of investigation, and the theory or model the vehicle of proof."[22] Indeed, Osiek and MacDonald take the model of honor/shame as a "key assumption" with which to interpret the evidence: references to the "character of the culture," or to the "Mediterranean world," appear to assert and account for differences between women and men.[23]

Tolbert raises another problem for using the analytic of honor/shame: "Concrete social relations may vary considerably from the symbolic constructions of gender upheld by social ideology."[24] In this case, the relations between men and women may have varied considerably from those upheld by the ideology of honor and shame. Osiek and MacDonald describe slaves as, "by definition," "totally lacking in honor."[25] On the other hand, the honor ascribed to wealthy women (and men) was routinely engraved in stone and displayed in public to recognize benefactors and office-holders. If slave women could not earn honor while many wealthy women did, then the construct honor/shame does not do enough to explain women's status. Schüssler Fiorenza has noted that the honor/shame system is only one feature of the "kyriarchal ethos of antiquity."[26] Other features include age, family, economic status, ethnicity, legal status, and sexual preference. Thus the dualistic construction of honor/shame in gender terms requires modification in an analytic framework that also includes factors such as legal status and access to socioeconomic resources. Analyzing these factors together would allow a better understanding of women's status.

HOUSEHOLDS

Some histories of religious groups describe women's status through use of a social model that locates women almost exclusively in a traditional household. For instance, John Elliott's analysis of the community addressed in 1 Peter has centered on the distinctive character of the group, and the author's descriptions of this character in terms of a household. "It is from a universal interest in the implications and applications of the household in a great variety of political, economic, social, and religious spheres of life that the image of the household of God in 1 Peter derives its socio-religious significance and its emotional

22. Mary Ann Tolbert, "Social, Sociological, and Anthropological Methods," in *Searching the Scriptures*, vol. 1, *A Feminist Introduction*, ed. Elisabeth Schüssler Fiorenza (New York: Crossroad, 1993), 266.

23. Osiek and MacDonald, *A Woman's Place*, 13 and16.

24. Tolbert, ""Social, Sociological, and Anthropological Methods," 265.

25. Osiek and MacDonald, *A Woman's Place*, 97. Imperial slaves should be an exception to this rule.

26. Schüssler Fiorenza, *Jesus*, 98.

power."[27] In Elliott's argument, the household provides the model for the group's organizational features, including authority, leadership, roles, relationships, and responsibilities.[28] In this traditional household model, women are seen as subordinate, whether they are free wives or slaves.[29] The ancient household was a primary institution of the imperial socioeconomic system.[30] Thus its political and economic significance in its historical context is crucial to reconstructing its use in 1 Peter. Elliott's analysis could be extended to critically examine slavery, marriage, and the imperial use of household in colonization. The correlations between women's socioeconomic status in the household and their religious status require more attention.

In modern socioeconomic theory, household has been distinguished from market, and historians have adopted these concepts. Ekkehard and Wolfgang Stegemann have contrasted the ancient "embedded" economy with the modern "detached" economy.[31] They name the household as "the most important ancient economic institution in which economic behavior was embedded."[32] Yet they also assert that the rights and powers that a head of the household had with respect to wife, children, and slaves cannot be claimed as "economic" matters. Thus "markets" appear prominently, in the title of a section, while marriage fails to rate notice as an economic institution. Given this understanding, it is not surprising that women do not appear in the labels on the diagram of the social pyramid (see Figure 1).[33] This analysis has the effect of producing the erasure of women in the economic system.

The omission of marriage from socioeconomic analysis has engendered a distinction between market and domestic economies that appears in neoclassical and Marxist socioeconomic theory.[34] Feminist economists have criticized forms of socioeconomic theory that replicate gender constructions unreflectively.[35]

---

27. Elliott, *Home for the Homeless*, 221.

28. Ibid., 188–89. The sense of religious group as civic assembly is not significant for Elliott's reconstruction.

29. Elliott does not distinguish between rhetorical goals of the author and possibilities for the historical situation that can be reconstructed from the letter.

30. See discussion of imperial ideology in Introduction.

31. Ekkehard W. Stegemann and Wolfgang Stegemann, *The Jesus Movement: A Social History of Its First Century*, trans. O. C. Dean (Minneapolis: Fortress Press, 1999), 18.

32. Ibid., 18.

33. Ibid., 72. Women do appear in the discussion, however, as belonging to the stratum of their husbands or fathers (66–67).

34. Hannelore Schröder, "The Economic Impoverishment of Mothers Is the Enrichment of Fathers," in *Women, Work and Poverty*, ed. Schüssler Fiorenza and Anne Carr (Concilium; Edinburgh: T. & T. Clark, 1987), 14. She also asserts that feminist economists' "analysis has to start with the domestic economy and

Household has become associated with women, domestic labor, childcare, unskilled labor, and consumption rather than production.[36] Women as workers are perceived as more concerned with family matters than men, thus less committed and less rational, transient, unskilled or semi-skilled. The classification of the work of motherhood as biological rather than socioeconomic has reified an essentialized view of the division of labor. And the historiography of (male) labor has paid little attention to the dependence of subsistence-level families on the labor of women and children within the household.[37] The postindustrial dichotomy of domestic and market with its attendant gender assumptions has thereby overdetermined historical reconstructions of ancient households. This has affected our understandings of household systems such as marriage and slavery.

Analysis of women's socio-religious status requires investigation of the socioeconomic status of women in marriage since both are linked to the household. Women's work, including the system of slavery, must be part of historical analysis of the household as an economic, social, or religious organization. The relationship between households and religious groups is not simple; accurate historical reconstruction requires attention to a wide variety of sources with focus on the distinctive features of the different sources.

The situation in the genuine letters of Paul should be investigated separately from the contexts of the letters penned by Paul's followers. Schüssler Fiorenza has argued that the structures of the traditional household were not those of the early missionary movement. The model Schüssler Fiorenza has elaborated for reconstruction of the missionary movement in the cities of Asia Minor features both missionary agents and local associations in house churches,

the domestic dominance fixed by marriage-, family-, and inheritance laws. The historical process is indispensable, for economy begins in the home (*oikos*)." Ibid., 13.

35. Based on her analysis of scholarship on person and choices, Paula England argues that the distinction between family and market owes its appearance in economic theory to hidden assumptions related to gender. England, "Separative and Soluble Selves: Dichotomous Thinking in Economics," in *Feminist Economics Today: Beyond Economic Man*, ed. Marianne A. Ferber and Julie A. Nelson (Chicago: University of Chicago Press, 2003), 33–48. Feminist ethnographers have introduced analyses of intrahousehold and interhousehold dynamics. "Subsistence farming was too often production when men did it and reproduction when women did it." Gracia Clark, "Introduction," in *Gender at Work in Economic Life*, ed. Gracia Clark (Walnut Creek, CA: AltaMira, 2003), xi.

36. M. Thea Sinclair, "Women, Work and Skill: Economic Theories and Feminist Perspectives," in *Working Women: International Perspectives on Labour and Gender Ideology*, ed. Redclift and Sinclair (London: Routledge, 1991), 3–13. Ava Baron, *Work Engendered: Toward a New History of American Labor* (Ithaca, NY: Cornell University Press, 1991) 6–15.

37. Baron, *Work Engendered*, 15. See discussion in preceding chapter.

with the full participation and leadership of women in both areas.[38] The way women are mentioned in the genuine Pauline correspondence indicates that the status of these women was equal to that of Paul, and that they were independent of Paul.[39] The titles Paul uses for women in the missionary movement and house churches do not refer to them with the terms that reflect their sexual status or gender roles, such as widow, wife, or virgin.[40] Also, the house church of Prisca and Aquila suggests that the house churches were organized as religious cults or private associations since the texts note Prisca and Aquila's travel but neither household nor family.[41] The distinctions between religious association and traditional household that are present in the Pauline correspondence are less clear in other sources.[42] Indeed, according to Elliott's study of 1 Peter (above), the household provides the model for a religious organization.

In harmony with Elliott, Osiek and MacDonald observe, "It is fair to say that by the latter decades of the first century, Christianity became grafted onto conventional patterns of family life in some church circles."[43] In contrast, Yuko Taniguchi has analyzed 1 Timothy and reconstructed a possible historical situation in which the author of 1 Timothy sought to impose household organization on a community operating according to the norms of a voluntary association.[44] This reconstruction depends on a contrast between the assembly rhetoric associated with an idea of egalitarian relationships among siblings versus the household rhetoric involving hierarchical order in terms of age, gender, and class.[45] Taniguchi applies socio-rhetorical-historical criticism to 1 Timothy in order to reconstruct the possible community and situation addressed by the letter.[46] In her interpretation, "the wo/men benefactors were leaders with authority in the democratic association of the *ekklesia*" (26). She further suggests that benefaction in the community could have created equal access to decision-making for all the members, including widows, elders, and

38. Schüssler Fiorenza, *In Memory of Her*, 168.

39. The women include Prisca, Apphia, Phoebe, Junia, and four more in Rom.16:6 and 12, plus Euodia and Syntyche.

40. Schüssler Fiorenza, *Memory*, 169.

41. Ibid., 180.

42. I return below to the question of whether group organization resembled either association or household.

43. Osiek and MacDonald, *A Woman's Place*, 233.

44. Yuko Taniguchi, *To Lead Quiet and Peaceable Lives: Rhetorical Analysis of the First Letter of Timothy* (Harvard University Th.D. Dissertation, 2002).

45. Ibid., 156.

46. In contrast to this method, traditional historical criticism positions the text of 1 Timothy as more transparent to reconstruction and reduces the level of conflict by adopting the author's perspective.

slaves (156). Taniguchi's study draws on a contrast between (free and slave) women's status in a voluntary association and such women's status in a household. The type of analysis performed by Taniguchi allows one to distinguish among rhetorical constructions embedded in the text and possibilities for historical reconstruction of the situation in which that text intervenes. The interpretation preserves tensions among proponents of different organizational systems in the religious movement. While the household has played a preeminent role in scholarship on women's status, an understanding of women's religious status requires study of voluntary associations as well.

ASSOCIATIONS

Philip Harland has studied associations in Asia Minor extensively, including early Christian and Jewish ones.[47] He argues persuasively for many lines of continuity among these groups. He does not, however, specifically inquire about the roles of patrons and of women. Many other interpreters have also emphasized the similarities between Christian and Jewish and other religious groups. Reggie Kidd's commentary has centered on wealth and class analysis in the Pastoral letters.[48] He concludes that the social setting of the community of the Pastorals was the "upper strata of the imperial municipalities."[49] His main concern is with the relationship between benefactors, conceived as wealthy male Christians, and the community of 1 Timothy as a voluntary association. In this discussion of women, the possibilities inherent in economic status are subordinated to women's status in the traditional household (100–106). Kidd assumes the presence of wealthy women but sees only men as patrons of early Christian and Jewish communities. However, it is not clear that patronage was restricted, and scholars have disagreed about the role of patrons.

Studies on the status of wealthy women as patrons have drawn on inscriptions from Asia Minor. These texts present numerous instances of office-holding by women. Tessa Rajak and David Noy have discussed benefaction by women who supported synagogues, and they assess women's roles: "The synagogue service is not the correct setting for that [functional] equality, and the contribution of women, just as that of men, must be envisaged as patronal and perhaps ceremonial rather than religious."[50] The authors do not explain

47. Philip Harland, *Associations, Synagogues and Congregations: Claiming a Place in Ancient Mediterranean Society* (Minneapolis: Augsburg Fortress Press, 2003).

48. Reggie M. Kidd, *Wealth and Beneficence in the Pastoral Epistles: A "Bourgeois" Form of Early Christianity?* (SBL Dissertation Series 122; Atlanta: Scholars, 1990).

49. Kidd, *Wealth and Beneficence*, 156.

their understanding of "religious," but the usage implies that a religious role is distinct from a patronal role.

William Countryman has advocated a similar assessment in his evaluation of the community of the Pastoral Epistles. He argues that the patronal role was limited to the donation of funds; donors abdicated administrative control.[51] Rajak and Noy argue that the evidence used to establish the role of the head of synagogue has been misinterpreted in some scholarship, and that this office, just as those in other associations in Greek and Roman cities, was "honor-driven."[52] It seems that having wealth was the primary qualification for the position. Indeed, scholars agree that high socioeconomic status was a routine prerequisite for office-holding in the ancient world.[53] However, it is not clear whether or not fulfilling the function of donor precluded the possibility of acting in other functions. The conclusion seems to rely on a modern assumption that these ancient people understood social roles as distinct from religious ones.

A discussion of women's religious patronage appears in the history by Osiek and MacDonald, who again provide a handy reference for trends in scholarship. This study recognizes as patrons the religious women Phoebe, Tavia, Alke, and some women in the audience of 1 Timothy.[54] In their detailed discussion of the source texts for "Christian women who host house churches," Osiek and MacDonald situate these patrons in a community organized along the lines of the household.[55] While they maintain that "in early Christianity there was little difference between the patronage of men and women" (219), they qualify this assessment elsewhere in their discussion of the activities of patrons (248). In their elaboration of the mechanics of patronage, presiding at the communal meal appears as an activity distinct from reading and teaching after the meal.[56] Referring to 1 Tim. 2:11-15, Osiek and MacDonald see women's teaching as eclipsed by "traditional norms that sought to silence

50. Tessa Rajak and David Noy, "*Archisynagogoi*: Office, Title and Social Status in the Greco-Jewish Synagogue," *Journal of Roman Studies* 83 (1993): 87.

51. L. William Countryman, *The Rich Christian in the Church of the Early Empire: Contradictions and Accommodations* (Lewiston, NY: Edwin Mellen, 1980), 164–65.

52. Rajak and Noy, "*Archisynagogoi*," 84–86.

53. The Roman system in the eastern Mediterranean could combine benefaction with minimum training for elite officials because slaves were an important source of expertise in administrative tasks. However, it does not follow that the duties of such offices were not considered political.

54. Osiek and MacDonald, *A Woman's Place*, 214–18.

55. Osiek and MacDonald shared Elliott's focus on women in the household. They develop a reconstructive model based on women's presence in the household as the "unifying element." Ibid., 243.

56. Osiek and MacDonald suggest that the presider at the communal meal might select the "invited expert" teacher and facilitate the conversation. Ibid., 163.

women in public functions."[57] Implied in this argument regarding women's teaching is that men patrons would not be restricted in the same sense. In this view, some religious leadership was open to women patrons, that which involved food and meals, while other areas, which involved reading, teaching, and preaching, were restricted. Thus these scholars envision a significant difference between women's and men's patronal leadership. The basis for this difference is not the capacity of the patron per se, but a gender ideal in which women are silent in public.[58] However, archaeological records suggest that wealthy women appeared frequently in public offices and monuments. Hence, one cannot assume that they did not do so also in religious assemblies.

The question of whether or how wealthy women's roles differed from that of men has appeared in studies of Asia Minor in the Roman era. Riet van Bremen has conducted an extensive study of women who held offices and provided benefaction in Roman Asia Minor.[59] She argues that representations of wealthy women patrons during the early empire were marked by the elite's self-representation as oriented toward family, in concert with the example set by the imperial family in Rome.[60] For both men and women, the vocabulary and images of family became the currency for establishing the legitimacy of leadership.[61] The representation of elite women in families in the imperial era is intertwined with the representation of ruling. Thus an analysis of women's patronage requires scrutiny of the overall sociopolitical context.[62]

57. The reconstructive model is one of decline for the status of women, "the restriction of women's leadership opportunities," as time went on. Osiek and MacDonald, *A Woman's Place*, 234. However, these authors also name a number of female teachers who appear in early Christian sources.

58. Iteration of women's silence in the biblical canon may testify to an ongoing controversy surrounding women's speech. Another possible reading of the same passages recreates them in a framework of conflict between the proponents of women's teaching authority and those who favored women's silent submission.

59. Riet van Bremen, *The Limits of Participation: Women and Civic Life in the Greek East in the Hellenistic and Roman Periods* (Amsterdam: J. C. Gieben, 1996).

60. Ibid., 165. Beth Severy explored imperial implications in household rhetoric in Roman sources, and suggested that portrayals of family life under the emperors arose from "the politicization of the family in the Augustan period, and continuing public status of the imperial family as an institution of the empire. The most important public figures of the day were evaluated and presented in the context of their familial relationships." Severy, *Augustus and the Family at the Birth of the Roman Empire* (New York: Routledge, 2003), 249.

61. Bremen, *Limits of Participation*, 163. The right to rule was based on ideological constructs and the "presentation of these aspects in a coherent self-image on the public stage."

62. Patronage by men in antiquity has been most often located in the context of friendships, civic organizations, and voluntary associations.

Studies on women's status have raised questions about the organizational structure of religious groups. Scholarship on "Christian" groups has been divided on whether their model of social organization more closely resembled a household or a voluntary association. The two forms of organization embody different views of the ekklesia in its internal relations and structures of authority and leadership. The sources indicate that the form of social organization was contested in some groups.[63] However, the ekklesia in the uncontested Pauline letters resembled associations to both insiders and outsiders.[64]

In sum, women's status has been inadequately theorized as determined by dominant cultural ideals, honor/shame, the traditional household, or gendered spheres of activity (such as patronage). We have seen that understanding the household context is critical for determining women's status in marriage and slavery. Since wealthy women were also patrons of religious associations, we also need to investigate the workings of patronage. Thus the question of women's religious status is complicated by the need to study socioeconomic institutions: marriage, slavery, and patronage.

SOCIOECONOMIC ANALYSIS

Steven Friesen has emphasized the need for socioeconomic analysis with his critique of use of the category "social status" in contemporary "capitalist criticism."[65] According to Friesen, mainstream New Testament studies discuss social status in terms of individuals and their social and psychological issues rather than the economic basis of social status.[66] Speaking of the field generally,

63. On 1 Timothy, see Taniguchi, *Quiet and Peaceable*.

64. Richard S. Ascough, "The Thessalonian Christian Community as a Professional Voluntary Association," *Journal of Biblical Literature* 119, no. 2 (Summer 2000): 311–28. Ascough has also suggested the term "elective social formations," in a talk at Harvard Divinity School, May 11, 2007. See the many essays in John S. Kloppenborg and Stephen G. Wilson, eds., *Voluntary Associations in the Graeco-Roman World* (London: Routledge, 1996). And most recently, Philip Harland, *Associations, Synagogues and Congregations*.

65. Stephen J. Friesen, "Poverty in Pauline Studies: Beyond the So-called New Consensus," in *Journal for the Study of the New Testament* 26, no. 3 (2004): 323–61. Capitalist criticism reflects the commitments of its interpreters, "from Diessmann's perspective of bourgeois industrial capitalism of the early twentieth century, to the new consensus perspective of bourgeois consumer capitalism in the late twentieth century. At both ends of the century, the dominant interpretations of Paul's assemblies fit comfortably with their respective contemporary, dominant, Western ideologies. As a result, the discipline of Pauline studies in the early twenty-first century appears to have no interest in why people were poor or how the Pauline assemblies dealt with economic injustice" (336). Exceptions include literature cited in the following section.

Friesen declares, "The discipline does not validate economic inquiry."[67] Fortunately, a few studies of women in religious groups have already begun the work of economic analysis.

Some scholars have subordinated gender in their socioeconomic analyses. Luise Schottroff has focused on the poor as a corrective to the histories of early Christianity from both socialist theorists and their antisocialist critics.[68] According to Schottroff, socialist theorists construct the religious groups as composed of the poor, but fail to see a revolutionary precursor to socialism. Antisocialists, on the other hand, ignore socialist scholarship and focus on the wealthy. "My critique is not directed against the assumption that rich women and educated men were part of the Christian communities but against the fact that, on account of them, the majority of the uneducated, poor, and weak (in the sense of 1 Cor. 1:26ff.) becomes invisible and the gospel of the poor and the option for women disappears."[69] A sustained focus on the poor, and concentration on Christians as revolutionaries, mark Schottroff's analysis. Her socioeconomic examination of differential access to resources has contributed many insights. However, this approach emphasizes access to wealth at the expense of gender analysis, a move that tends to eclipse investigation of the full range of possibilities for women's status in religious groups.

A weakness in Schottroff's approach appears in her discussion of slave women. For instance, where the text of the Acts of the Apostles indicates that Lydia's entire household was baptized (Acts 16:15), Schottroff accepts the author's representation of the slaveholder's dominance. She assumes that female slaves would have experienced Christian slaveholders as liberating. "A Christian owner, female or male, would hardly have been able to prevent them from living in sexual abstinence, in marital fidelity, or in divorce. What the ancient church has to say about Christian female slaves matches this picture. When they belonged to a Christian owner, they could expect to be granted free time and sexual independence."[70] However, support for this opinion is absent. In contrast, Jennifer Glancy's work has argued persuasively that Christian

66. Ibid., 334. Wayne Meeks's work on early urban Christians contextualizes religion in a study of society that emphasizes adherents' social formation and belief. Meeks cites Max Weber and Moses Finley for the development of the category "social status," which is crucial to his analysis. See Wayne Meeks, *The First Urban Christians: The Social World of the Apostle Paul* (New Haven: Yale University Press, 1983), 53.

67. Friesen, "Poverty in Pauline Studies," 335.

68. Luise Schottroff, *Lydia's Impatient Sisters: A Feminist Social History of Early Christianity*, trans. Barbara and Martin Rumscheidt (Louisville: Westminster John Knox, 1995), 150.

69. Ibid., 150.

70. Ibid., 126.

slaveholders would not have viewed the beating or sexual use of a slave as immoral.[71]

Schottroff's conception of the "option for the poor" and women in biblical texts derives from her subordination of gender in a liberation-theological perspective based on Marxist class analysis. Kwok Pui-lan has noted that an adequate analysis should include the phenomenon of "indigenous elites employed as colonial agents."[72] Even as a convert, a slaveholder retained the privilege protected by the Roman Empire that allowed her to dominate slaves. This example illustrates the need to rethink socioeconomic concepts so that they include gender, access to wealth, legal, and colonial status as interlocking oppressions.

In other approaches to the history of religious women, the model used to represent the socioeconomic system of the Roman Empire cannot account for nuances present in evidence about the Roman system. Ivoni Richter Reimer's reconstructions of women's socioeconomic status have provided many valuable references for this study even though her concern for "what the story teaches us" concedes too much influence to the rhetorical shaping of women in Luke-Acts.[73] She portrays Prisca of Ephesus as an artisan-class tentmaker and missionary alongside Paul.[74] Her model of the Roman economy features a split between a few elite and masses of the poor; this model is the basis for her critique of exegetes who place Prisca and Aquila among the "well-to-do," in contrast to early exegetical tradition.[75] Reimer refers to inscriptions and other material remains to reconstruct persuasively the context and socioeconomic status of female laborers in the eastern Roman Empire. In her view, early Christian women were offering support in their homes and doing missionary work; they were independent heads of churches and active in trades.[76] All belonged to low socioeconomic levels. Her reconstruction of women depends on a socioeconomic model that does not account for middle levels of property ownership. Thus Reimer does not explore the possibilities for propertied women and their access to patronage in religious associations.

71. Glancy, *Slavery in Early Christianity*, 39–70, 130–56.

72. Kwok Pui-lan, "Roundtable Discussion: Anti-Judaism and Postcolonial Biblical Interpretation," *Journal of Feminist Studies in Religion* 20, no. 1 (2004): 99–106, quotation on 105.

73. See the account of Sapphira's moral culpability in Ivoni Richter Reimer, *Women in the Acts of the Apostles: A Feminist Liberation Perspective*, trans. Linda M. Maloney (Minneapolis: Fortress Press, 1995), 14–16.

74. In common with Schottroff, Reimer reads the Alexandrian text of Acts as more primary and less misogynist than the Western text. Reimer, *Women in the Acts*, 197–99.

75. Ibid., 199–200.

76. Ibid., 250–52.

Finally, another group of publications conceives gender unreflectively as secondary status. James Malcolm Arlandson emphasizes women's socioeconomic status in his study of rising and falling motifs in Luke-Acts.[77] Following the Lukan author, Arlandson writes of Prisca as a teacher of Apollos but fails to describe her as a leader or "religionist."[78] He does not consider the possibility of women's religious leadership. Commenting on Luke 8:1-3, Arlandson views with disfavor "the idea that the women are patrons of Jesus and the twelve, as if Jesus and the twelve depended on them. Jesus and the twelve have a special place in the kingdom; it is not likely that they would be depicted as permanently depending on anyone—male or female—but God."[79] Arlandson's view of women's secondary status seems to accompany a stereotypical view of religious practice. "Jewish women hearing of Mary sitting at Jesus' feet may have been surprised, since it was indeed rare for women to do this. But Gentile women hearing of Mary would not have been surprised, since in their social experience women followed itinerant philosophers."[80] This perspective suggests that Jewish women were less likely to be educated than other women, but Arlandson offers no support for this view. This example again illustrates the need to read a text's rhetoric critically for gender, access to wealth, and race or ethnicity.

The main element still missing from this body of scholarship is an investigation of women's status with an adequate analytical socioeconomic model. Schottroff, Reimer, and Arlandson are concerned to show how religious conversion alleviates the harsh conditions suffered by the masses of poor women depicted in biblical texts.[81] This goal curtails the possibility of directing sufficient critical attention to women's status, since men remain at the center of biblical theological activity. Why were women seen as lower status (if, or when, they were)? On what basis was status conceived? What were the structures of domination that determined and perpetuated women's socioeconomic situation? How were relations of power maintained? And, how do the answers to all these questions change for wives, widows, slave women, wealthy women, Romans, and provincials?

I have argued that a critical analysis of women's religious status requires investigation of the principal institutions that affected women in religious

---

77. James Malcolm Arlandson, *Women, Class, and Society in Early Christianity: Models from Luke-Acts* (Peabody, MA: Hendrickson, 1997).

78. Ibid., 125, 146, and 193.

79. Ibid., 163 n. 14.

80. Ibid., 138.

81. None focus on historical reconstruction of the possibilities for women's leadership.

associations: marriage, slavery, and patronage. While scholarship has not ignored these institutions entirely, we have not yet developed frameworks adequate to theorize gender in socioeconomic analysis. The analysis must also allow us to think about how women's status depended on the ways economic institutions overlapped and intertwined. For instance, how did a woman's household or legal status affect her patronage? Furthermore, study of these institutions must be contextualized in an analysis of the larger political, social, and economic situation in colonized Asia Minor. Reconstruction of the socioeconomic history of women requires development of a socioeconomic model that foregrounds and integrates gender, differential access to economic resources, as well as marital, legal, ethnic, and colonial status.

Perusal of a recent publication on socioeconomics and early Christianity demonstrates the need for a specifically materialist socioeconomic framework. The argument in Bruce Longenecker's *Remember the Poor* is based on socioeconomic analysis and, in this respect, represents a positive step for biblical studies.[82] Longenecker builds on a theme of "elite acquisitiveness" in his description of the Roman economy. Although Longenecker implies systemic exploitation, that critique is softened by its characterization as acquisitiveness. "[F]or our purposes, the sole feature that needs to be highlighted is the acquisitive character of power in advanced agrarian cultures in general, with the elite being well-placed to use their power to acquire the resources of others." One might deduce from this articulation that socioeconomic inequities resulted principally from greed, theft, and corrupt magistrates. Materialist analysis shifts attention to political and socioeconomic systems. "One of the key concepts of historical materialism is this recognition that the production of life is a *systemic* process, one that takes place through a system of related activities. Historically, these activities have taken the form of divisions of labor or relations of production, organizations of state and of consciousness or culture."[83] A feminist materialist analysis of the Roman economy investigates how precisely the elite exploited others and extracted surplus through such *systems* as slavery, the household, and patronage. Longenecker's discussion of "the economic attractions of Paul's communities" could be nuanced by addressing how gender, marital status, and legal status (among other factors) overlapped to produce socioeconomic status.[84] In kyriarchy, we have a framework adequate to perform

82. Bruce Longenecker, *Remember the Poor: Paul, Poverty, and the Greco-Roman World* (Grand Rapids: Eerdmans, 2010), 19–35.

83. Rosemary Hennessy and Chrys Ingraham, "Reclaiming Anticapitalist Feminism," in Hennessy and Ingraham, eds., *Materialist Feminism: A Reader in Class, Difference, and Women's Lives* (New York: Routledge, 1997), 4.

robust analysis of the Roman Empire since kyriarchy predicates a materialist feminist analytical framework.

CONCLUSION

In this chapter I have reviewed studies of texts about women's religious status in Asia Minor in the first two centuries of the common era. A few scholars have proposed that wealthy women held positions of religious leadership in antiquity while the majority maintain that women's secondary status precluded or limited such leadership.

Scholars have discussed women's subordination in terms of dominant cultural values, honor/shame, household roles, and patronage. However, none of these has proven complete because none has fully investigated socioeconomic aspects of women's status in households and patronage. While some studies have included socioeconomic analysis, each omits some factors crucial to the determination of women's status. Thus the question of wealthy women's religious leadership remains open because prevailing frameworks have not developed a robust analysis of gender.

Histories of women's secondary status have relied on analytical models in which gender appears to be fixed in the landscape of the historical milieu. In contrast, the approach I proposed in the preceding chapter in the framework of materialist feminism views gender as a fluid variable, and thus asks of each historical source, "How does this source present or construct gender?" In addition, since gender is just one of the preconstructed systems operational in kyriocentrism, a materialist feminist approach simultaneously investigates other ascriptions of status, whether configured as race, ethnicity, class, wealth, age, or legal status. Modeling social relations as kyriarchy allows analysis of multiple factors of oppression in an interlocking system of material economic and political relations. Thus the analytical question is more accurately framed as, "How does this source represent gender in interaction with wealth, ethnicity, marital, and legal status in material relations?"

Rosemary Hennessy's materialist feminist theory predicts that investigation of particular historical economic and political relations will uncover contradictions and ambiguities that the iteration of kyriocentric ideology obscures (since competing ideologies are always present). More specifically for this study, the theory hypothesizes that analysis of presentations of women's status in marriage, patronage, and slavery with respect to kyriarchy will reveal

---

84. Longenecker, *Remember the Poor*, 259–78.

that women's status varied with their positions in these institutions as gender interacted with wealth, ethnicity, marital, legal, and occupational status. The following chapters pursue this investigation.

2

Wealthy Women and Household Status

I have argued that determinations of women's religious status depend on understanding women's status in such socioeconomic institutions as the household, patronage, and slavery. In this chapter I investigate relationships among household position, socioeconomic status, and religious status for (relatively) wealthy women who lived in Asia Minor in the first two centuries of the common era.[1] Studies of households have contributed through analysis of women's status in terms of honor/shame, family relationships, or gendered spheres of activity, yet we still need a more comprehensive understanding of how women's socioeconomic positions varied within households. In contrast to most of the earlier studies, this one draws upon inscriptions and iconography as well as literary texts, and it highlights differences in representations of women with respect to their households. Instead of harmonizing different portrayals of wealthy women, my approach highlights tension and variation in order to make status distinctions more visible.

Understanding women's religious status depends on understanding their status in households since some religious groups met in households and some texts associate household organization with the organizational structures of religious groups.[2] The household was the primary socioeconomic unit throughout society. In a preceding chapter I discussed affinities between the household and imperial politics in terms of governing hierarchies and the Augustan propaganda of paternalism and concord or peace. Household relations were also fundamental to the legal regulation of property transfer in marriage and inheritance.[3] Taking note of these political and legal aspects of the

---

1. By "households with property," and "wealthy women," I refer to people who occupied a middle position on Friesen's poverty scale, somewhat above subsistence level but well below imperial elites (discussed in the preceding chapters). This group had the resources to carve funerary monuments and to leave records of their property transactions in legal sources.

2. I return to this in the following discussion.

household both underscores the importance of determining women's household status and foreshadows some of the complexities that arise in this investigation. Accurate interpretation of texts that associate women's status in religious groups with households must take into account socioeconomic, political, and legal dimensions of households. Thus I seek to analyze the sources with reference to the model of kyriarchy, a comprehensive representation of Roman systems.

In kyriarchal structures of socioeconomic and political status, women who had access to socioeconomic resources enjoyed a relatively high (elite) position. I will argue that socioeconomic status varied further within this group with factors such as age, legal and marital status, ethnicity, education, and training. Where legal status can be determined, the women in this chapter were freeborn (but the sources do not always distinguish between freeborn and freed persons). Nearly all freeborn women married early in their childbearing years.[4] Demographic studies indicate that elite women often survived their older husbands to become widows.[5] I examine representations of propertied wives and widows in order to investigate relationships between women's household status and their socioeconomic status. Analysis of these representations suggests possibilities for historical understandings of wealthy wives and widows in religious texts.

My sources for the study of wealthy wives and widows include iconography, inscriptions, and literary texts. I have selected texts that indicate that wealthy women's household status impacted their religious status. I highlight the two letters of Ignatius to religious groups in Smyrna and the status of freeborn women in households.[6] In these texts, we see both unmarried women in households without men as well as married women in their husbands' households.[7] In order to interpret these texts, I have chosen inscriptions and images that portray wealthy women's households in antiquity. I analyze representations of freeborn wealthy women in households in funerary inscriptions, funerary iconography, Xenophon's *Oikonomikos*, and legal

3. Octavian (Caesar Augustus) himself was adopted by Julius Caesar, a move that facilitated the transfer of privileges, property, and status.

4. Ann Ellis Hanson, "Widows Too Young in Their Widowhood," in *I, Claudia II: Women in Roman Art and Society*, ed. Diana E. E. Kleiner and Susan B. Matheson (Austin: University of Texas Press, 2000), 151.

5. See the discussion in Hanson, "Widows Too Young," 150–51.

6. These are Ignatius' *To the Smyrneans* and *To Polycarp*.

7. While 1 Timothy is another text that discusses both wives and widows, the household situation of the widows in this text is somewhat less clear than it is in the two letters of Ignatius to Smyrna. However, it is possible that one could make an argument for that text very similar to the one I make for the letters to Smyrna.

"confession" inscriptions.[8] I discuss the representations that originate in the same historical context as the Ignatian texts in order to understand wealthy women's status in households in Smyrna.

I begin with the socioeconomic status of elite women in households, drawing on inscriptions and iconography, and then I move on to interpretations of wealthy women's household and religious status in the letters of Ignatius to Smyrna.

Representations of Households

In the following section, I analyze portrayals of women in iconography and inscriptions from Asia Minor and describe how these sources present wealthy women with respect to households. The investigation emphasizes contrasts in portrayals of wives and widows; these contrasts show how martial status significantly determined household status.

Names and Iconography

Analysis of inscribed representations of freeborn wives from Asia Minor allows us to develop a richer understanding of the possibilities for historical reconstructions of households and the status of wealthy wives. Many of these representations are funerary monuments inscribed with names and household relationships; some stones depict the deceased in scenes from life or myth. Scholarship on funerary monuments has identified conventions of naming and iconography.[9]

8. Other studies that use these sources include Paul Zanker's study of "middle-class" self-representation in western Asia Minor, which draws on funerary commemorations, inscriptional, and iconographic: "Bürgerliche Selbstdarstellung am Grab im römischen Kaiserreich," in *Die Römische Stadt im 2. Jahrhundert nach Christ* (Köln: Rheinland, 1992). Sarah Pomeroy discusses women's socioeconomic status in her commentary on Xenophon, *Plutarch's* Advice to the Bride and Groom *and* A Consolation to His Wife: *English Translations, Commentary, Interpretive Essays, and Bibliography* (New York: Oxford University Press, 1999). The "confession inscriptions" form an important source for studies of legal structures in Asia Minor. See Angelos Chaniotis, "Under the Watchful Eyes of the Gods: Divine Justice in Hellenistic and Roman Asia Minor," in *The Greco-Roman East: Politics, Culture, Society*, ed. Stephen Colvin (Cambridge: Cambridge University Press, 2004).

9. See Johanna Fabricius, *Die hellenistischen Totenmahlreliefs: Grabrepräsentation und Wertvorstellungen in ostgriechischen Städten* (München: Dr. Friedrich Pfeil, 1999). Dale Martin, "The Construction of the Ancient Family: Methodological Considerations," *Journal of Roman Studies* 86 (1996): 40–60; "Slave Families and Slaves in Families," in *Early Christian Families in Context: An Interdisciplinary Dialogue*, ed. David L. Balch and Carolyn Osiek (Grand Rapids: Eerdmans, 2003), 207–30. Marielouise Cremer,

A household that lived in the Roman province of Bithynia appears on this tombstone dated to 111–112 c.e.

ἔτους απρ΄, μηνὸς Δίου· Σιμισσι-
μει καὶ τούτου γυνὴ Σιμιοκενίς, θυγάτηρ Λεθυαίου, οἰκέται [οἰκηταί?] Ἐρένας καὶ τού-
των υἱοὶ Τόκαλος καὶ Μόκων καὶ Καλός,
θυγάτηρ Κηνις καὶ Κουζαλα ἀνέθηκαν
ἀρετῆς χάριν. οἱ παράγονζες [παράγοντες?]
χαῖρε.

The year 181, the month of Dios. Simissimei and his wife Simiokenis, daughter of Lethuaios, inhabitants of Erena, and their sons Tokalos and Mokon and Kalos, daughter Kenis and Kouzala erected [this memorial] on account of [their] virtue. Passersby, farewell.[10]

This simple inscription is conventional in depicting the order of precedence within the household: husband, wife, sons, and then daughters. Simiokenis can name her father, and so was freeborn, and perhaps came from a memorable family. In contrast, her husband's name appears without a patronymic, which suggests that he had a lower status, perhaps as a freed slave. Even though the source portrays Simiokenis' social status higher than Simissimei's, the wife's name follows her husband's. And the daughters follow the sons. Conventions of naming established the precedence of husbands, and males generally.[11]

Many funerary monuments depict households in the motif of meal scenes. A stele erected for Telesphoros dates to the Trajanic era (about 100 c.e.) in northwest Asia Minor.

ὑπόμνημα Τελεσφόρου ὃ ἐποίησεν
αὐτῷ ἡ γυνὴ Χρήστη μνήμης χάριν.

Hellenistisch-römische Grabstelen im nordwestlichen Kleinasien, vol. 1, *Mysien* (Asia Minor Studien Band 4.1; Bonn: GMBH, 1991).

10. *SEG* 35.1326, 38.1279.

11. Ignatius followed this convention when he greeted "households of brothers with wives and children."

The tomb of Telesphoros, which his wife Chreste made for him as a memorial.[12]

Figure 3. Interior, black and white. Funerary stele, showing a couple above, a funerary banquet below, separated by a Greek epitaph of Telesphoros by his wife Chreste. Imperial Roman, 1st half 1st c.e. to 1st quarter 2nd ce.[13]

12. IK 18.453. Ernst Pfuhl and Hans Möbius, *Die ostgriechischen Grabreliefs* (Mainz am Rhein: Von Zabern, 1977–79), no. 1603. While the stone was said to be found near Smyrna, Cremer places it with other monuments from a workshop near Kyzikos because of the unusual depiction of a visible naked foot of the reclining male figure also found on KB 5, 8, and 9, and KSt 28, 41, and 42. Cremer, *Hellenistisch-römische Grabstelen*, KB 3, 165.

13. From Cyzique. Marble 67 x 46 x 9.5 cm. MA2857. Photo Credit: Les frères Chuzeville. Musée du Louvre, Paris, France. © RMN-Grand Palais / Art Resource, NY

Two engraved images accompany this inscription (see Figure 3). The upper panel shows the couple in bust form, with Chreste dressed in a *stolatus*, an adoption in the provinces of the Roman iconography for a matron.[14] The *stola* symbolized a wife's status as a married prosperous woman; poorer women, freed women, and women with low-status occupations did not wear this garment.[15] In the lower meal scene, Chreste wears the *himation*, an outer garment common in local Hellenistic Greek custom for representing wifely modesty. Here, she sits on the left, with her left hand holding up the outer fold of the garment to keep it wrapped over her right arm and chest.[16] She cannot move even an arm without disrupting her costume. In contrast, the male figure in the meal scene reclines on his left elbow, dominating the center of the scene. Typically, his left hand holds a bowl or cup, while his right arm rests on his right leg or raises an object. The three-legged table with food on it is placed in front of him. The reclining man, seated woman, and table are the basic elements of the funerary meal scene that represented a household.[17]

The man generally faces the viewer while the woman is seen from her side, her gaze directed to the interior of the scene. While the wife sometimes holds a child or an instrument, she is usually passive. Clothing and posture indicate her status and personality as a matron. Chreste's figure is oriented vertically at the side of an oblong panel. The larger horizontal dimension is occupied by the reclining Telesphoros. In this example, the tomb and memorial belong to Telesphoros so we expect his figure to dominate, but the meal scene in this format recurs widely.

A nearly identical inscription accompanies the meal scene for Markion, dated to the first or second century of the common era, in the environs of Miletos. (See Figure 4.)

ὑπόμνημα Μαρκίωνος
ὃ ἐποίησεν αὐτῷ ἡ γυνὴ
μετὰ τῶν τέκνων μνήμης
χάριν.

14. Ibid., 96.

15. Ibid., 95.

16. This is the posture of *pudicitia*.

17. Pfuhl and Möbius, *Die ostgriechischen Grabreliefs*, 73. Johanna Fabricius, *Die hellenistischen Totenmahlreliefs*. In Chapter Five, I discuss the slaves who frequently appear in the margins of these portraits.

The tomb of Markion, which [his] wife with children made for him as a memorial.[18]

MiSt 35

Figure 4. A Stele for Markion and Wife.[19]

18. IK 18.289. Cremer, *Grabstelen*, MiSt 35, plate 22. Museum Bursa (Inv. Nr. 2571, alt 246).181.

19. Cremer, Grabstelen, MiSt 35, plate 22. Funerary meal scene. 60 x 35 x 7 cm. Museum Bursa Museum (Inv. Nr. 2571, alt 246). Reproduced by permission of Bursa Museum.

The iconography of the couple is typical for a number of tombstones. A male figure reclines in the center of the scene on a couch with a high back; a laden table stands before him. A woman sits in three-quarter profile on a stool at the left side of the couch. A male slave is shown as a small figure standing to the right of the table. A small server stands beneath the woman's stool. The scene represents a household hierarchy: husband, wife, slaves. The size of the figures, their clothes, and placement signal their relative household precedence.

Meal scenes were popular in the Greek East from the Hellenistic era through the Imperial. The motifs heroicize the dead, particularly the reclining male holding a cup of wine.[20] On some stones, the man extends a wreath toward the head of the woman, symbolically crowning her as a heroine.[21] The conceit of the hero is not limited to the most elite socioeconomic strata: a household involved in raising and/or selling pigs includes a meal scene on its tombstone (see Figure 5).

20. Cremer, *Grabstelen*, 117.

21. For example, the tomb of Soteris, mother of three children, from the second century C.E. in Bithynia. Cremer, *Grabstelen*, 66.

Figure 5. A Stele for a Swine-Herding Household.[22]

The meal scene depicts a reclining man raising a cup, but there are a few differences from those above. Here the woman holds a child in her lap and a dog replaces the slaves. The pigs underneath are the clue to the household business. There is no inscription.

In all these presentations, the husband is constructed as the foremost figure of the household. This presentation would carry less impact if he were portrayed alone; the presence of wife and slaves (and the implements mentioned below) contribute different dimensions to his household leadership.

Interestingly, there are several tomb reliefs from Asia Minor in the middle of the second century c.e. that portray women reclining as men do in the more

22. Pfuhl and Möbius, Die ostgriechischen Grabreliefs, no. 1165, plate 174, in Denizli.

conventional meal scenes. Chryseas seems to have been a widow when she died at age 71 (see Figure 6).

Χρυσέα Ἀνδρέα
ἐτῶν οα'· χαῖρε.

Chryseas Andreas, 71 years old. Farewell.[23]

H 8

Figure 6. Funerary Monument of Chryseas.[24]

23. *SEG* 42.1138. Cremer, *Grabstelen*, H8, 96–98.

24. Cremer, *Grabstelen*, H8, plate 29. Well preserved stele, 35 x 26 cm. Findspot unknown. Private collection. Photo reproduced by permission of Rudolf Habelt, Bonn, Germany. Marielouise Cremer,

Another tombstone shows Trophime, who was just twenty when she died; she is identified as a daughter, but not as a wife.[25] These women recline at a banquet; table and food are placed in front of the couch. Chryseas holds a cup in one hand while the other rests on her hip. No other figures in the scene distract from the attention on her. The scene is identical to those used for men.[26] The iconography of the reclining figure identifies these women as dominant in their own households.

Significantly, the inscriptions present neither Trophime nor Chryseas as married.[27] Many wives became single women through death or divorce. Papyri and demography studies indicate that Egyptian and Judean wives divorced their husbands (as Roman wives did), and that many wives became widows.[28] In the Egyptian census data, a woman might be known as a χήρα ("widow"), no matter how her marriage ended.[29] Charlotte Methuen's study of "widow" in ancient contexts found that it connotes a woman who did not live with a man.[30] Hereafter, I follow the convention in the sources and refer to these single women (like Trophime and Chryseas) as widows.

Thus far, we have seen that meal scenes portray the subordination of wealthy wives through passive clothing and posture, the placement of her figure to the side, her distance from the banquet food and table, and the lack of engagement with the viewer in her gaze. The focus in these images remains on the husband, his primacy, his name, his occupation, his activity, and his leadership in the household. In contrast to wives portrayed as matrons, some

Hellenistisch-römische Grabstelen im nordwestlichen Kleinasien. Part 1–2. Asia Minor Studien, vol. 4, 1–2 (Bonn 1992) H7 (Stele der Trophime); H8 (Stele der Chryseas).

25. Pfuhl and Möbius, *Die ostgriechischen Grabreliefs,* 2019, pl. 293. Cremer, *Gabstelen,* H 7.

26. Johanna Fabricius has discussed this phenomenon in the context of Hellenistic depictions of reclining Rhodian women. She attributes the masculine depiction to the social prominence and wealth of Rhodian women (whose prosperity declined under the Romans). Fabricius, *Die hellenistischen Totenmahlreliefs,* 183–90.

27. Cremer presents a third reclining women, Epicharis; she also appears as unmarried. Cremer, *Grabstelen,* 2, pl. 29. Permission granted courtesy of H.P. Willi Publishing.

28. Papyri from Asia Minor would not have survived the centuries as they have in the dry deserts of Judea and Egypt. Scholarship includes Hannah Cotton, "A Cancelled Marriage Contract from the Judean Desert (XHev/Se Gr. 2)," *Journal of Roman Studies* 84 (1994): 64–86.

29. Ann Hanson has argued that many single women did not remarry but appear in the census data living in households dominated by adult women, usually relatives. If males are present, they are minors. Hanson, "Widows Too Young," 152.

30. Charlotte Methuen has investigated the meaning of "widows," in religious texts and suggests that it carries the connotation of a woman who did not live with a man. Methuen, "The 'Virgin Widow': A Problematic Social Role for the Early Church?" *Harvard Theological Review* 90, no. 3 (1997): 286.

wealthy widows appear without men; these unmarried women are presented with motifs that connote dominance in the household.

A different set of motifs from Asia Minor represents women and men through reference to activities or occupations in households.[31] Throughout Phrygia, tombstones were carved to resemble doors, that is, portals to the world of the dead.[32] The doors are divided into panels. Simple bold engravings outline objects that accompany the names of the dead: spindle, distaff, comb, and mirror for wives; pruning hook, ax, plow, and whip for husbands. While the objects representing women are drawn from this narrow range, the objects representing husbands could vary with their occupations. Examples from Akmonia include: a shoe or leather worker (125–150 c.e.), a blacksmith (150–200 c.e.), a stonecutter (second to third century), and a farmer (150–180 c.e.).[33] While men seem to be represented by their actual work activities, wives are represented in a more idealized and generic mode of iconography.[34]

The asymmetrical representations of household members on Phrygian door tombs repeat in other depictions from Asia Minor. A stone from first-century (c.e.) Smyrna shows a man holding a carpenter's hammer (Figure 7). A small dog balances the scene and looks toward the man. The inscription under this image mentions his wife, Trophime.

Φεράγαθες Κορ-
διανοῦ χρηστὲ χ[αῖ]-
ρε. Τροφίμη Φεραγά-
θου χρηστὴ χαῖρε

Farewell good Pheragathos, son of Kordianos. Farewell good Trophime, wife of Pheragathos.[35]

---

31. Some artisans were owners of successful workshops and belonged to the economic strata of the middle group that was relatively wealthy.

32. Marc Waelkens, *Die kleinasiatischen Türsteine: Typologische und epigraphische Untersuchungen der kleinasiatischen Grabreliefs mit Scheintür* (Mainz am Rhein: P. von Zabern, 1986).

33. Waelkens, *Die kleinasiatischen Türsteine*, 420, 411, 417, and 404, respectively.

34. Some interpreters suggest that references to wool work actually refer to feminine virtue rather than to women's work. See Gloria Ferrari, *Figures of Speech: Men and Maidens in Ancient Greece* (Chicago: University of Chicago Press, 2002), 11–60.

35. IEry 529. Pfuhl and Möbius, *Die ostgriechischen Grabreliefs*, 1168, pl. 175. Berlin, Pergamon-Mus. Inv. Nr. Sk. 789.

Figure 7. A Stele for Pheragathes.[36]

Pheragathes appears with an occupational identity as well as canine company, whereas Trophime appears only in the inscription. To the illiterate, she remains unknown.

These three examples typify a reluctance to portray the wives of prosperous households as active, working, contributing to the livelihood of the household. Wives are absent from funerary work scenes.[37] The focus in these images

36. Interior, black and white. Funeral stele of a blacksmith (lower section). Roman, 1st c.e.ntury c.e. From Smyrna/Izmir (Turkey). The deceased (Pheragathos, son of Skopelianos) is shown holding in his left hand a pointed double-headed hammer, along with his daughter (Trophime). Marble, 50 × 34 × 5 cm. Inv. SK 789. Photo credit: bpk, Berlin / Staatliche Museen / Johannes Laurentius / Art Resource, NY.

37. See Pfuhl and Möbius, *Die ostgriechischen Grabreliefs*, 1169, 1171.

remains firmly on the husband: his primacy, name, occupation, activity, and his leadership in the household. The conventions of representation position wives as stock characters sitting passively in the margins or offstage. Depictions of passive wives display the wealth and status of the husband's household.[38]

Iconography from Asia Minor portrays wifely subordination in scenes on funerary monuments. While men are depicted engaged in occupations, wives are not presented as actively working (although a wife may be portrayed with a child nearby). Portrayals of wives present their household status as distinct from their husband's, and subordinate to his. These idealized wives appear as passive, marginalized, and dependent. The woman in this kyriarchal representation is also known as a Roman *matrona* or Greek *kyria*, the lady of a wealthy household.

LEGAL STATUS

Some inscriptions from Asia Minor present women in terms different from those of the matron. I discuss these representations in order to examine the ways in which wealthy women's household status was linked to political and legal standing. The available sources present women's civic status in terms of their occupations, and citizenship, and legal liability. These are particularly important because this aspect of women's lives has received much less attention than their family roles and the matron ideal.[39]

An inscription from Mysia that probably dates to the second century A.D.orns the tomb of Eutychias.

38. Natalie Kampen's analysis of reliefs from Ostia made several important suggestions about the relationships between iconography, gender, and social status, which I discussed in the introduction (see Kampen, *Image and Status: Roman Working Women in Ostia* [Berlin: Mann, 1981] and "Social Status and Gender Gender in Roman Art: The Case of the Saleswoman," in *Roman Art in Context: An Anthology*, ed. Eve D'Ambria [Englewood Cliffs, NJ: Prentice Hall, 1993]). Kampen's analysis attends to occupational categories and socioeconomic strata; she does not focus on household status in particular. For Asia Minor, it seems that representational conventions also vary with marital status. This observation emerges from a comparison of the depictions of wives with those of single women and widows and is developed further in the following.

39. Women's citizenship is discussed by Cynthia B. Patterson, "'Hai Attikai': The Other Athenians," in *Rescuing Creusa: New Methodological Approaches to Women in Antiquity*, ed. Marilyn B. Skinner (Lubbock: Texas Tech University Press, 1987), 49–67. Léopold Migeotte's study of public subscriptions characterizes the many women donors as "en fait les citoyennes," since donations involved defense and rebuilding of cities. See Migeotte, *Les Souscriptions Publiques dans les Cités Grecques* (St. Jean Chrysostome, Québec: Les Éditions du Sphinx, 1992), 371. See, for example, *SEG* 29.1097, dated to Ephesus 30 B.C.E., in which eight of thirteen women contributed their funds independently.

[Εὐ]τυχίας ὃ κατεσκεύ[ασεν]
[ἑαυ]τῇ καὶ τοῖς ἑαυτῆς γο[νεῦσι]
καὶ τοῖς τέκνοις· τοῖς [δὲ λοι]-
[πο]ῖς ἀπαγορεύω· ὃς δ' ἂν [τολ]-
[μήσῃ] ἕτερον καταθέσθαι ν[εκρὸν],
[δώσει τῷ ἱε]ρωτάτῳ συνεδρίῳ τῶν
[γ]ναφέων (δην.) ‚αφ'.

Eutychias prepared [the tomb] for herself and her parents and children; I forbid any others. Anyone so reckless as to put another body [here] will give to the most glorious association of fullers 1500 *denari*.[40]

This inscription presents the usual formula that identifies Eutychias as a fuller, that is, she was involved in the trade of cleaning fabric (usually wool) as a step in the production of clothing. Since Eutychias identifies her parents and her children, she was freeborn. She does not mention the father of her children, and she paid for the monument herself; this suggests that she was a widow in control of financial resources, and the socioeconomic head of her household.

This inscription honors Antiochis who lived in Lycia in the first century C.E.

Ἀντιοχὶς Διοδότου
Τλωὶς μαρτυρηθεῖ-
σα ὑπὸ τῆς Τλωέων
βουλῆς καὶ τοῦ δή-
μου ἐπὶ τῇ περὶ
τὴν ἰατρικὴν τέ-
χνην ἐνπειρίᾳ
ἔστησεν τὸν ἀν-
δριάντα ἑαυτῆς.

40. IK 18.211. J. P. Waltzing, *Étude historique sur les corporations professionelles chez les Romains depuis les origines jusqu'à la chute de l'Empire d'Occident*, 4 vols. (Louvain: C. Peeters, 1895–1900; reprint Bologna: Forni, 1968), 136. Inscriptions relating to associations in the Greek East peaked in the second century C.E. See Onno van Nijf, *The Civic World of Professional Associations in the Roman East* (Amsterdam: Gieben, 1997), 24.

Antiochis, daughter of Diodotus, citizen of Tlos, recognized by the council and the people of Tlos for her practice in the medical art, has set up this statue of herself.[41]

Antiochis erected her own statue, was freeborn, and a citizen. The presentation of her father's name and her city duplicate the way that inscriptions identify male citizens. The text honors her for her esteemed position in the community. She proclaims economic power in citing her own sponsorship of the memorial. The city government would have approved the placement of the statue.[42] The text emphasizes her citizenship, rather than her role in a household.[43] Like Eutychias, she appears as a widow.

The presentation of Antiochis in terms of citizenship resembles that of Momo from Macedonia in northern Greece. Macedonia lies between Asia Minor and Corinth on the path that travelers took along the Aegean coast. Greece shared social and political institutions with Asia Minor. In Macedonia of the second century, Momo identified herself through her city.

> Μωμω Μεστου θυγά-
> τηρ, Γαζωρία, Οὐ<ε>-
> νερία τῇ θυγατρὶ
> ἑαυτῆς καὶ Γαΐῳ
> Τορκάτου καὶ ἑαυ-
> τῇ {ς} · ζώσῃ {μνη}-
> {ς} μνήμης χάριν.
> ἔτους ϛορ' τοῦ βϞσ'.

Momo, daughter of Mestos, Gazorian, for her daughter Oueneria, and Gaios, son of Torkatos, and herself, still alive. A farewell memorial. In the year 144/45 c.e.[44]

---

41. TAM 2.595. H. W. Pleket, *Epigraphica II: Texts on the Social History of the Greek World* (Leiden: Brill, 1969).

42. Discussed further in the following chapter.

43. The inscription is not a funerary monument like the others I cite. The genre would influence the representation. It seems to belong to the category of honorary inscriptions except that honorary inscriptions typically detail a benefactor's contributions and their titles or offices.

44. *SEG* 30.599.

Momo includes her citizenship and her father's name, indicating that she was freeborn. The inscription represents Momo's household as comprised of her daughter and Gaios. Since Gaios was freeborn and his name appears after Momo's daughter, he may have been Momo's son-in-law or grandson. In any case, the position of Momo's name at the beginning of the text and in the nominative case presents her as the one who paid for the tomb and the inscription, the most prominent member of this household, as well as a citizen of Gazoros.

These three brief inscriptions depict single women identifying themselves by their cities, occupations, legal status, and households. They are freeborn daughters and mothers, but none mentions a husband. Their prominence is expressed in the position of their names, their financial ability, their community membership and recognition. The memorials present the single women with the socioeconomic status of a head of a household. One belonged to an association and two others belonged to the citizenship of cities. At least two were widows (with children).

Momo and other Macedonian women may have been known by a title specific to their civic status, "widow citizen." An article published in a Greek journal discusses an inscription recently found in Dion in lower Macedonia, but the inscription itself has not yet been published.[45] According to Miltiade Hatzopoulos, the inscription is dated to the Hellenistic era and lists sixty-eight names.[46] Of these, five appear under the rubric χῆραι πολίτιδες, "widow citizens." Hatzopoulos considers whether the five widows were members of a religious association or heads of citizen households involved in a civic recruitment.[47] The two suggestions are not mutually exclusive, however, since groups such as the *gerousia* (association of elders) had political as well as religious functions in the cities.[48]

The title "widows" also appears in a list of newly minted citizens. Like the list from Dion, this inscription is dated to the Hellenistic era, early in the third century B.C.E. It comes from the city of Ilion in Asia Minor. This complete list

45. D. Pandermalis, "Dion 2000," in Το αρχαιολογικο εργο στη Μακεδονια και Θρακη 14 (2000): 381–82.

46. Miltiade B. Hatzopoulos, *Revue des Études Grecs* 112 (1999): 639–40 (no. 349).

47. Miltiade B. Hatzopoulos, *Revue des Études Grecs* 115 (2002): 672 (no. 254) for the interpretive suggestions. Other sources from Macedonia indicate that widows conducted transactions without guardians (*kyrioi*).

48. An inscription that falls within my target parameters documents collective political activity by "the women, Greek and Roman" of Akmoneia early in the first century C.E. MAMA 11. Peter Thonemann, "The Women of Akmoneia," *Journal of Roman Studies* 100 (2010): 163–78.

is quite long and much is damaged. Widows appear as a distinct category of citizens in lines 59–61.

χῆρα[ι]· Εὐμενὶς Μικ[ίν]γου — Στρατο[νίκη] Ἀπολλοφάνου — Πόα Ἀριστομάχ[ου]
Ἀριστοδάμα Ἰδαίου — Φιλίννα Ποτάμωνος — Μανία Ἀνδρέου — Εὔκλεια
Βακχίου — Ναννὶς Πολυμήδου[49]

The text presents eight women under the heading, "widows." These names are preceded and followed by traditional household listings, in which women are included as wives, mothers, and daughters. Each widow's name is followed by a name in the genitive case, probably her father or former husband, whereas the other women in the inscription are represented by first name only. This latter group is symbolically included in a man's household already; each follows the name of a man, and the text delineates her family or relationship to him. It seems then, that naming conventions present each of these widows as a head of household: the second name in the genitive identifies a man who headed her former household. The same convention holds for men: each name is followed by the patronymic, the man's father's name, the head of his former household.

The inscriptions from Dion and Ilion predate the target parameters of this study in the imperial era. Nonetheless, they suggest precedence for interpreting the status of women such as Eutychias, Antiochis, and Momo in the Greek East. For Antiochis and Momo, the city name gives not only her place of residence but also tells her reader that she claims a recognized political status there.[50] The monuments present Eutychias and Antiochis with civic identity through their occupations and their access to financial resources. The portrayal differs from that of wives in that the single women are seen as members of a city rather than as members of a man's household. Both the earlier citizenship lists as well as the later funerary monuments present widows as heads of households through

---

49. IK 3.64. BÉ (1992), no. 377. See discussions of the demographics in: Pierre Brulé, "Enquête Démographique sur la Famille Grecque Antique," *Revues des études anciennnes* 92 (1990): 233–58; Linda-Marie Günther, "Zur Familien- und Haushaltsstruktur im Hellenistischen Kleinasien," *Studien zum antiken Kleinasien* 2, no. 1–2 (1991–92): 23–42.

50. Many urban inhabitants as well as the inhabitants of rural villages were identified as *katoikoi* and *paroikoi*, rather than as citizens. Michael Rostovtzeff, *The Social and Economic History of the Roman Empire*, 2 vols. (Oxford: Clarendon, 1957), 255–57 and 654–55, n. 2.

the same set of iconographical and inscriptional conventions with which they present male heads of households.

One inscription shows that it was also possible for a woman to be represented as a wife and as a citizen and as achieving occupational success.

Chrysopolis describes herself a citizen of Nicea in her funerary epigram dated to the second century C.E. The text emphasizes her civic identity by positioning it as the first word of the inscription.

Νεικαίης πάτρης με πολεῖτιν ὁρᾷς παροδεῖτα |
Χρυσόπολιν, τὸ πάλαι πολλοῖς θεάτροις ἀρέσασαν· |
ἄνδρα δὲ Λονγεῖνον ἐπὶ ξενίῃ προλιποῦσα |
ὧδ' ἐλθοῦσ' ἔθανον προπετῶς θερμοῖσι λυθεῖσα· |
μοῦνος Ἰουλιανὸς δι' εὐσεβίην δέ μ' ἔθαψε. |

Λονγεῖνος Χρυσοπόλει συνβίῳ μνήμης χάριν |
ζησάσῃ κοσμίως ἔτη μη'.
Χαίρετε.

Passerby, you see me, a citizen of my hometown, Nicea, Chrysopolis, who used to please [audiences] in many theaters; [now I am] abandoning my husband Longinus as a foreigner, since I have gone and died, having succumbed quickly to fever; Julianos alone buried me, on account of piety.

Longinus, in memory of Chrysopolis, [his] spouse. She lived decently for forty-eight years. Farewell.[51]

After her citizenship, Chrysopolis' voice (from the grave) highlights her occupational fame and success: she performed in many theaters.[52] It is not clear whether or not she was freeborn. The inscription identifies her husband very briefly, without his father's name, occupation, or citizenship. The memorial presents Chrysopolis as more prominent than her husband.

51. IK 31.17.

52. The presence of Homeric usage of the verb λυθεῖσα in the epigram suggests that the dramatization of epic poetry was among the performances in Chrysopolis's repertoire. See *Steinepigramme aus dem griechischen Osten*, ed. Reinhold Merkelbach and Josef Stauber (Stuttgart: B. G. Teubner, 1998–2002), 242. Other editors have suggested she was a dancer or a mime. *SEG* 39.1139.

There is a clear contrast between the representation of Chrysopolis and the representation of the matron/kyria described in the previous section. Chrysopolis herself is described through her city and her work.[53] She is not presented with the conventions of a wife's socioeconomic status seen elsewhere. She is neither passive, nor dependent, nor identified through her husband. This example shows that it was possible to present wives who were not seen as matrons. Except for marital status, the representation of Chrysopolis resembles that of the citizen physician Eutychias (above) who was honored by her city.

I turn now to another aspect of women's legal status, their legal liability. These inscriptions are especially interesting because few sources exist for investigating women's legal status in Asia Minor.[54]

The confession inscriptions number over 140; they originated in Lydia and Phrygia between the first and third centuries C.E..[55] According to Eckhard Schnabel's study, the basic structure of the confession genre includes these elements: the name of the person who committed a wrongdoing; the specific offense; the reaction of the deity; punishment by the deity; redressal of the crime; public confession; acknowledgment of the power of the deity; erection of the stele inscribed with the story; and often, a commitment to praise the deity or a warning to others.[56] The gods force the confession through tragic events. The texts present a great deal of very specific information, forming a public record of crime and punishment. Angelos Chaniotis characterizes the wrongdoing: "offences commonly prosecuted by property and criminal law, such as theft, the neglect to pay a debt, cheating, insult, slander, injury, adultery and sorcery."[57] These inscriptions represent a significant portion of

---

53. Her citizenship suggests she was freeborn but the lack of a patronymic and her occupation both raise doubt about her birth status.

54. See discussion in Riet van Bremen, *The Limits of Participation: Women and Civic Life in the Greek East in the Hellenistic and Roman Periods* (Amsterdam: J. C. Gieben, 1996), 197–202.

55. The texts are available in G. Petzl, *Die Beichtinschriften Westkleinasiens* (Epigraphica Anatolica 22; Bonn: Habelt, 1994). Many more await publication according to Angelos Chaniotis, "Under the Watchful Eyes of the Gods: Divine Justice in Hellenistic and Roman Asia Minor," in *The Greco-Roman East: Politics, Culture, Society*, ed. Stephen Colvin (Cambridge: Cambridge University Press, 2004), 3. Scholars have debated the type of legal proceedings represented in these inscriptions (Chaniotis, 28–29). The confessions are similar to other inscriptions that call on deities when invoking curses or making vows (6–11). The priests of the temples intervened to settle disputes as arbitrators and administrators of oaths. They also collected fees and received property that were necessary to effect reconciliation with the god (34).

56. Eckhard J. Schnabel, "Divine Tyranny and Public Humiliation: A Suggestion for the Interpretation of the Lydian and Phrygian Confession Inscriptions," *Novum Testamentum* 45, no. 2 (2003): 160–88.

57. Chaniotis, "Watchful Eyes," 4.

the workings of the justice system, particularly in a society with little law enforcement. The inscriptions show how women with property were held liable for household crimes.

This engraving dates to 114/15 c.e. and comes from northeast Lydia.

Μεγάλη Μήτηρ Ἀναεῖτις Ἄζι-
τα κατέχουσα καὶ Μεὶς Τιαμου
καὶ αἱ δυνάμεις αὐτῶν. Ἑρμογέ-
νης καὶ Ἀπολλώνιος ὁ Ἀπολλωνίου Μίδου ἀπὸ Σύρου Μανδρῶν
πλαζομένων χοίρων τρειῶν Δημαινέτου καὶ Παπιου ἐξ Ἀζί-
των καὶ προσμιγόντων αὐτῶν
προβάτοις τοῦ Ἑρμογένου καὶ Ἀ-
πολλωνίου, παιδίου αὐτῶν βόσ-
κοντος πενταετοῦς, καὶ ἀπαγα-
γόντων ἔσω, ζητοῦντος οὖν τοῦ
Δημαινέτου καὶ τοῦ Παπιου οὐ-
κ ὡμολόγησαν διά τινα ἀχαριστί-
αν. ἐπεστάθη οὖν τῆς θεοῦ τὸ σκῆ-
πτρον καὶ τοῦ κυρίου τοῦ Τιαμου
καὶ μὴ ὁμολογησάντων αυτῶν ἡ
θεὸς οὖν ἔδειξεν τὰς ἰδίας δυ-
νάμις καὶ ἱλάσοντο αὐτὴν τελευ-
τήσαντος τοῦ Ἑρμογένου ἡ γυνὴ
αὐτοῦ καὶ τὸ τέκνον καὶ Ἀπολλώνιος ὁ ἀδελφὸς τοῦ Ἑρμογένου καὶ
νῦν αὐτῇ μαρτυροῦμεν καὶ εὐλο-
γοῦμεν μετὰ τῶν τέκνων.
ἔτους ρϟθ'.

[A lunar symbol.] Great are Mother Anaitis who occupies Azita and Meis of Tiamos and their powers. Hermogenes and Apollonius from Syros Mandrou, when three pigs belonging to Demainetus and Papias from Azita wandered off and got mixed up with the sheep belonging to Hermogenes and Apollonius while a five-year-old boy was pasturing them, and they were herded back inside, so Demainetus and Papias were looking for them, [but] they did not confess through some ingratitude. The staff of the goddess and the lord of Tiamos was therefore set up, and when they did not confess the goddess duly showed her powers, and when Hermogenes died, his wife and the child and Apollonius, brother of Hermogenes, implored mercy and now bear witness to her and with the children sing her praises. In the year 199 [114/15 C.E.].[58]

This inscription is memorable for its narration and detail. The text seems to argue extenuating circumstances—the pigs wandered off (by themselves), the five-year-old shepherd was too young to be responsible—nonetheless, Hermogenes' theft results in a severe penalty. After his death, propitiation of the goddess falls to his wife and child and the other thief. His widow replaces Hermogenes in his legal status as the responsible party. It falls on her to make amends: to name the wrongdoer and the offense, perform the public confession, inscribe and erect the stele, acknowledge the power of the goddess, implore her mercy, and sing her praises. The widow performs these actions to protect her household and avert further punishment.

In this representation of the operations of the criminal justice system, the widow bears the same responsibility as her husband, had he lived, and Hermogenes' co-conspirator (his brother Apollonius). As a wife, she was not named in the theft, but as a widow, she is held responsible in her new role as head of the household. The widow inherits the household's legal status. She negotiates relationships with other households and the temple. The inscription does not present her as needing a guardian when she negotiates relationships between her household and the community.

Widows bear the legal status of men in the situations represented in other inscriptions from this group as well. For example, Apaphias failed to fulfill her vow to Men and was punished.[59] She is identified as a daughter; no husband appears in the text. One man seems to have disappeared after committing perjury; his ox and donkey died, then his daughter.[60] The remaining household, mother and four sons, propitiate the god through public confession and praise.[61] Ammia paid a fine to the god through the priests to make amends for her

---

58. TAM 5.1.317. Petzl, *Die Beichtinschriften Westkleinasiens*, 68. The translation follows Stephen Mitchell, *Anatolia: Land, Men, and Gods in Asia Minor* (Oxford: Clarendon, 1993), 192.

59. Petzl, *Die Beichtinschriften Westkleinasiens*, 65.

60. *TAM* 5.1.464.

61. Physical separation could effect divorce in the Roman world.

household debts.[62] These widows represented their households in terms of legal liability.

Legal liability itself did not depend on marital status in this group of inscriptions. Some married women were also held accountable for wrongdoing. Syntyche made amends after her thirteen-year-old son was punished because she had failed to proclaim the power of the god.[63] The socioeconomic status of these households is not clear. However, it is clear that women engaged in these proceedings as disputants, wrongdoers, victims, payers, and confessors. Furthermore, in this system of religious justice and community relations, widows are represented with legal, religious, and socioeconomic responsibility for their households.

This body of confession inscriptions has contributed to the portrayal of the legal status of widows in western Asia Minor. The inscription quoted is especially interesting in its depiction of a change of status from wife to widow. I move now to the status of women in a literary source, Xenophon's *Oikonomikos*. In this text the woman is a wife; her status as a widow is not addressed.

XENOPHON'S OIKONOMIKOS

Xenophon's *Oikonomikos* is a treatise on household management that depicts the operation of a rural estate in an agricultural economy dependent on slave labor. The text dates to the fourth century B.C.E. However, Cicero later translated the text from Greek to Latin so that Romans could benefit from its advice as well. Galen of Pergamon knew this text in the second century C.E.[64] Thus Xenophon's depiction of the household represents an understanding of the household that can be reconstructed for the historical context of Asia Minor in the first two centuries of the common era.

In the *Oikonomikos*, the husband presents elite marriage to his wife as an economic partnership: "at present we two share this estate. I go on paying everything I have into the common fund; and you deposited into it everything you brought with you. There is no need to calculate precisely which of us has contributed more, but to be well aware of this: that the better partner is the one who makes the more valuable contribution" (7.13).[65] The husband highlights

---

62. *SEG* 34.1219. A daughter of Apollonius paid a fee to propitiate the gods in Petzl, *Die Beichtinschriften Westkleinasiens*, 33.

63. *SEG* 37.1001. Petzl, *Die Beichtinschriften Westkleinasiens*, 59.

64. Pomeroy, *Plutarch's* Advice to the Bride and Groom, 93. Cato, Columella, and Jerome also knew the text (71–73).

the ways in which the wife adds value to the estate: through her own education so that she can keep inventory and accounts; through training slaves, which increases their value (7.41); supervision of work; nursing sick slaves; and in her care for the household property. Even taking exercise makes her more attractive to her husband and, presumably, makes her more fit to bear and raise children, "to support the partners in their old age" (7.20). With these assignments, "a wife who is a good partner in the estate carries just as much weight as her husband in attaining prosperity" (3.15). In Xenophon's ideal elite marriage, the economic value of a wife's work equals that of her husband, their respective tasks differ by nature and law (7.20–31), and, together they share the rewards. The economic partnership seems rational and fair: separate work, equal value, and shared benefit.

Even as Xenophon's husband recognizes the value of his wife's work, the treatise omits mention of exchange value gained by the wife. The cash value of her dowry is minimized; honor, instead of saved value, constitutes her security for old age (7.42–43). According to Sarah Pomeroy, "Patriarchy literally means 'the rule of fathers'; [it] functions not only as a social system, but also as an economic system in which the male who heads the *oikos* [household] appropriates the labour of his wife, children, and slaves."[66] The husband also assumes leadership in decision-making, in religion, and in knowledge. He characterizes his wife as a girl of fifteen at the time of her marriage (7.5). He sacrifices and prays before beginning to teach her the duties of household management. She follows him by offering the same prayers (7.8), agreeing to all he says (7–10), and then obeying his instructions (10.13). The text does not address the possibilities of the wife having a different religion or her own managerial knowledge and style. Nor does it address dissolution of the partnership or the woman's widowhood.

Xenophon's text portrays a wealthy wife as vital to the household's economic functions; this portrayal stands in contrast to the funereal iconography from Asia Minor. Her status in the text during the discussion of marriage remains lower than her husband's and she is clearly dependent on his expertise. The marriage is depicted as a partnership, with the husband represented as the preeminent partner through his leadership and prominence in speaking. The wife will exercise these skills in her management of slaves and children, but this is reported in the text only indirectly, when the wife receives instruction. Since she speaks very little and listens rather than acts, the treatise

65. Xenophon, *Oeconomicus*, 7.13. Translation in Pomeroy, *Plutarch's* Advice to the Bride and Groom, 141.

66. Pomeroy, *Plutarch's* Advice to the Bride and Groom, 58–59.

presents a diminished portrayal of the wife's work activities. Although the wife here is portrayed as active in comparison to the representations on memorials above, she continues to be viewed as a subordinate character, clearly secondary to her husband.

The text indicates that the husband's preeminence in the household is based on his experience and knowledge. The husband's acquisition of the knowledge of farming is actually the topic of the treatise. Xenophon's characters discuss marriage and slavery as the central relationships in the household. The husband's success in estate management and his prosperity depend on his ability to manage these household relationships well. The treatise focuses on this challenge through best management practices. The portrayal of wifely obedience, efficiency, and thrift elevates his status. Throughout, the characters assume that the farmer husband has primary responsibility for the property. In spite of clear status differentiation, Xenophon insists that the contributions of husband and wife to the estate can be equal in value. However, it seems that the husband controls the property of the estate (7.3, 15–17; 9.16). The question of the wife's claim to property or exchange value does not arise.

Xenophon's differentiated representations of the household status of wives and husbands on the rural estate may seem to fit an analytical separation of market and home in economic models. The categories of classic economic theory support analysis based on a distinction between private/home and public/market economies. Was the ascription of secondary status to wives related to the idea that her activities took place in the residence, contextualized as part of the household economy, whereas the husband's work was public, contextualized in the city or market economy? Historians have looked to archaeology for evidence of gendered spheres of activity in the ancient urban economy.

Archaeological remains from around the Mediterranean suggest that little physical space (if any) distinguished "residence" from "workplace."[67] At Pergamon in Asia Minor, excavators uncovered an entire neighborhood; it consists of two peristyle houses, three courtyard-style houses, one simple apartment, and fourteen rooms that might have been shops or workshops or storerooms. Built on a slope, buildings mingle together with shared walls, few right angles, and small units next to large.[68] For a similar pattern of building in Pompeii, Wallace-Hadrill has suggested that the building pattern fits the

67. The distinction belongs to an economic analysis that separates private from public, and domestic economy from market.

68. Monika Trümper, "Material and Social Environment of Greco-Roman Households in the East: The Case of Hellenistic Delos," in *Early Christian Families in Context*, ed. D. Balch and C. Osiek, 35–37.

social structure of a wealthy household surrounded by its dependents—client, freed, or slave—and their workspaces. He describes these cellular neighborhoods as "essentially mixed in nature, between grand houses and blocks of flats and little shop units on the one hand, and buildings that formed focuses of local communal life on the other—baths, clubs, and corporation."[69] These archaeological interpretations have not supported a hypothesis that wives and husbands focused their activities in different areas of urban spaces.[70] Archaeological remains have limited use in indicating how spaces were used at different times of the day or week and the relative status of the persons who used them. A minimal claim notes simply that it has not been established that gendered workspaces or spheres of activity accompanied differences in household status.

Xenophon elaborates gendered hierarchical roles for this elite household to prosper in an agricultural economy.[71] I noted above that funerary iconography and inscriptions ascribe occupational activities to the head of the household, whether male or female. It seems that a woman's position as either wife or widow determined representations of her work. Conversely, representations of activities contributed to constructions of household status.

Xenophon's literary treatise associates male ownership and control with ascription of secondary status to elite wives. He assigns asymmetric relations to labor, property, and socioeconomic status. This literary portrayal resonates with the representations of the matron/kyria. In common with iconographic and inscriptional sources on marriage, this literary household features gendered division of labor; Xenophon both delineates and subordinates the woman's activities. Inscriptional sources indicate that a wife's status changed when her husband died; Xenophon's literary portrayal does not address this possibility even as it points out the wife's youth compared to her husband.[72]

"Even within insulae with the most lavish and distinguished houses, living units of different kinds are densely interwoven" (26).

69. Andrew Wallace-Hadrill, "*Domus* and *Insulae* in Rome: Families and Housefuls," in *Early Christian Families*, ed. Balch and Osiek. "The absence of traces of internal sanitation and cooking facilities makes it likely that public baths, and nearby cookshops and bars, formed a key focus of communal life" (13). The mixing of socioeconomic levels reflected hierarchically oriented institutions such as patronage, and also appeared in the mixed composition of associations of all kinds.

70. See, for example, Miriam Peskowitz's conclusion based on her study of archaeological remains from Palestine of Roman times. Peskowitz, "'Family/ies' in Antiquity: Evidence from Tannaitic Literature and Roman Galilean Architecture," in *The Jewish Family in Antiquity*, ed. Shaye J. D. Cohen (Atlanta: Scholars, 1993), 9–36.

71. In this agricultural economy, small landholders might belong to the local elite. The majority of agricultural workers lived close to subsistence and did not own the land.

SUMMARY AND COMPARISON

There is a marked contrast between the representations of household wives and single women in these sources. Iconography portrays wifely subordination in scenes on funerary monuments through passive clothing and posture, the placement of her figure to the side, her distance from the banquet food and table, and the lack of engagement with the viewer in her gaze. While men are depicted engaged in occupations, wives are not presented as actively working. Wives are not shown working in workshops although archaeologists suggest that workshop and household space overlapped. The focus in all the images remains on the husband, his primacy, his name, his occupation, his activity, and his leadership in the household. A treatise on household management presents the husband's preeminence as based on his knowledge and his responsibility for the household property. Portrayals of wives present their household status as distinct from their husband's, and subordinate to his. These idealized wives appear as passive, marginalized, dependent, obedient, and financially subservient. The woman in this kyriarchal representation is also known as the matron/kyria, the lady of a wealthy household. This figure of the matron/kyria contrasts with the figure of the widow.

In comparison, representations of widows emphasize their social standing in the cities through association memberships, citizenship, occupational achievement, and control of economic resources. They appear as active, working, and the most prominent member of their households. Confession inscriptions present widows with legal, religious, and socioeconomic responsibility. Widows are presented as heads of households, executing financial decisions, managing their property, and engaging in legal actions. Funerary iconography presents them with the same motifs used for men, and they may have constituted a distinct category of citizens.

In this comparison of wealthy women, socioeconomic status varies with household position. The representations distinguish the socioeconomic position of wealthy widows from that of wealthy wives. The portrayals associate subordinate socioeconomic status with the marital status of wives.

It is important to note that not all wealthy wives appear as matrons. There is a clear contrast between the representation of Chrysopolis and the

---

72. Dominic Rathbone has hypothesized that older women in Roman Egypt did not remarry because they could and did lead independent lives. See "Poverty and Population in Roman Egypt," in *Poverty in the Roman World*, ed. Margaret Atkins and Robin Osborne (Cambridge: Cambridge University Press, 2006), 104–5.

representation of the matron/kyria described above. Chrysopolis herself is described through her city and her work. She is neither passive, nor dependent, nor identified through her husband. This example shows that it was possible to represent wives who were not seen as matrons. The depictions of matrons conceal their work and contributions to the household.

I turn now to the literary texts of Ignatius and historical reconstruction of the religious status of the women in Smyrna. I have shown that a wealthy woman's household status has tremendous consequences for her socioeconomic status. For these ancient women, marital status cannot be reduced to sexual status.

HOUSEHOLD AND RELIGIOUS STATUS IN IGNATIUS

Some of the most noteworthy references to women in religious texts of Asia Minor occur in the two letters Ignatius wrote from Troas to people in Smyrna. In the letter addressed to "the *ekklesia*" in Smyrna,[73] Ignatius greets three groups of households: "my brothers, along with their wives and children, and the virgins who are called widows, [and] the household of Tavia" (*Smyrn.* 13.1–2).[74] Similarly, in his letter to Polycarp and other Smyrneans,[75] Ignatius refers to these groupings: wives and husbands, widows, and "the wife of Epitropus,[76] along with the entire household of her and her children" (5.1, 4.1, 8.2). This letter additionally includes references to celibates[77] and female slaves (5.2, 4.3).

With respect to household status, Ignatius groups women in Smyrna as either wives, widows and virgins in (a) household(s), single women who own or manage households, or household slaves.[78] In his advice to his fellow bishop, Ignatius directs Polycarp's attention toward different concerns for each group of women. This different treatment for each household group indicates that

---

73. Ignatius has high praise for this group, "the church of God the Father and the beloved Jesus Christ which is in Smyrna of Asia, which has been shown mercy in every gracious gift, filled with faith and love, and lacking no gracious gift, a church that is most worthy of God and bears what is holy" (Ign. *Smyrn.* Insc.).

74. English translation: Bart Ehrman, trans, *Apostolic Fathers*, vol. 1 (Cambridge, MA: Loeb Classical Library/Harvard University Press, 2003).

75. Ignatius uses the plural form of *you* from *Pol.* 6–7.

76. It is not clear whether this is a proper name or the man's office.

77. William R. Schoedel, *Ignatius of Antioch: A Commentary on the Letters of Ignatius of Antioch* (Hermeneia; Philadelphia: Fortress Press, 1985), 273.

78. These groupings are not exclusive; some women may belong to more than one. However, these are the groupings that Ignatius constructs. I focus on these slaves in the fifth chapter.

Ignatius associates these women's religious status with their household situation.[79]

One might object that these women differ with respect to their sexual status rather than their household status. Nonetheless, since households were the basic economic institution of society, exploration of marriage as a sexual relationship does not exhaust the significance of the categorization of women with respect to households. We must also investigate marriage as an aspect of the socioeconomic dimensions of households.

WIVES

Here Ignatius speaks of wives and husbands:

τοῖς ἀδελφαῖς μου προσλάλει, ἀγαπᾶν τὸν κύριον καὶ τοῖς συμβίοις ἀρκεῖσθαι σαρκὶ καὶ πνεύματι. ὁμοίως καὶ τοῖς ἀδελφοῖς μου παράγγελλε ἐν ὀνόματι Ἰησοῦ Χριστοῦ, ἀγαπᾶν τὰς συμβίους ὡς ὁ κύριος τὴν ἐκκλησίαν. . . . πρέπει δὲ τοῖς γαμοῦσι καὶ ταῖς γαμουμέαις μετὰ γνώμης τοῦ ἐπισκόπου τὴν ἕνωσιν ποιεῖσθαι, ἵνα ὁ γάμος ᾖ κατὰ κύριον καὶ μὴ κατ' ἐπιθυμίαν.

Instruct my sisters to love the Lord and to be satisfied with their husbands in flesh and spirit. So too enjoin my brothers in the name of Jesus Christ to love their wives as the Lord loves the church. . . . It is right for men and women who marry to make their union with the consent of the bishop, that their marriage may be for the Lord and not for passion. (Ign. Pol. 5.1–2)

In this passage, Ignatius himself seems to direct our attention to the sexual aspects of marriage. According to Margaret MacDonald, Ignatius draws from the same tradition found in the Letter to the Ephesians.

In both Ephesians and Ignatius' letter to Polycarp we see the symbol of the church-bride serving as a metaphor for the whole community and acting as a guide to relations between the married couple. The reference to "flesh and spirit" in Ignatius, Letter to Polycarp 5.1, means

---

79. One might argue that he also singles out one woman by affection; he twice remembers "Alke, a name dear to me" (Smyrn. 13.2 and Pol. 8.3). He omits both household reference and religious advice for Alke.

that there is no question of the symbol of the woman church being used in relation to "ascetic, spiritual" marriages. The importance of a wife's chastity within marriage is forcefully conveyed. Like the wife who is ever content with her one true husband, the church-bride is faithfully united with Christ.[80]

MacDonald notes that the ideal articulated in these passages "encompasses ethics which permeated Greco-Roman society."[81] The female church-wife is passive, subordinate, dependent, and obedient to her Lord-husband.[82] The woman's role resembles that of the matron/kyria in the households discussed above.MacDonald's interpretation emphasizes the sexual aspect of the relationship between wives and husbands, and this is the dimension that Ignatius himself emphasizes when he discusses engaged couples a few lines later in the letter. However, there were also socioeconomic dimensions to marriage that remain to be investigated. We need to explore the implications of Ignatius' move to imbue the socioeconomic dimensions of marriage and household relationships with theological significance.

Interpretations of religious texts could benefit from analysis of gender stereotypes in addition to investigation of socioeconomic dimensions of households. For instance, Bruce Winter has drawn on excerpts from a number of ancient sources to delineate two types of women: the traditional wife who resembles the matron described above, and the "new Roman woman" who was her opposite in sexual behavior. "Both in ostensibly factual texts and in imaginative writing a new kind of woman appears precisely at the time of Cicero and Caesar: a woman in high position, who nevertheless claims for herself the indulgence in sexuality of a woman of pleasure."[83] Winter attributes

80. Margaret Y. MacDonald, *Early Christian Women and Pagan Opinion: The Power of the Hysterical Woman* (Cambridge: Cambridge University Press, 1996), 233–34.

81. Ibid., 236.

82. MacDonald characterizes this articulation as an effort "to encourage marital behavior that could not lead to the slander of the community" (237). In other words, society also knew the matron's opposite in another type of idealized woman characterized by her household relationships. "I argue in this book that, for a variety of reasons, the early church threatened images of the ideal woman that existed in the ancient Mediterranean world." Rather than adhering to notions of the ideal wife and mother, the early Christian woman (in public opinion) "combined secret religious rites with unchastity" (7).

83. Bruce W. Winter, *Roman Wives, Roman Widows: The Appearance of New Women and the Pauline Communities* (Grand Rapids: Eerdmans, 2003), 21, citing Elaine Fantham and others, *Women in the Classical World: Image and Text* (Oxford: Oxford University Press, 1994), 280.

the appearance of this wanton wife to a change in legal and socioeconomic status.

> What could have given rise to such a change in the traditional behavior of married women? Wives still brought to marriage the all-important dowry but could now retain their own property. It was also possible for them to terminate the marriage, and receive back a portion of, or the whole dowry.[84]

Whereas the matron was idealized as dependent, passive, obedient, and financially subservient, the "new Roman woman" is presented as financially independent, sexually assertive, and in "revolt" against her husband's (inequitable) moral standards.[85] Categorization of wives according to this dichotomy leaves little space to negotiate complexities in our sources, such as a woman depicted as both wealthy and chaste.

William Shoedel's interpretation of the passage in Ign. *Poly.* 5.1–2 hypothesizes that a concern for sexual ethics lies behind Ignatius' instructions to wives in 5.1b. He articulates this view in his commentary for the Hermeneia series.

> The presumed reference to the immorality of slaves may have prompted this special section on marriage in general. . . . The appearance of a strict sexual ethic in such groups is probably best explained as a corollary to marginal status in society. The group requires coherence to survive, and control of sexuality is a vital factor in maintaining such coherence.[86]

However, control of women's sexuality was rather common, not a characteristic peculiar to the defensive posture of a marginal group. If sexual ethics were the main concern, one would expect to see an emphasis on the husband's behavior. This is the case with the rules for the association cited by Schoedel: "A man [is not to take] another woman in addition to his own wife. . . ."[87] While the rule for this association is extended to women as well, it is the

---

84. Ibid., 21.
85. Ibid., 22.
86. Schoedel, *Ignatius of Antioch*, 272.

men who are addressed first and at length. However, Ignatius addresses wives first, so the relevance of the parallel is not certain.

Schoedel's commentary also goes beyond analysis of sexual ethics. He notes that for Ignatius, "marriage, a matter of the 'flesh,' receives a religious interpretation and becomes also a matter of the 'spirit.'"[88] It seems that this move harmonizes well with Ignatius' preoccupation with a bishop's authority evidenced throughout the letter. Ignatius tells wives that he approves of marriage in the spirit (as well as the flesh), advising them to be content with marriage as a spiritual state. Schoedel hypothesizes that Ignatius' cautious attitude toward celibacy is due in part to "the potential challenge it poses to episcopal authority."[89] Women might see celibacy as a higher spiritual calling. So Ignatius advises them that marriage, too, is spiritually satisfying in that the woman images the church (to her husband's lordship.) Ignatius' direction for engaged couples, that they seek the bishop's consent for marriage, evinces the same concern for the bishop's authority. Marriage and household become subject to the control of religious authorities.

Ignatius must have seen traditional kyriarchal marriage and households as intrinsic to a well-organized social grouping, whether city or church. According to Schoedel, Ignatius was comfortable thinking with the institutions and organizational tools of the Greek city.[90] Perhaps Ignatius had belonged to the ruling elite of his city. Shawn Carruth has argued that "[Ignatius'] use of the idealized qualities of the city to praise the churches he addresses reflects an understanding of how those ideals should work toward establishing good order and unity in a city's population. And Ignatius appears to think those ideals could work in the churches as well."[91] Ignatius uses the term *ekklesia*, (civic) assembly, for the groups he addresses. He does not seem to imagine the church as a household,[92] but he could have followed political theorists in reinforcing

87. *SIG* 3.985. Robert Grant, ed., *Hellenistic Religions: The Age of Syncretism* (New York: Liberal Arts Press, 1953), 28–30.

88. Schoedel, *Ignatius of Antioch*, 272.

89. Ibid., 272. This interpretation is also espoused by David G. Hunter, *Marriage, Celibacy, and Heresy in Ancient Christianity* (Oxford: Oxford University Press, 2007), 92. Temporary sexual asceticism often accompanied women's religious leadership in antiquity. See Celia Schultz, *Women's Religious Activity in the Roman Republic* (Chapel Hill: University of North Carolina Press, 2006), 76; Elisabeth Schüssler Fiorenza, *In Memory of Her: A Feminist Theological Reconstruction of Christian Origins* (New York: Crossroad, 1982), 278.

90. Schoedel, *Ignatius of Antioch*, 14, n. 70 and 71.

91. Shawn Carruth, "Praise for the Churches: The Letters of Ignatius of Antioch," in *Reimagining Christian Origins*, ed. Elizabeth A. Castelli and Hal Taussig (Valley Forge, PA: Trinity, 1996), 295–310, 303.

the household's kyriarchal relations in order to strengthen political relationships within and between the churches.[93] A series of stacked hierarchical structures forms an ideal(ized) chain of command. In Ignatius' understanding, households will be models of kyriarchal concord if wives accept the spiritual lordship of their husbands. Imperial ideology linked concord in household with concord in cities and empire. Just as Livia took on the persona of the goddess Concordia, the responsibility for household concord fell to the wife.

A sound interpretative strategy distinguishes Ignatius' instructions from the historical situation of the addressees in Smyrna. It is possible that the wives to whom Ignatius refers regarded some other values as greater than concord, or, they may have rejected kyriarchal social organization as the best route to concord.

I noted above a wife who was represented in terms of civic status and occupational success and contrasted this representation with that of the matron in a kyriarchal household. This alternative motif for a wife's representation is significant for understanding the historical context in Smyrna. It indicates that kyriarchal social organization was not the only way to represent wealthy households and marriages. Some wives and husbands in the historical context had access to non-kyriarchal models to represent marriage and household. Ignatius, however, seeks to strengthen the imperial kyriarchal understanding of marriage and household in religious terms by advising wives to accept the spiritual lordship of their husbands.

Interpreters have proposed several possibilities for reconstructing the historical situation in Smyrna. Christine Trevett expands on Schoedel's views, arguing that Ignatius understood celibacy as a challenge to episcopal authority.[94] Wives may have been practicing marital celibacy, or avoiding

---

92. Compare "the household of God" imagery employed by the authors of 1 Timothy and 1 Peter. See Schoedel, *Ignatius of Antioch*, 22–23. However, MacDonald and Harry O. Maier take the kyriarchal household as the model organizational structure for the groups addressed by Ignatius. MacDonald, *Early Christian Women*, 36; Harry O. Maier, *The Social Setting of the Ministry as Reflected in the Writings of Hermas, Clement and Ignatius* (Waterloo, ON: Wilfrid Laurier University Press, 2002), 47.

93. Maier has written, "Ignatius' conception of community leadership . . . is best understood as reinforcing social impulses inherent in a situation in which the hierarchically ordered Graeco-Roman household was adopted as a means of church organization." Maier, *Social Setting*, 181.

94. "Episcopal control was what Ignatius wanted to see—over baptisms, eucharists, *agapés* (*Smyrn.* 8), matters of money, widows and here, marriage." Christine Trevett, *Christian Women and the Time of the Apostolic Fathers (A.D. c 80–160): Corinth, Rome and Asia Minor* (Cardiff: University of Wales Press, 2006), 183. See also Maier, *Social Setting*, 179. Maier's study leads him to declare: "Ignatius's conception of the church is not merely where two or three are gathered, but where the bishop or one whom he appoints presides (*Trall.* 3:1; *Smyrn.* 8:1–2); . . ." (179).

marriage for the sake of celibacy.[95] Ignatius presents celibacy as part of the religious self-understanding of some in Smyrna who "honor the flesh of the Lord by maintaining a state of purity" (*Poly.* 5.2). Margaret MacDonald argues that women ascetics in Corinth left marriage through divorce in pursuit of religious purity.[96] More recently, David Hunter has contrasted the value placed on celibacy with the ideal of marriage promoted in the household codes (especially in the Pastoral Letters).[97] Harry Maier also remarks on an interest in sexual abstinence from marriage in religious texts of second-century Asia Minor (particularly in the *Acts of Thecla*).[98]

Trevett presents a majority opinion: "It is probable that life without marriage or abstention from sex within marriage were hot topics in Smyrna in Ignatius' time."[99] These reconstructions agree that some women in religious groups sought to avoid sexual relationships, either by avoiding marriage or by seeking celibate marriages. However, the ancient understanding of marriage for a wealthy woman also included the aspects of her socioeconomic status as a wife in her husband's household, so an interpretation limited to sexual dimensions of household relationships leaves aside a vital factor in understanding the household.

A consideration of wealthy women's socioeconomic household status enriches the picture of the historical context. Since a widow might own and control property, including her own household, a marriage-free state for wealthy women entailed more than celibacy. To be unmarried also meant to control the household's resources and management, to have civic status, and

95. See notes in preceding on the formation of a spiritual ascetic elite. Trevett also implies that some may have divorced in order to remarry for social advantage. "Marital rectitude was flourished, rhetorically and philosophically, and it conferred *dignitas*. Yet, in reality, social climbing through marriage for advantage was common in the second century, both among the better classes and among freedpersons." Trevett, *Christian Women*, 184.

96. MacDonald, *Early Christian Women*, 137. Elisabeth Schüssler Fiorenza's interpretation of 1 Peter has suggested that wives in religious groups divorcing their husbands was an issue for the audiences of this letter in Asia Minor in the late first century. See "Empire and the Rhetoric of Subordination," in *The Power of the Word: Scripture and the Rhetoric of Empire* (Minneapolis: Fortress Press, 2007), 178–79. Antoinette Clark Wire has argued that divorce by wives was a significant phenomenon in the religious community in Corinth in the middle of the first century. See *Corinthian Women Prophets: A Reconstruction through Paul's Rhetoric* (Minneapolis: Fortress Press, 1990), 84–85.

97. David G. Hunter, *Marriage, Celibacy, and Heresy in Ancient Christianity: The Jovinianist Controversy* (Oxford: Oxford University Press, 2007), 90–96.

98. Harry O. Maier, "Heresy, Households, and the Disciplining of Diversity," in *A People's History of Christianity*, vol. 2, *Late Ancient Christianity*, ed. V. Burrus (Minneapolis: Fortress Press, 2005), 218.

99. Trevett, *Christian Women*, 184.

legal and religious responsibility. As the head of a household, widows could also serve as leaders of *ekklesia* groups based in their houses.

Scholars have analyzed Ignatius' rhetoric in terms of sexual status. In this view, Ignatius understood celibacy as a threat to the bishop's leadership from a spiritual elite. However, Ignatius' rhetoric could also be understood in terms of socioeconomic status. For wealthy women, being marriage-free entailed a higher socioeconomic status than marriage did. A widow's leadership of a religious group presented a challenge to episcopal authority in the same way that an ascetic elite did.

WIDOWS

Ignatius' treatment of widows supports the idea that he was concerned with leadership based in socioeconomic household status. He sends a greeting to "virgins called widows" (*Smyrn.* 13.1). He also writes:

Χῆραι μὴ ἀμελείσθωσαν· μετὰ τὸν κύριον σὺ αὐτῶν φροντιστὴς ἔσο. Μηδὲν ἄνευ γνώμης σου γινέσθω μηδὲ σὺ ἄνευ θεοῦ τι πρᾶσσε.

Do not allow the widows to be neglected. After the Lord, it is you who must be their guardian.[100] Let nothing be done apart from your consent, and do nothing apart from God. (Ign. *Pol.* 4.1)

The Greek term translated as "widow" (χήρα) denotes a woman who lived without a man.[101] While many commentators have interpreted this passage in terms of charity, Elisabeth Schüssler Fiorenza has suggested that Ignatius is concerned with supervision of the widows:

In the papyri, the Greek word used here [φροντιστής] refers to the guardian or trustee of women who could not represent themselves in law courts. The word can, moreover, connote the managerial administration of a household or association. In an inscription from

---

100. In the Loeb edition, Ehrman translates φροντιστής as a verbal form: "It is you who must be mindful of them." Ehrman, *Apostolic Fathers*, 315.

101. Methuen, "'Virgin Widow,'" 285–88. See also Gustav Stählin, "χήρα," *Theological Dictionary of the New Testament* 9.440–65. It seems that these women lived together since Ignatius greets households in this section. Schüssler Fiorenza, *In Memory of Her*, 313.

Pamphylia, a φροντιστής of the synagogue is mentioned.[102] Whether the word implies the legal tutorship and administration of the widows' affairs, or is used here in a more generalized sense, in any case it enforces the control of the bishop over the widows, and seeks to curtail their independence.[103]

Ignatius' concern for the authority of the bishop shaped his attitude toward widows' households. Ignatius instructs Polycarp to take on the role of guardian of the widows. Thus Polycarp is to act as the male head of household, as fathers and husbands did for daughters and wives. However, as we have seen, a wealthy widow herself could act as head of the household. Analysis of representations of wealthy women's household status indicates that similar conventions determined the socioeconomic leadership of heads of households, whether they were men or widows. As Harry Maier has noted, "there was a house-church setting in which patrons of the church had a central role of leadership."[104] Since Ignatius seeks to consolidate leadership under a bishop, he advises the bishop to take on the role of *kyrios* with respect to widows. A wealthy widow's religious self-understanding as marriage-free could have included socioeconomic leadership (as well as celibacy) and needed to be controlled.

Among women with households, Ignatius names Tavia and the wife of Epitropus. Tavia seems to be a widow with property while the wife of Epitropus may be a prominent woman whose husband was not affiliated with the religious group. Schüssler Fiorenza has suggested that Alke had a prominent religious status in Asia Minor as well since her name was still known in the middle of the second century.[105] The affection Ignatius conveys suggests that Alke provided him with hospitality in her household or a similar form of personal support. These three women seemed to have had access to some wealth. Since Ignatius names these women individually they must be prominent in the *ekklesia*, but Ignatius omits information about their relationships to the *ekklesia* as well as their specific religious status. Nonetheless, Ignatius singled out these women and left clues to their socioeconomic status so that their names have become part of the history we can reconstruct of women's religious leadership.

102. *JHS* 1908:194, 29. In a bilingual inscription from Bithynia, φροντιστής translates the Latin *tutor* in IK Iznik 1141. The term refers to a city's agent/manager or curator in *SEG* 13.258. Discussion in Bremen, *Limits of Participation*, 231–33.

103. Schüssler Fiorenza, *In Memory of Her*, 314

104. Maier, *Social Setting*, 156.

105. Schüssler Fiorenza, *In Memory of Her*, 247–48.

In summary, two letters from Ignatius to religious assemblies in Smyrna distinguish among women in terms of household groupings and religious status: wives with husbands, women with households, and widows (including virgins). Ignatius attempts to persuade his audience to share his view of women's religious subordination: he instructs the bishop to manage widows (after the Lord) and he presents kyriarchal household and marriage as a religious ideal.

Ignatius also refers to a group of celibates: it is not clear whether these persons are female, male, or both, nor whether or how they overlap with the first three groups.[106] Interpreters have suggested that religious women sought to avoid sexual relationships, and this has been discussed fruitfully in terms of sexual asceticism and social oppression.[107]

My argument has emphasized dimensions of households that encompassed social, economic, and legal relationships. For wealthy women, socioeconomic household status might vary significantly with marital status. Thus religious women's marriage-free status entailed socioeconomic leadership as well as sexual asceticism. Insofar as socioeconomic leadership allowed religious leadership, women's religious status was inseparable from their socioeconomic status.

The next chapter explores wealthy widows' exercise of leadership more specifically with investigation of their socioeconomic status in the system of patronage.

CONCLUSION

Well-known scholarship discusses the affinity of religious women for a marriage-free state in terms of sexual status. In this socioeconomic study,

106. Ehrman's translation of "τις" as "he" might obscure the indefinite grammar of the pronoun: "If anyone is able to honor the flesh of the Lord by maintaining a state of purity, let her/him do so without boasting." Cf. Ehrman, *Apostolic Fathers*, 316–17.

107. I noted above interpreters' references to the formation of a spiritual ascetic elite in Ignatius' *Letter to Polycarp*. Some years ago, Schüssler Fiorenza suggested: "While the a-sexual and a-familial ethos of early Christianity is often misunderstood as antisexual and antiwoman, it actually is an indication of a 'role-revolt' which allowed women to 'legitimately' move out of the confines of the patriarchal family and to center their life around the spiritual self-fulfillment and independence that gave them greater respect, mobility, and influence." Schüssler Fiorenza, *In Memory of Her*, 90. Virginia Burrus has written, "Even male authors in the ancient period share the awareness that sexually ascetic women escape certain forms of physical suffering and social oppression through the rejection of marriage. . . . Female ascetics express little interest in bodily intactness or cloistered privacy, topics which loom large in male discussions of female virginity." V. Burrus, "Word and Flesh: The Bodies and Sexuality of Ascetic Women in Christian Antiquity," *Journal of Feminist Studies in Religion* 10 (1994): 31–32.

however, I argue that an adequate analysis of religious status must adjust the framework to include the socioeconomic dimensions of marriages and wealthy households.

We notice that Ignatius associates women's religious status with their household status. His address distinguishes household groups of women and he gives instructions based on women's marital or household status. Interpretation of these texts depends on understanding women's status in households. In order to do this, I sought out sources that are particularly rich in their presentations of women in households. Since the household was an institution with socioeconomic and political dimensions, I have investigated the sources on households using the analytical model of kyriarchy.

My analysis emphasized two types of representation of elite women: wives who resembled Roman matrons, and widows who were heads of households. Marital status emerged as a critical determinant of status for wealthy women. The portrayals communicate status with Roman and provincial identifiers, women's relation to work and economic agency, and civic and legal standing. Wifely subordination and passivity enhanced the status of her household whereas a wealthy widow might refer to occupation and citizenship to display her status. Household and marital status were critical to a woman's socioeconomic status. While a feminine ideal of the matron accompanied portrayals of women's secondary status, an ideal of political and economic leadership accompanied portrayals of the head of the household. Representations of wealthy widows indicate that wealth and marital status had a significant impact on the relationship between gender and ascriptions of political and economic status.

Ignatius' advice that the bishop establish himself as a guardian of wealthy widows draws on an ideal of feminine subordination to ascribe a secondary status to these widows. However, the historical possibility of wealthy widows' socioeconomic leadership is still apparent. Ignatius' advice to wives to accept the spiritual lordship of their husbands would reinforce women's secondary status in the household. In his instructions about wives and widows, Ignatius sought to strengthen kyriarchal social organization in the religious group. Ignatius associated women's religious status with their household status and he sought to manage both.

Scholarship has established that wealthy heads of households served as patrons of religious groups that met in their houses (as I discussed in the preceding chapter). In the following chapter, I investigate the status of wealthy widows in the institution of patronage in order to understand further the proclivities for their religious leadership.

3

Women Patrons

In the preceding chapters, I have begun investigating the question of wealthy women's religious leadership in Asia Minor in the first two centuries of the common era. I presented an approach based on historical materialist feminism, drawing on the model of kyriarchy to analyze sources about women's religious status. The advantage to this approach emerges clearly in the conclusion showing the association of marital status with socioeconomic status for wealthy freeborn women: representations of married women emphasized their secondary status in the household whereas wealthy widows were presented in terms of their cities, associations, and occupations. A wealthy widow's religious status depended on her socioeconomic leadership as the head of a household. Ignatius saw these women's leadership as a threat to the bishop's leadership of the religious association. Could wealthy widows serve as leaders also through their patronage of religious groups?

Studies of wealthy women's leadership of religious groups in Asia Minor in the first two centuries of the common era have emphasized the female figures in several texts and an inscription: Phoebe appears in Paul's Letter to the Romans, an inscription from Smyrna honors Rufina, and Tryphaena plays a major role in the *Acts of Thecla*.[1] In this chapter, I discuss interpretations of these texts, beginning with patronage itself. For all the sources, inscriptional and literary, I analyze the representations in terms of the materialist feminist model of kyriarchy. I seek out interlocking constructions of difference in terms of wealth, marital and legal status, age, and ethnicity.[2] These distinctions

---

1. Respectively, Romans 16:1-2, *CIJ* 2.741, and the *Acts of Paul and Thecla*. Although Phoebe herself was from Greece, we know of her through Paul, who was from Asia Minor; analysis of her history thus falls within the parameters of this study.

2. Readers may be surprised that I do not distinguish among religious groups. It seems that "religion" was not a distinct category in antiquity, nor were "Christian" and "Jewish" distinct ethnicities in the first centuries. I address this in preceding chapters.

are crucial in elaborating the production(s) of patronage through the Roman Empire's socioeconomic and political systems in Asia Minor. Through the use of historical materialist feminism, my analysis incorporates socioeconomic dimensions of patronage, leadership, and religious groups; this approach leads to a more complete reconstruction of the historical possibilities for women such as Phoebe, Rufina, and Tryphaena.

Scholars have debated the significance of the two nouns that Paul applies to Phoebe: *prostatis* and *diakonos*. Investigation of these terms has raised questions about wealthy women's religious leadership as patrons. First, we examine the institution and ideology of patronage in Asia Minor. Studies of elite women in Asia Minor have drawn primarily from honorary inscriptions. This genre of inscriptions presents prominent people in the cities in Asia Minor during Roman rule. I discuss honorary inscriptions that are significant for investigating wealthy women's socioeconomic status as patrons, including one that presents Rufina as a wealthy Jewish widow with a title of religious leadership. Literary texts also present portrayals of women's patronage and religious status. Scholarship on wealthy widows in religious groups has focused on women in the Apocryphal Acts, particularly the figure of Tryphaena in the *Acts of Paul and Thecla*. I analyze this literary depiction and compare it to the portrayals presented in the epigraphic sources. As the final step of this investigation of women's religious leadership in patronage, I return to Phoebe in Paul's Letter to the Romans and seek to understand her status and activities. Interpretation of Phoebe's religious status hinges on understanding wealthy widows' status in patronage.

CRITICAL FEATURES OF PATRONAGE

In the Roman Empire, vertical relationships of patronage controlled access to goods and resources. Terry Johnson and Christopher Dandeker have argued that patronage should be analyzed as a social system, a complex and hierarchically organized series of relationships.[3] A more complete analysis also emphasizes its economic dimensions. Richard Saller writes that "according to the ideology in Roman society, public figures, from municipal administrators to the emperors, were not only expected, but were supposed to use their positions to bestow *beneficia* on friends."[4] This phenomenon was not confined to Romans; Saller also cites Greek author Plutarch as evidence. Patronage played a role in

3. Terry Johnson and Christopher Dandeker, "Patronage: Relation and System," in *Patronage in Ancient Society*, ed. Andrew Wallace-Hadrill (London: Routledge, 1989), 219–42.

social structures, military and legal systems, and the hierarchy of political and religious offices. Particularly for Asia Minor, Rome maintained control of the population by making clients of local leaders rather than by the presence of standing armies.

Inscriptions of Asia Minor created during the early centuries of Roman imperial rule highlight local urban and provincial elite patronage. The political economy became more integrated in this period. "Not only did rich Romans own land in all the provinces, but increasingly rich provincials became Romans."[5] Members of the elite increased their wealth under imperial rule.[6] Elites from cities and provinces of Asia Minor joined the rank of the Roman Senate through patronage.[7] "For the Vedii Antonini [of Ephesus], as for other elite *gentes* in the cities of the Roman Empire, patronage and benefaction were duties that could advance family status from one of local to imperial importance."[8] Vedius I and Vedius II served as patrons of local associations, magistrates, and priesthoods.[9] Ambassadorships allowed them to establish friendship with emperors.[10]

Vedius III and his wife, Flavia Papiane, solicited the emperor's approval for a new council building (*bouleuterion*),[11] which they decorated with commemorations of their relationship with imperial families.[12] Flavia Papiane served as high priest(ess) of Asia, and Vedius III entered the Roman senate.[13] In Ephesus, the Vedii concentrated their patronage in the Koressos neighborhood.[14] They financed buildings and workers' associations located here or nearby: food workers, temple builders, teachers, and wool weavers.[15]

---

4. Richard P. Saller, *Personal Patronage Under the Early Empire* (Cambridge: Cambridge University Press, 1982), 30. Also, Peter Garnsey and Richard Saller, *The Roman Empire: Economy, Society and Culture* (Berkeley: University of California, 1987), 125.

5. Keith Hopkins, "Rome, Taxes, Rents and Trade," in *The Ancient Economy*, ed. Walter Scheidel and Sitta von Reden (Edinburgh: Edinburgh University Press, 2002), 206.

6. This increased wealth is "generally veiled by a prevailing aristocratic ideology, which reports cruelty and persecution by emperors." Hopkins, "Rome, Taxes," 206.

7. Saller, *Personal Patronage*, 143.

8. Angela Kalinowski, "The Vedii Antonini: Aspects of Patronage and Benefaction in Second-Century Ephesus," *Phoenix* 56 (2002): 144.

9. *IEph* 728.

10. Kalinowski, "Vedii," 145.

11. *IEph* 460.

12. Kalinowski, "Vedii," 141–44.

13. *IEph* 729, 732.

14. Kalinowski, "Vedii," 134–35.

15. *IEph* 728, 3075, 2065, 727.

Through vertical relationships of patronage, these workers in Ephesus had access to the influence of imperial elites in Rome.

For members of the Vedius Antonini family of Ephesus, municipal and provincial patronage could help men rise to the Roman senate, but women like Flavia Papiane could not join the senate in their own right. This restriction on Papinae reproduces that of the elite of the empire, since only men served as emperors and other military leaders. Certain aspects of political processes appear to have been closed to women, such as membership in the council and the administrative office of secretary.[16] Steven Friesen's study of hundreds of honorary inscriptions from Ephesus found gendered patterns among benefactors: male offices included Asiarch and the Kuretes, and female offices included the priest(ess) of Artemis.[17] Wealthy women who survived their families had narrower opportunities for patronage than similarly positioned wealthy men, who could try to improve their rank. Elisabeth Schüssler Fiorenza has hypothesized that such wealthy women might establish relationships with voluntary associations, thereby gaining "recognition and public honor in return for their benevolence."[18] Scholarship has accepted that wealthy women were honored as patrons and benefactors in Asia Minor.[19] At the same time, a debate continues about women's status with respect to their clients. Did the ideal of femininity that barred women's access to the highest ranks also constrain the manner in which women enacted their patronal activities? I return to this question later.

16. Sviatoslav Dmitriev, *City Government in Hellenistic and Roman Asia Minor* (Oxford and New York: Oxford University Press, 2005). Dmitriev devalues positions held by women by grouping them in a family context, comparing them with offices held by children, and describing the offices as those "that could be bought," and those of no administrative importance (46–56, 178–88). His authority for the last claim is Magie, *Roman Rule*. See 182, n. 223. An up-to-date systematic study is still needed. Inscriptions that cite familial connections are not evidence that women held offices "simply by virtue of their belonging to leading families" (183) any more so than for men. Nonetheless, men held the most prestigious office and they could hold government offices. Steven Friesen, "Myth and Symbolic Resistance in Revelation 13," *Journal of Biblical Literature* 123, no. 2 (2004): 303.

17. Steven Friesen, "Ephesian Women and Men in Public Office During the Roman Imperial Period," in *100 Jahre Österreichische Forschungen in Ephesus. Akten des Symposions Wien 1995* (Wien: Österreichische Akademie der Wissenschaften, 1999), 112. These data are based on a study of hundreds of inscriptions and coins, most from Ephesus. Elsewhere, Friesen suggests that the deification of Livia in 41 c.e. occasioned the new pattern in provincial high priesthoods. Friesen, *Twice Neokoros: Ephesus, Asia, and the Cult of the Flavian Imperial Family* (Leiden: Brill, 1993), 88–89.

18. Elisabeth Schüssler Fiorenza, *In Memory of Her: A Feminist Theological Reconstruction of Christian Origins* (New York: Crossroad, 1982), 182–83, 249.

19. On women patrons in North Africa, see Emily A. Hemelrijk, "City Patronesses in the Roman Empire," *Historia* 53, no. 2 (2004): 209–45.

The sources for patronage in Asia Minor are chiefly honorary inscriptions, a different genre from the funerary monuments and legal material used in the preceding chapter. The genre of these honorary inscriptions circumscribes our information about women in religious and civic organizations.[20] The historical record is virtually silent about the many women (and men) whose participation in such associations was less illustrious than the few they honored. The genre of the sources also limits what we can know about the activities of the women who were honored. Honorary inscriptions typically praise a sponsor for her financial generosity; thus the women who appear here belonged to socioeconomic strata situated in the higher levels of society. Their wealth allowed them to stand as patrons or benefactors in relation to religious and civic groups.[21]

This brief introduction to patronage provides historical context for the discussion that follows. I return to patronage in Asia Minor after a close look at the scholarship about Phoebe's religious status.

PHOEBE

Discussions of women's patronage of religious associations have centered on the figure of Phoebe mentioned in Romans 16. Around the middle of the first century, Paul sent a long list of greetings that began with this recommendation:

Συνίστημι δὲ ὑμῖν Φοίβην τὴν ἀδελφὴν ἡμῶν, οὖσαν καὶ διάκονον τῆς ἐκκλησίας τῆς ἐν Κεγχρεαῖς, ἵνα αὐτὴν προσδέξησθε ἐν κυρίῳ ἀξίως τῶν ἁγίων, καὶ παραστῆτε αὐτῇ ἐν ᾧ ἂν ὑμῶν χρῄζῃ πράγματι, καὶ γὰρ αὐτὴ προστάτις πολλῶν ἐγενήθη καὶ ἐμοῦ αὐτοῦ.

I commend to you our sister Phoebe, minister of the church at Cenchreae, so that you may welcome her in the Lord as is fitting for the saints, and help her with anything she may require from you, for she has been a patron of many and of myself as well. (Rom. 16:1-2)

These verses come at the conclusion of Paul's letter to the Romans. Scholars debate whether this chapter of Romans was originally part of a letter headed to

---

20. The same problems with interpretation, such as omissions, genre inflection, and rhetoricity, occur with all sources. I have discussed these in the introduction.

21. Unfortunately, few sources remember the many persons who served organizations in other roles.

Ephesus, or whether it appeared as it does now, in a letter intended for Rome.[22] In either case, commentators agree that Phoebe delivered the letter.[23]

Phoebe is the only person whom Paul describes as both *diakonos* and *prostatis* in his letters (translated "minister" and "patron" above).[24] Paul mentioned many titles of religious status in Romans 16 without gender specification: both women and men are known as co-workers (16:3, 9), apostles (16:7), workers (16:6, 12), and compatriots (16:7, 11). Paul uses both the masculine grammatical form for Phoebe (διάκονος) and feminine forms (προστάτις and ἀδελφή). Thus Paul does not correlate men and women with the grammatical gender of these terms. His use of grammatical gender corresponds to the use of titles and occupational terms in many other ancient sources.[25]

Paul does not specify Phoebe's marital or family status, but it seems that she was a widow since no husband is mentioned.

Since Paul describes Phoebe with several terms, and two of these have been debated extensively in scholarship, I discuss them separately, taking up *prostatis* first, and then *diakonos*.

"PROSTATIS"

Phoebe is the only person identified as a patron in Paul's writings. Paul uses a substantive form of the cognate verb (προΐστημι) in Rom. 12:8 as "leader,"[26] and in 1 Thess. 5:12, it means "to be in charge of."[27] The lexicon translates the masculine form of the noun with "ruler," "administrator," "presiding officer," and "patron."[28] Both of Paul's uses refer specifically to leaders of the groups he

---

22. Werner Georg Kummel, *The New Testament: The History of the Investigation of Its Problems* (New York: Abingdon, 1972), 316–20. Peter Lampe, *From Paul to Valentinus: Christians at Rome in the First Two Centuries* (Minneapolis: Fortress Press, 2003), 153–64. Lampe's careful reading argues persuasively that Romans 16 was original with Romans 1-15.

23. Robert Jewett, assist. by Roy D. Kotansky, *Romans: A Commentary* (Hermeneia; Minneapolis: Fortress Press, 2007), 942–43.

24. I cite the large body of scholarship on Phoebe in the following sections as I elaborate on Phoebe's role.

25. Suzanne Dixon, "Exemplary Housewife or Luxurious Slut? Cultural Representations of Women in the Roman Economy," in *Women's Influence on Classical Civilization*, ed. Fiona McHardy and Eirann Marshall (London: Routledge, 2004), 56–74.

26. εἴτε ὁ παρακαλῶν ἐν τῇ παρακλήσει, ὁ μεταδιδοὺς ἐν ἁπλότητι, ὁ προϊστάμενος ἐν σπουδῇ, ὁ ἐλεῶν ἐν ἱλαρότητι.

27. Ἐρωτῶμεν δὲ ὑμᾶς, ἀδελφοί, εἰδέναι τοὺς κοπιῶντας ἐν ὑμῖν καὶ προϊσταμένους ὑμῶν ἐν κυρίῳ καὶ νουθετοῦντας ὑμᾶς.

addresses, "the *ekklesia*" (1 Thess. 1:1), and the "one body" (Rom. 12:8) "called to be saints" (Rom. 1:7). If Phoebe were said to be *prostatis* of Cenchreae, the translation should certainly be "president" of the assembly. However, because she enacts this leading role with respect to "many" and to Paul himself, NRSV translates *prostatis* as "benefactor." Since Paul has already referenced her leadership of the assembly at Cenchreae with the term *diakonos* (minister), one wonders whether members of the assembly of Cenchreae are among the "many" who receive Phoebe's patronage. If so, perhaps we should also understand her to be "administrator" or "presiding officer" of an assembly.[29]

R. A. Kearsley has improved our understanding of the institution of patronage. She studies two women whom first-century inscriptions name as patrons, Junia Theodora from Greece and Claudia Metrodora from Asia Minor.[30] Kearsley reconstructs the situation and activities of these women and also discusses Phoebe, concluding that "although a lack of information prevents any exploration of Phoebe's social and family background, nevertheless the evidence of the inscriptions discussed above indicates that women of wealth could and did hold influential positions in the society of Paul's lifetime, and that the title *prostatis* and cognate words designated such actions."[31] Kearsley enumerates the political, commercial, and legal dimensions of women's patronage and the recognition they received from grateful clients (individuals and cities).[32] The women Kearsley studies were Roman citizens who operated in civic contexts; their patronage entailed political, commercial, and legal dimensions. Kearsley's examples suggest that Phoebe's patronage might entail some political, commercial, and legal dimensions as well, but Phoebe's sphere of operation differed, so the relevance of the analogy needs more investigation.

Robert Jewett has recently reconstructed Phoebe's role. Describing her activities within a house church, he notes:

Recent studies . . . of the leading role played by upper-class benefactors, both male and female, in early Christian communities provide the social background of the description of Phoebe's status.

28. LSJ, "προΐστημι."

29. As suggested by Elisabeth Schüssler Fiorenza, "Missionaries, Apostles, Coworkers: Romans 16 and the Reconstruction of Women in Early Christian History," *Word & World* 6, no. 4 (1986): 426.

30. R. A. Kearsley, "Women in Public Life in the Roman East: Iunia Theodora, Claudia Metrodora and Phoebe, Benefactress of Paul," *Tyndale Bulletin* 50, no. 2 (1999): 189–211.

31. Ibid., 202.

32. Ibid., 194–97.

The host or hostess of house churches was usually a person of high social standing and means, with a residence large enough for the church to gather, who presided over the eucharistic celebrations and was responsible for the ordering of the congregation. The fact that Paul mentions Phoebe as a patroness "to many, and also to me" indicates the level of material resources that would support this kind of leadership role.[33]

In Jewett's reconstruction, Phoebe provides socioeconomic leadership, presiding at eucharistic meals and organizing the ekklesia. Paul mentions only an "assembly at Cenchreae," not an assembly meeting in a house, as he reports elsewhere.[34] So Jewett's reconstruction of Phoebe's hospitality remains uncertain. However, Kearsley's analogy to Theodora suggests that patrons did provide hospitality. At the time that Paul writes, Phoebe is leaving Cenchreae, so perhaps it would be strange if Paul said that the group gathered in her house. Nonetheless, Paul still describes Phoebe as *diakonos* of the assembly of Cenchreae. Thus Paul implies that Phoebe's role included religious as well as socioeconomic leadership.

Jewett's interpretation goes on to underscore Phoebe's orientation toward a religious goal. In Jewett's understanding of Phoebe and Paul's relationship, Paul commends Phoebe as a patron of the Spanish mission (Romans 15).[35]

The Roman recipients of the letter would understand her to be recommended as the patroness of the Spanish mission, which Paul had announced in the preceding cheaper. As a missionary patroness "of many" and therefore a person of substantial wealth, the churches of Rome would have no fear that cooperation with her would require onerous financial obligations on their part. They would be honored by the prospect of involvement with a person of this high social status.[36]

---

33. Jewett, *Romans*, 947.

34. Rom. 16:3-5, 23; 1 Cor. 16:19; Philem. 2.

35. Whelan joins the minority opinion that argues that the destination of Romans 16 is Ephesus, not Rome. Thus she does not imagine a role for Phoebe in Paul's plans for a missionary trip to Spain.

36. Jewett, *Romans*, 948.

In Jewett's reconstruction, Paul's commendation provides testimony to Phoebe's wealth or perhaps a testimony to her desire and ability to provide patronage. Jewett argues that Paul's commendation would have helped Phoebe in her role as a missionary patron. Jewett imagines her role as more financial and social than missionary since he also argues that she was not herself a traveling missionary.[37] For Jewett, Phoebe's patronal religious leadership, hosting, and organizing was based in Cenchreae; in Rome, she would provide financial support and social cachet. So Jewett does not address why Phoebe's patronal role would change from Cenchreae to Rome, nor does he make it clear why Paul refers to Phoebe as a *diakonos*.

According to both Kearsley and Jewett, Phoebe enjoys high social standing relative to Paul and supports him financially.[38] Jewett suggests that Phoebe has agreed to underwrite Paul's mission to Spain. If this is the case, and the status differential between the two is the usual one for patrons and clients, why would Paul write a letter of commendation for the more socially prominent Phoebe? Caroline Whelan's study of ancient patronage has proposed that Paul draws on his reservoir of friends in Rome, asking them to receive Phoebe as one of the community as a favor to him.[39] Whelan notes that, "as a Christian missionary, Paul would inevitably have built a large body of friends and followers throughout the Roman Empire. In Romans 16 Paul is exploiting this network of 'clients' on behalf of Phoebe, introducing her to his network of connections and thereby reciprocating her benefactions to him and his [*sic*] church."[40]

Whelan highlights the reciprocity and mutual obligation inherent in the patron–client relationship. Phoebe would receive hospitality and, once she established new patronal relationships, gratitude.[41] Whelan also discusses the economic and social benefits Phoebe would have provided for Paul and for others. She adds, "To treat Phoebe, therefore, 'merely' as a financial benefactor, if that is what she was, is to misunderstand the nature of benefaction in antiquity. Benefaction included not just financial support, but also allowing clients access to one's social and economic resources."[42] Whelan's explication of the mutuality of Paul and Phoebe's relationship explains an aspect of Paul's commendation of Phoebe, but not Phoebe's religious status.

37. Ibid., 945.

38. Kearsley, "Women in Public Life," 202; Jewett, *Romans*, 946–47.

39. Caroline Whelan, "*Amici Pauli*: The Role of Phoebe in the Early Church," *Journal for the Study of the New Testament* 49 (1993): 67–85.

40. Ibid., 84

41. Ibid., 84.

42. Ibid., 84.

After having discussed the interpretations of Jewett and Whelan, Carolyn Osiek suggests that Phoebe and Paul collaborated: "Whether one considers Romans 16 as addressed to Rome or to Ephesus will necessarily influence one's interpretation of Phoebe's role. But whichever it is, it is likely that Paul is not just commending Phoebe to a new group, but is participating in some greater plan, which may have been initiated not by Paul but by Phoebe."[43] In Osiek's proposal, the mission is a joint enterprise.

Sojung Yoon has also questioned the view of Phoebe's patronal role as "a mere helper and financial supporter of Paul" in Rome since she is also a diakonos.[44]

> Considering the fact that Paul never identifies any other Christian leader as superior to him or having authority over him, including James, Cephas, and John (Gal 2:6, 9), Phoebe's status in the church at Cenchreae must have been considerable. This may also be the reason why Paul downplays her role as προστάτις, "even of me." . . . Phoebe's leadership and influence within the church at Cenchreae may have led Paul to fear her capacity as a potential competitor for influence and allegiance in Rome.[45]

According to Yoon, Paul provides Phoebe with an introduction to people he knew in Rome because Phoebe was traveling to Rome as a religious leader. Besides financial support, Phoebe's activities could have included introducing audiences to the mission and to letters from Paul and others. Yoon's reconstruction highlights the need to investigate the religious activities and leadership capacities of wealthy women who engaged in patronage.

Since Phoebe had the financial resources to engage in patronage and to have many clients, she seems to have been a member of the small percentage of the population who lived well above subsistence.[46] Women had access to wealth in several circumstances: if freeborn, a woman may have been born or married into an elite family; or, she may have acquired access to wealth as a freed slave

43. Carolyn Osiek, "Diakonos and Prostatis: Women's Patronage in Early Christianity," *Hervormde Teologiese Studies* 61, no. 1–2 (2005): 365.

44. Sojung Yoon, "Phoebe, a Minister in the Early Christian Church," in *Distant Voices Drawing Near*, ed. Holly E. Hearon (Collegeville, MN: Liturgical, 2004), 31.

45. Yoon, "Phoebe," 31.

46. Steven J. Friesen, "Poverty in Pauline Studies: Beyond the So-called New Consensus," in *Journal for the Study of the New Testament* 26, no. 3 (2004): 323–61.

in a lucrative occupation. I address slave women's socioeconomic and religious status in the following chapter.

In sum, research on patronage has gone far beyond the translation of *prostatis* as (a modern) "benefactor." Kearsley, Jewett, Whelan, Osiek, and Yoon have all suggested that Phoebe's activities extended beyond that of a financier, but consensus on the shape of that has not become clear.[47] However, since the text combines the description of Phoebe as *diakonos* with *prostatis*, I turn first to a more detailed look at this term before returning to patronage.

"Diakonos"

In addition to characterizing Phoebe as *prostatis*, Paul also introduces her as "*diakonos* of an assembly." John Collins's extensive study of the use of *diakonia* and its cognates in various historical contexts has concluded that the base idea is of a "go-between" who conveys messages and acts as another person's agent.[48]

> Because the root idea expressed by the words is that of the go-between, the words do not necessarily involve the idea of "humble activity" at all, and never express the idea of being "at the service of" one's fellow man with what that phrase implies of benevolence; in commonly signifying that an action is done for someone, the words do not speak of benefit either to the person authorizing the action or to the recipient of the action but of an action done in the name of another.

According to Collins, while *diakonos* has been translated as "servant," neither menial service nor benevolence belongs to its semantic range. Rather, he argues, "A substantial part of Christian usage [of the term] relates to the passing on of revelation."[49]

In Paul's letters, the vocabulary of the *diakonos* word group occurs most frequently in 2 Corinthians[50] wherein the "words are saying something about

---

47. Other commentaries have less basis in the historical context. Some translate *prostatis* as "helper."

48. John N. Collins, *Diakonia: Re-interpreting the Ancient Sources* (New York: Oxford University Press, 1990), 194.

49. Collins, *Diakonia*, 217.

50. 2 Corinthians accounts for 20 of 35 uses by Paul. Another 9 of the 35 occur in Romans. (Paul accounts for 35 of the 100 occurrences of the word group in the Christian Testament.)

the communication of the gospel rather than about service to the Lord or to the brethren."[51] Collins adds that use of the noun did not originate with Paul. "Given the currency of the term in many religious situations, including that of divine message," Collins believes that both Paul and his adversaries would have used it.[52] Paul uses the term of himself and Apollos in the sense of "servants of both God and the Church as they use their gifts to bring the latter to faith" (1 Cor. 3:5).[53] Similarly, in 1 Cor. 16:15-18, the ministry of Stephanas and his companions must be "sustaining the community of Corinth in the word of God."[54] In general, *diakonoi* were agents or envoys, usually in a religious context and involved in speaking roles. For Paul (and perhaps his competitors), a *diakonos* was a missionary preacher, a persuasive messenger acting as an agent of God in spreading the word and teaching in the assembly.[55]

Collins devotes only one paragraph of his study to Phoebe's status. For Rom. 16:1, he translates *diakonos* as "emissary," rather than "minister,"[56] an unexpected move since Collins emphasizes the term's connotations of divinity, agency, and message, especially as the term is used in biblical texts.[57] In contrast, Reimund Bieringer has discussed Phoebe in the context of Paul's understanding of himself as *diakonos* in 2 Corinthians.

> Some might claim that Paul would not have applied *diakonos* to Phoebe in the exact same sense as he would have applied the term to himself, for, they might continue, no one except the apostles appointed by the risen Christ was actually *diakonos* in the same sense as Paul. Even if this is correct, this does not mean that Paul could

---

51. Collins, *Diakonia*, 206.

52. Ibid., 207.

53. H. W. Beyer, "διακονος," TDNT, 2:89.

54. Collins, *Diakonia*, 224.

55. Paul may refer to women and men *diakonoi* in the letter to the Philippians. In Phil. 1:1, Paul names the *diakonoi* of the assembly as those among the addressees (along with *episkopoi* and holy ones). Near the end of the letter, he names particular persons, who may be those same ministers: Euodia and Syntyche, "for they have struggled beside me in the work of the gospel," and Clement and other "co-workers" (Phil. 4:2-3).

56. "She is the community's emissary—no doubt also the bearer of Paul's letter—but the precise nature of her business is unknown; to judge from the vagueness of the request to help her in whatever she might need, the business may not have been with the Roman community at all." Collins also translates *prostatis* as "helper," instead of "patron" or "president." Collins, *Diakonia*, 225.

57. And, Paul uses the same words to describe women and men: workers, co-workers, compatriots, and apostles.

not also have applied fundamental elements of his *diakonia*-theology to the *diakonia* of Phoebe. Moreover, if Paul wanted to make a clear distinction between his being *diakonos* and that of Phoebe's, it would be surprising that he uses the same terminology for both.[58]

Philology supports applying to Phoebe the same understanding that has developed from studying the use of *diakonos* in Paul and other ancient sources,[59] that of a missionary preacher (of Cenchreae).[60] Probably she was the founder of the assembly there. Since Paul trusted her to deliver his letter to assemblies in Rome, it seems that he understood her to be a persuasive teacher of the gospel.[61]

We can compare the missionary relationship between Phoebe and Paul to Paul's relationships with Titus and Timothy. Margaret Mitchell has made a persuasive case that Paul's use of Titus (2 Corinthians) and Timothy (1 Thessalonians) follows epistolary and diplomatic conventions.[62]

> Is it not more likely the case that in certain instances Paul sent envoys or letters (or both) to represent him because he thought that they might be more effective than a personal visit in dealing with a particular situation that was facing a church? . . . The same possibility, that the letter (and envoy, in some cases) was not an inadequate substitute for the more desirable Pauline physical presence but was in fact deemed by him a superior way to deal with

58. Reimund Bieringer, "Women and Leadership in Romans 16: The Leading Roles of Phoebe, Prisca, and Junia in Early Christianity," http://eapi.admu.edu.ph/eapr007/bieringer.htm, accessed 26 March 2008. English translation by Wolf Diedrich of Reimund Bieringer, "Febe, Prisca en Junia. Vrouwen en leiderschap in de brieven van Paulus," in *Paulus, Verslagboek Vliebergh-Sencie-leergang*, ed. Frans Van Segbroeck, Bijbel 2003 (Leuven-Voorburg: Vlaamse Bijbelstichting-Acco, 2004), 157–202.

59. Elsewhere in Romans, *diakonos* is predicated of rulers (13:4, Roman authorities), who Paul calls *diakonoi* of God. The genitive, "of God," refers to origin or the one who authorizes the agents. In Rom. 15:8, *daikonos* is predicated of Christ, "*diakonos* of circumcision" (in the genitive). Paul is consistent in using *diakonos* to refer to the religious agency of leaders who exercise speaking authority.

60. As argued by Schüssler Fiorenza, "Missionaries," 420–33.

61. Jewett describes Paul's use in Romans and 1 and 2 Corinthians as references to missionaries. "However, in light of the possessive qualification, "deacon *of* the church in Cenchreae," it seems more likely that she functioned as a local leader rather than as a traveling missionary" (945). Yet, Phoebe clearly intends to travel and to deliver a message.

62. Margaret M. Mitchell, "New Testament Envoys," *Journal of Biblical Literature* 111, no. 4 (1992): 641–62.

a given situation, is likely true also for Galatians, surely for Romans, and perhaps for 1 Thessalonians and 1 Corinthians.[63]

According to Mitchell, Paul's descriptions of the missions of Timothy and Titus fit conventions expected for envoys in terms of "commissioning formulas" and "the double-sided role of the envoy" as a go-between to affirm mutual goodwill.[64]

Mitchell's analysis suggests that Phoebe travels to Rome ahead of Paul not as a substitute for Paul's presence but as a more effective agent than Paul himself could be. Phoebe's situation resembles that of Titus and Timothy in that Paul's commendation serves to introduce her, her credentials, and her mission. Yet, Phoebe's situation is also dissimilar to that of Paul's envoys. Unlike the conventional "return of the envoy" narrated in 2 Corinthians 7 and 1 Thessalonians 3,[65] Paul makes no mention in Romans of Phoebe's return nor that he expects she will communicate her findings with him. Thus it seems that Phoebe is not an envoy of Paul as Timothy and Titus were, even though she carries the letter.[66]

I investigated freeborn wealthy women's literacy, education, and training through an examination of inscriptions in the first chapter. It is reasonable to assume that Phoebe was the daughter of a wealthy family who had been trained to speak and to argue persuasively before an audience according to contemporary rhetorical conventions of composition. Paul would have been seen as wise to entrust his letter to an educated woman such as Phoebe, who would be sure to present a persuasive case for a mission to the Gentiles. The historical possibilities support Mitchell's suggestion that Phoebe had a background useful for becoming an effective missionary agent.

This focus on texts about Phoebe raises questions about wealthy women's status that warrant further pursuit. If a wealthy widow did not host a house church, what sort of patronage did she provide? Seeking to understand more precisely Phoebe's activities, I draw on inscriptions to inquire about other

63. Ibid., 642.

64. Ibid., 652, 660.

65. Ibid., 653–61.

66. Some may object that Paul's commissioning of Phoebe as an envoy differs in Romans from that in 2 Corinthians and 1 Thessalonians because he has not yet visited the Roman assemblies. Yet, he already has relationships with many of them: there are at least fifteen friends and co-workers personally known to Paul among those to whom he sends greetings in Romans 16. He could ask that they communicate to Phoebe their goodwill towards him. Such a request might be expected when he asks that they receive Phoebe "in the Lord in a manner worthy of the saints."

possibilities for the religious leadership of a wealthy widow. Interpretation of the inscription about Rufina informs this discussion. I then turn to inquire about the portrayal of Tryphaena in a literary text. This variety of literary and epigraphic sources allows me to compare the types and develop a more complete reconstruction of wealthy widows' activities. Finally, I return to Paul's characterization of Phoebe as *prostatis* and *diakonos* to elaborate understanding of her patronal religious status.

WEALTHY FREEBORN WOMEN AND PATRONAGE

WEALTH AND LEADERSHIP

In order to envision more clearly and completely the possibilities for elite women's status and activities, I turn now to inscriptions that depict wealthy widows within social groups. The inscriptions belong to the same cultural milieu in which Phoebe and other people mentioned in Paul's letters lived: the early imperial era (first and second centuries c.e.) in Greece and western Asia Minor. The possibilities for women's leadership emerge from study of material culture, civic processes, education of elite women, associations as clients, and the religious dimensions of patronage. Examination of these texts adds richness to the picture of the historical political socioeconomic contexts of patronage.

Some studies of Roman social history have characterized benefaction and patronage as different socioeconomic interactions.[67] They base this distinction on two problematic premises: overdrawn contrasts between public and private relationships and a reading of honorific inscriptions as mirrors of benefaction relationships. The contrast between public and private casts benefaction as a civic relationship and patronage as private relationship. However, Onno van Nijf has noted that "the ancient sources appear to offer no support for any conceptual distinction between generosity towards cities and generosity towards smaller groups such as civic subdivisions and collegia."[68] Benefaction

67. For example, Johnson and Dandeker, "Patronage: Relation and System," 239. It seems that historians working primarily in Greek sources tend to emphasize benefactor (translating εὐεργέτης) while Latinists prefer patron (translating *patronus*). Rosalinde A. Kearsley notes that *patronus* appears in Greek inscriptions at Ephesus as a Latin loan word. Kearsley, *Greeks and Romans in Imperial Asia: Mixed Language Inscriptions and Linguistic Evidence for Cultural Interaction Until the End of A.D. III* (Bonn: Habelt, 2001), 151.

68. Onno van Nijf, *The Civic World of Professional Associations in the Roman East* (Amsterdam: Gieben, 1997), 80–81.

for a city and patronage for an association are more aptly viewed as two points on a continuum of well-known societal relationships.

In some interpretational frameworks, benefaction appears to be a lopsided exchange of material benefits for honors.[69] However, these honors affirmed benefactors in their positions of socioeconomic prominence and leadership, which allowed them to (continue to) accumulate wealth. Simply put, both benefaction and patronage involved asymmetrical relationships and exchanges.[70] While I use benefaction and patronage interchangeably, I prefer the vocabulary of *patron* and *client* because I want to emphasize the relationship between the two parties.

Historians have relied on careful analysis of inscriptions for essential material for reconstruction of the possibilities for wealthy women's patronage.[71] In the preceding chapter, I argued that wealthy widows exercised socioeconomic leadership as heads of their households. The following inscriptions focus on the status of widows in patronage.

This inscription from Termessos in Pisidia dates to the second century of the common era. The material context of patronage and some of its political dimensions can be seen from analysis of the text honoring Atalante.

μηνὸς Σωτηρίου δεκάτη γ΄ ἐν τῇ ἐν-
νόμῳ ἐκλησία ἔδοξε τῶι δήμωι προ-
βούλων γνώμηι· ἐπεὶ Ἀταλάντη, Π[ι]-
ατηραβιος Πιλλακοου Κιννουνιος θυγάτηρ, χήρα, εὐγενεία καὶ σωφροσύνη κε-
κοσμημένη καὶ πᾶσαν γυναικείαν ἀρε-
τὴν ἀποδεικνυμένη, ἀκόλουθα πονοῦ-
σα τοῖς προγόνοις αὐτῆς πολλάκις τὴν
πόλιν πεφιλοτειμημένοις ἔν τε ἀναλώ-
μασιν ἐπισημοτάτοις καὶ ἐν προχρήσεσιν
ἀργυρίων καὶ ἐπιδόσεσιν καὶ δωρεαῖς καὶ ἱε-
ρωσύναις, ἐπηνγείλατο σειτοδείας πολ-

69. Stephan Joubert, *Paul as Benefactor: Reciprocity, Strategy and Theological Reflection in Paul's Collection* (Tübingen: Mohr Siebeck, 2000). Bruce Winter, *Seek the Welfare of the City: Christians as Benefactors and Citizens: First-Century Christians in the Graeco-Roman World* (Grand Rapids: Eerdmans, 1994).

70. Richard Saller, "Patronage and Friendship in Early Imperial Rome: Drawing the Distinction," in *Patronage in Ancient Society*, ed. Andrew Wallace-Hadrill (London: Routledge, 1989), 49–62.

71. Riet van Bremen, *The Limits of Participation: Women and Civic Life in the Greek East in the Hellenistic and Roman Periods* (Amsterdam: J. C. Gieben, 1996).

λῆς οὔσης εὐθηνίαν παρασσχέσθαι τῷ
πλήθει πληροῦσά τε τὴν φιλοτειμίαν δ[α]-
ψιλῆ ταύτην παρέχεται ἀπὸ μηνὸς Ἰδα-
λιανίου τοῦ ἐπ' ἔτους· δεδόχθαι τετει-
μῆσθαι αὐτὴν ὑπὸ τοῦ δήμου εἰκόνι
χαλκῇ καὶ χρυσῷ στεφάνῳ ἀνατεθῆναί
τε τὴν εἰκόνα ἐν ἐπισήμῳ τῆς πόλεως
τόπῳ πρὸς τῇ Ἀττάλου στοᾷ κατὰ τὸν
τῆς μεσημβρινῆς εὐθείας τοῖχον ὁδοῦ,
ἐφ' οὗ καὶ ἆθλα ἀνάκειται τῶν νεικησάν-
των παίδων ἐν γυμνικῷ ἀγῶνι, ὃν ἔθη-
κεν παιδονομῶν Ἑρμαῖος Οπλονος,
συνκεχωρῆσθαι δὲ καὶ τοῖς τεχνεί-
ταις ἐν τῷ αὐτῷ τόπῳ ἀναστῆσαι ὃν πε-
φιλοτείμηνται ἀνδριάντα τῆς Ἀταλάν-
της, καθὼς ἡτήσαντο, ἐπιγραφῆναί τε
τῷ μὲν τοῦ δήμου ἀνδριάντι τόδε τὸ
ψήφισμα, τῷ δὲ τῶν τεχνειτῶν, ἣν ἂν
αὐτοὶ θελήσωσιν ἐπιγραφήν.

In the month of Soterios, the thirteenth day in the regular assembly,
it was resolved by the people, on the proposal of the council. Since
Atalante, daughter of Piaterabis, daughter of Pillakoas, daughter of
Kinnounis, a widow, adorned both with nobility and with a sense
of what is right, and who reveals to the full the quality of a woman
emulating by her exertions the accomplishments of her progenitors
in their ambitious services towards the city, both in expenditure of
no mean kind in advancing money and in public subscriptions and
gifts and priesthoods, has promised in time of great grain shortage
to provide an ample supply for the *plebs*, and in fulfillment of her
generous promise she provides grain unstintingly from the month
Idalianos of the present year. It was resolved that she shall be honored
by the people with a bronze statue and a golden crown and that the
statue shall be set up at a prominent location in the city, near the *stoa*
of Attalos, in front of the wall facing south, where also the prizes are
placed that were won by the youths in the gymnastic games which
Hermaios, son of Hoplon, organized when he was *paidonomos*. And
also that the artisans shall have permission to set up, at the same spot,
a statue of Atalante, as they requested; and that in the statue set up

by the people this decree shall be inscribed, but in that of the artisans any inscription they shall want.[72]

The text's author explicitly identifies Atalante as a widow, a freeborn woman, and emphasizes women in her genealogy. This wording highlights gender precisely in order to declare that Atalante has matched or even exceeded the benefaction of her ancestors. Some of those referred to are men, since the author uses the masculine plural form for "progenitors." Atalante's identification as a widow suggests her financial independence as the head of a household.[73]

Atalante could afford grain (or had an enormous stockpile) while others could not.[74] The gift and the honors of which the passage speaks are predicated on this inequity. Erection of this testimonial may have functioned to encourage her to continue providing grain, but such gifts did not result in closing the gaps between socioeconomic strata. Paul Veyne has argued that it was much less expensive for the elite to provide such goods than it would have been to make structural changes allowing the majority of the population to live above subsistence level.[75]

Veyne and others have said that the cities of Asia Minor were dependent on wealthy patrons to make up for budgetary shortfalls.[76] However, Hertha Schwarz has recently argued that historians have heavily underestimated the capacity of civil governments to raise revenues and finance public amenities.[77] Analyzing one facet of elite patronage, Arjan Zuiderhoek found that elite contributions toward building programs are best characterized as "the icing on the richly decorated cake of civic life in Roman Asia Minor."[78] Thus, while inscriptions such as those honoring Atalante highlight the material gulf between

---

72. *TAM* 3.1.4. Translation from van Nijf, *Civic World*, 113. The artisans' inscription is *TAM* 3.1.62.

73. See the preceding chapter on the socioeconomic status of unmarried women.

74. The socioeconomic model proposed in the preceding delineates several levels between these two extremes. The dichotomy functions in the construction of patronage.

75. Paul Veyne and Oswyn Murray, *Bread and Circuses: Historical Sociology and Political Pluralism* (London: Penguin, 1992), 56.

76. Ibid., 132. At one time, this was taken to be the explanation for the perceived anomaly of the public role of wealthy women.

77. H. Schwarz, *Soll oder Haben? Die Finanzwirtschaft Kleinasiatischer Städte in der Römischen Kaiserzeit am Beispiel von Bithynien, Lykien und Ephesus (29 v. Chr.–284 n. Chr.)* (Bonn: Habelt, 2001). Cited in Arjan Zuiderhoek, "The Ambiguity of Munificence," *Historia* 56, no. 2 (2007): 212 n. 54.

78. Arjan Zuiderhoek, "The Icing on the Cake: Benefactors, Economics, and Public Building in Roman Asia Minor," in *Patterns in the Economy of Roman Asia Minor*, ed. Stephen Mitchell and Constantina Katsari (Swansea: Classical Press of Wales, 2005), 178.

elites and plebs (and plebs' vulnerability), economic necessity alone does not explain wealthy women's roles in civic patronage.

The dedication to Atalante gives a sense of the political process behind awards of civic honor. The city's democratic political institutions deliberated and voted on the wording of the inscription that mentioned Atalante's previous contributions, her family's civic participation, and her current deeds. They also determined the type of monument and its exact location.[79] Associations, such as artisans' groups, needed approval, for example, if they wished to erect a statue in the city.[80] Honorific inscriptions and statues littered the landscape of ancient cities. The second inscription mentioned above, in which artisans honor Atalante, has also been located, so presumably there were also two statues in her honor.[81] Repetitions reiterated the connections among elites, wealth, and honor. Atalante's history and presence merges with the city's own public genealogy, geography, political groups, economic activity, social memory, and self-representation.

A notion of leadership emerges in the portrayal of Atalante's patronage. First are the ways in which the parties are named. Clients appear as groups, anonymous crowds: council, people, assembly, plebs, and artisans. Atalante's individuality is emphasized through the specification of her genealogy. Other individuals mentioned in the inscriptions were also patrons: Attalos gave the stoa, and Hermaios sponsored the gymnastic games. The inscription further singles out Atalante by listing her virtues, her history of benefaction, and the awards of statue and crown. The crowds would literally look up from the words inscribed on the statue base to Atalante represented in her statue. Patrons often received a title or office such as *paidonomos* for Hermaios. Atalante's crown contributes to her visual prominence. Simply by naming the two principal parties as "the people" and "Atalante," the wording of the text emphasizes Atalante as unique and remarkable, a person who stood out in a crowd.

Other aspects of the depiction of patronage in the inscription also put Atalante forward as a leader. Group actions are represented as unanimous. In a similar way, both Romans and provincials voiced support for the emperor by unanimous acclamation on special occasions.[82] The participants would have

---

79. "The *stoa* of Attalos bordered on the city's *agora*, and was one of the most prominent constructions in that area." Bremen, *Limits of Participation*, 189.

80. "Access to public places for the purpose of setting up honorific inscriptions was, so it seems, jealously guarded by means of formal rules and informal conventions." Van Nijf, *Civic World*, 115.

81. The inscription is *TAM* 3.62.

82. Clifford Ando, *Imperial Ideology and Provincial Loyalty in the Roman Empire* (Berkeley: University of California Press, 2000), 199–205.

associated unanimous acclamation with affirmation of leadership. The text presents the group action to be a reasonable result of democratic processes of discussion and voting. This sense of rationality naturalizes Atalante's patronage and the institution of patronage in general. Furthermore, like legal documents, this acclamation is written. Epigraphical writing has a sense of both permanence and legality. These traits adhere to Atalante's patronage and establish the individual patron forever as a natural leader justly chosen. Since Atalante shares her prosperity with the people, she also participates in the leadership rationale voiced by Caesar Augustus: the prosperity that flowed to all (allegedly) during his reign vindicated his rise to power and exemplified divine authorization for his rule.[83] In all of these ways, Atalante's honorary inscription presents leadership tightly wrapped up with patronage.

Inscriptional representation of Atalante suggests that patronage could involve complexities that went far beyond an exchange of honor and money. Patronage through public subscriptions, gifts, and priesthoods was not necessary because of financial shortfalls in the cities, nor did patronage effect structural changes in the economic disparity between wealthy and poor. The institution of patronage was intertwined with the production of political and social ideology around wealth, decision-making, leadership, and visual prominence. Atalante appears without common markers of family status, husband, father, and children, but is presented as a freeborn woman identified through her female lineage. It seems the distinctions she achieved as a patron were not surpassed by those of her male ancestors. As an elite widow benefactor participating in civic events in Asia Minor, her patronal roles were not determined by gender subordination.[84]

This analysis of the presentation of Atalante's patronage has delineated characteristics of the kyriarchal relationship between patron and clients in order to investigate the socioeconomic status of women patrons in the cities of Asia Minor. The clients named in the inscription are the people of the city and the artisans. In cities throughout Asia Minor, artisans formed associations and honored the patrons of their associations. Since many religious groups

---

83. Ibid., 14–15, 278–96, 311–12.

84. Carolyn Osiek has made a similar point: "The prohibition of women from the elective process, however, by no means kept them out of politics or the patronage system. We are accustomed to thinking systemically about women in this society in terms of gender dichotomies in a gender-based hierarchical structure. But in face of evidence, we can only conclude that women of sufficient social status in the Roman world exercised a great deal of freedom and power with regard to business and social activities." Osiek, "Diakonos," 358–59.

organized themselves as associations, I continue the investigation of women's status as patrons by focusing on texts about women's patronage of associations.

Religious groups organized themselves as associations, as did other groups gathered around commonalities of occupation or social status.[85] In his study of occupational associations, van Nijf found that patrons' generosity allowed them to establish their social superiority inside the group.[86] A corollary to this statement would imply that persons with established social superiority in the group were often generous patrons. That is, those named as officers or honored by associations seem to have been those who supported the association with their socioeconomic status. Women were among these patrons.

Extensive research on women and associations has identified this inscription in which an association of teachers honored Pontia Apelliane in second-century Ephesus.

κατὰ τὰ δόξαν-
τα τῇ φιλοσε[βά]-
στῳ βο[υλῇ]
Πον[τίαν]
Ἀπελ[λι]ανὴν
ἐτ[είμ]ησαν
τὴν
[λ]αμπαδάρχισσαν
τῆς θεοῦ
οἱ περὶ τὸ Μουσε[ῖον]
παιδευταὶ
λαμπαδαρχή-
σασαν ἐπὶ ἀρχόν-
των Ἑρμίππου
καὶ Ἐλπιδηφόρο[υ,]
ἀνασταθεῖσαν

85. See John S. Kloppenborg and Stephen G. Wilson, eds., *Voluntary Associations in the Graeco-Roman World* (London: Routledge, 1996). Philip Harland, *Associations, Synagogues and Congregations: Claiming a Place in Ancient Mediterranean Society* (Minneapolis: Augsburg Fortress Press, 2003). The vocabulary for associations was not consistent.

86. Onno van Nijf, "*Collegia* and Civic Guards: Two Chapters in the History of Sociability," in *After the Past*, ed. Willem Jongman and Marc Kleijwegt (Leiden: Brill, 2002), 329. Associations drew their membership from economically successful persons of the urban middle strata; this group occupied a level between the small ruling oligarchy and the lower "classes." Van Nijf, "*Collegia*," 335.

ἐπὶ Ἀμφείονο[ς]
καὶ Ἰουλίου.

According to the decree of the patriotic ("emperor-loving") council, the teachers of the Mousieon honored Pontia Apelliane superintendent of the torch-race[87] of God and set up [this memorial] during the rule of Ampheiono and Ioulios since she supervised the torch-race during the rule of Ermippos and Elipephoros.[88]

The inscription indicates that the city council approved this honor. As in the text about Atalante, the wording establishes leadership by naming Pontia Apelliane, ascribing her title, repeating it in verbal form, specifying the legality of the memorial, and reproducing all of this in a permanent record. Nothing in the writing refers to Pontia Apelliane's family status, nor does the statement use vocabulary associated with femininity. Marital status is not part of the presentation of leadership and honor.

Torch races took place during religious festivals.[89] Such festivals included processions, banquets, and contests. Pontia Apelliane's title and activities suggest that she was a patron of the teachers' association and that she represented or led them during processions or ceremonies. She may have provided prizes for a race or hosted a banquet. Studies of similar inscriptions can inform interpretation.

Scholarship on other texts about associations suggests possibilities for envisioning Pontia Apelliane's patronal leadership. During special events, associations of all kinds paraded, probably with special banners and statuary.[90] According to Simon Price, processions produced ideological maps that linked together a city's disparate public centers and personnel.[91] In various ways processions displayed social hierarchies. During the funeral march for Apollonis, "the presidents and the eponymous magistrates are to follow the cortège, as also are the boys, ephebes [young men], citizens, and all free males in the city; likewise unmarried girls, female citizens, and the remaining free women who live in the city."[92] Ephebes took pride of place in the procession of C. Vibius

87. In the classical era, this race featured runners who carried lit torches at the festivals of fire gods.
88. *IEph* 3068.
89. The Panathenaea in ancient Athens included a torch race. "Greek religion," *Encyclopædia Britannica* 2009. Encyclopædia Britannica Online, http://www.search.eb.com/eb/article-65478.
90. Van Nijf, *Civic World*, 200.
91. S. R. F. Price, *Rituals and Power: The Roman Imperial Cult in Asia Minor* (Cambridge: Cambridge University Press, 1984), 110–11. Festive rituals served the interests of both elites and non-elite groups, according to Arjan Zuiderhoek, "The Ambiguity of Munificence," Historia, 56, no. 2 (2007): 213.

Salutaris at Ephesus (104 C.E.) discussed by Guy Rogers.[93] The procession of Demosthenes at Oinoanda aligned office-holders with precision: the festival president led, followed by the priest and priestess of the imperial cult, then the priest of Zeus, festival officials, and other civic officials.[94] Van Nijf summarizes the overall effect: "Such ritual occasions are not only a model *of* society, they are also set up as a model *for* society. The details of the idealized image are dictated by the interests of the members of the ruling elite. They set themselves apart from the others and define, through ritual, the relationships among the groups that made up society."[95] A procession or ceremony accompanying the torch race would have displayed Pontia Apelliane's leadership in the teachers' association.

Other highly visible events portrayed in conjunction with women's patronage include banquets, distributions, and public seating. The details of Aba's donations appear in an inscription from Histria in second-century Moesia (the western shore of the Black Sea).[96] The group with highest status, including council members and elders, received an invitation to a banquet and a distribution of money. The second group received an allotment of wine. The general citizenry seems not to be mentioned, but the inscription is damaged and partially unreadable. Implicitly, Aba held the highest status in the group, since she provided the gifts. In the second century C.E., Menodora of Sillyon (in Pamphylia) distributed drachmas according to rank in the city: members of governing councils received between 77 and 86, their wives 3, citizens 9, and freedpersons and other residents 3 drachmas each.[97] Surveys of inscriptions

92. E. Schwertheim, "Ein postumer Ehrenbeschluss für Apollonis in Kyzikos," *Zeitschrift für Papyrologie und Epigraphik* 29 (1978): 213–28 (plates 11, 12), lines 42–47. G. H. R. Horsley, trans., *New Documents Illustrating Early Christianity: A Review of the Greek Inscriptions and Papyri Published in 1979* (North Ryde, Australia: The Ancient History Documentary Research Centre, Macquarie University, 1987),12. The inscription comes from Kyzikos in Mysia, in the second quarter of the first century C.E.

93. Guy M. Rogers, *The Sacred Identity of Ephesus: Foundation Myths of a Roman City* (London: Routledge, 1991).

94. This procession was founded during the reign of Hadrian (124/5 C.E. perhaps). Rogers, *Sacred Identity*, 189.

95. Onno van Nijf, "Local Heroes: Athletics, Festivals and Elite Self-Fashioning in the Roman East," in *Being Greek Under Rome: Cultural Identity, the Second Sophistic and the Development of Empire*, ed. Simon Goldhill (Cambridge: Cambridge University Press, 2001), 332. Thus elites were able to represent a subdued population to their Roman overlords. Demosthenes dictated twenty whip carriers to ensure good order in the theatre. "Festive euergetism thus helped to legitimize an increasingly oligarchic political system, that was securely locked into an all-embracing imperial system" (333).

96. Histria 57. From 150 to 200 C.E. in Moesia.

97. Van Nijf, *Civic World*, 162–65; Bremen, *Limits of Participation*, 108–12.

suggest that banquet activity frequently illustrated the same pattern of rank, as did distributions in the western empire.[98]

Inscriptions found in theaters throughout western Asia Minor indicate that status was on display in seating arrangements at contests and entertainment venues.[99] The same seems true for associations. For example, the synagogue of Jews at second-century Smyrna honored Tation's patronage by giving her a gold crown and a seat of honor.[100] The gold crown and reserved seat were some of the highest honors awarded to patrons and benefactors.[101] Both practices are widely attested in the Greek East through commemorative inscriptions and inscriptions reserving places in theaters, odeums, and stadiums. The texts present the patronage of Aba, Menodora, and Tation in concert with political and social hierarchies in their cities and associations. Banquets, distributions, and seats are three aspects of the portrait of patronage that display rank and leadership. Thus the textual representation of patronage visualizes the patron's leadership at meals, entertainments, and association meetings.

Scholarship on texts about women's patronal leadership of religious associations has focused on an inscription about Rufina, a Jewish woman.

In a way similar to Pontia Apelliane, Rufina is depicted with a title of leadership of an association. In this case, the association is religious or ethnic instead of occupational.

'Ρουφεῖνα 'Ιουδαία ἀρχι-
συνάγωγος κατεσκεύα-
σεν τὸ ἐνσόριον τοῖς ἀπε-
λευθέροις καὶ θρέμασιν·

98. Price, *Rituals and Power*, 113. Van Nijf, *Civic World*, 152–54, 161–65.

99. Provincial events shared this characteristic with spectacles in Italy: "Romans paraded their rank whenever they appeared in public, and nowhere more conspicuously than at public spectacles in theatre, amphitheatre and circus. . . . Putting everyone in his proper place was a visual affirmation of the dominance of the imperial social structure, and one calculated to impress the bulk of the population of the empire." Peter Garnsey and Richard Saller, *The Roman Empire: Economy, Society and Culture* (Berkeley: University of California, 1987), 117.

100. *CIJ* 738. Τάτιον Στράτωνος τοῦ 'Εμπέδωνος τὸν οἶκον καὶ τὸν περίβολον τοῦ ὑπαίθρου κατασκευάσασα ἐκ τῶ[ν ἰδ]ίων ἐχαρίσατο τ[οῖς 'Ιο]υδαίοις. ἡ συναγωγὴ ἐ[τείμη]σεν τῶν 'Ιουδαίων Τάτιον Σ[τράτ]ωνος τοῦ 'Εμπέδωνος χρυσῷ στεφάνῳκαὶ προεδρίᾳ. "Tation, daughter of Straton, son of Empedon, having erected the house and the walls of the courtyard with her own funds, gave them to the Jews. The synagogue of the Jews honored Tation, daughter of Straton, son of Empedon, with a gold crown and a seat of honor."

101. Joan Breton Connelly, *Portrait of a Priestess: Women and Ritual in Ancient Greece* (Princeton: Princeton University Press, 2007), 204–5.

μηδενὸς ἄλου ἐξουσίαν ἔ-
χοντος θάψαι τινά. εἰ δέ τις τολ-
μήσει, δώσει τῷ ἱερωτάτῳ τα-
μείῳ ,αφ' καὶ τῷ ἔθνει τῶν Ἰουδαίων ,α. ταύτης τῆς ἐπιγραφῆς
τὸ ἀντίγραφον ἀπόκειται
εἰς τὸ ἀρχεῖον.

Rufina, a Jewish woman, head of the synagogue, built this tomb for her freed slaves and the slaves raised in her house. No one else has the right to bury anyone (here). Anyone who dares to will pay 1500 denaria to the sacred treasury and 1000 denaria to the Jewish people. A copy of this inscription has been placed in the (public) archives.[102]

The inscription comes from second-century Smyrna on the west coast of Asia Minor.[103] Bernadette Brooten has suggested that Rufina's name perhaps indicates her status as the daughter of a leading Roman family.[104] The text presents her as slaveholder and as the builder and owner of the tomb, indicating that she had access to wealth that she used at her own discretion. Since most wealthy women married, Rufina seems to have been a widow. Her freed slaves remained members of her household. Her title in the synagogue is associated elsewhere with patronage.[105] Thus, she appears to have been a wealthy widow patron of a religious association. Since anyone who violated the tomb would owe a fine to the Jewish people, the synagogue association had an ongoing interest in the memorial.

Brooten characterized the head of a synagogue's exercise of leadership as administrative and exhortative.[106] In contrast, Tessa Rajak and David Noy have argued that head of the synagogue was an honorary position for wealthy

102. CIJ 741. Translation based on Ross S. Kraemer, ed., Maenads, Martyrs, Matrons, Monastics: A Sourcebook on Women's Religions in the Greco-Roman World (Philadelphia: Fortress Press, 1988), 218.

103. Tessa Rajak and David Noy date this inscription to the third century c.e. or later. See Rajak and Noy, "Archisynagogoi: Office, Title and Social Status in the Greco-Jewish Synagogue," Journal of Roman Studies 83 (1993): 90.

104. Bernadette J. Brooten, Women Leaders in the Ancient Synagogue: Inscriptional Evidence and Background Issues (Chico, CA: Scholars, 1982), 32.

105. Rajak and Noy, "Archisynagogoi," 87–89. Bernadette J. Brooten, "Female Leadership in the Ancient Synagogue," in From Dura to Sepphoris: Studies in Jewish Art and Society in Late Antiquity, ed. Lee I. Levine and Ze'ev Weiss (Portsmouth, RI: Journal of Roman Archaeology, 2000), 217.

106. Brooten, Women Leaders, 32.

donors.[107] Recently, Lee Levine reviewed the research and argued that biblical texts clearly portray synagogue heads as leaders of associations.[108] "In summary, the New Testament evidence attests to a prestigious office associated with a leadership role within the synagogue in the political and especially religious realms."[109] In this comment, Levine is referring to Jairus in Mark 5:21-43 and Luke 8:40-56, to the religious leader in Luke 13:14, and to several references in the Acts of the Apostles (18:8, 17).

Levine draws on the biblical texts to investigate the significance of the inscriptions that refer to the head of a synagogue.[110]

> Clearly, these inscriptions indicate that an *archisynagogue* was not infrequently an important donor to the synagogue. However, as noted, it would be a major—and unwarranted—leap to assume, on the basis of this evidence, that this philanthropic dimension was a sine qua non for becoming an *archisynagogue* or that an *archisynagogue* functioned only in this capacity. What may have been common and, in many cases, even expected was not necessarily the sole or determinant factor in defining one's position.[111]

Besides the financial role of the head of the synagogue, Levine argues that there were religious dimensions to the office of synagogue head, as "the one in charge of worship."[112]

So Levine's assessment follows the interpretation of the title that Brooten suggests.

> Heads of the synagogue seem to have had responsibility for inviting members of the congregation to read from Scripture and to preach. Exhorting and teaching, as well as, together with the presbyters,

---

107. Rajak and Noy, "*Archisynagogoi*," 88–89. They also argue that the head of the synagogue need not be Jewish. For a recent review of the scholarship and sources, see Lee I. Levine, *The Ancient Synagogue: The First Thousand Years*, 2nd ed. (New Haven: Yale University Press, 2006), 412–53.

108. Levine, *The Ancient Synagogue*, 416.

109. Ibid., 419.

110. For men with the same title as Rufina, see *CIJ* 766, Akmonia, first century C.E.; *CIJ* 1404, Jerusalem, before 70 C.E. As discussed elsewhere, women are underrepresented in sources.

111. Levine, *The Ancient Synagogue*, 424.

112. Ibid., 416–17.

collecting money to be sent to the Patriarch, occur in the ancient sources as activities of the *archisynagogos*. The *archisynagogos* seems to have been the leading synagogue functionary, judging by the fact that the title occurs at the head of ancient lists of synagogue officials, as well as by the etymology of the word itself (*archos*, chief, ruler).[113]

Brooten's evaluation in this passage emphasizes the religious spiritual leadership of the heads of synagogues in addition to their financial and administrative leadership.

Levine raises a question about the status and activities of the head of the synagogue for Rufina in particular, but his argument seems inconsistent. On one hand, Levine asserts that women participated in worship by reading the Torah in congregational worship (506–7). "There is certainly the possibility that most, if not all, the titles that appear in over a score of Diaspora inscriptions are those of functioning women officials" (511). On the other hand, Levine's reconstruction concludes that Jewish communities "resisted contemporary influence . . . in the denial of any liturgical function to women."[114] In reasoning to this conclusion, Levine stresses "women's generally inferior public status in antiquity" (505). This assumption about women's secondary status seems to contradict Levine's admission of the possibility of "functioning women officials." The leadership status of Jewish women such as Rufina constitutes grounds for questioning "women's generally inferior public status."

Furthermore, inscriptions depict educated women competing in public, and patronal women's leadership in processions and at festivals, banquets, and other events. The best historical reconstruction indicates that Rufina was a wealthy Jewish widow in a religious office functioning as a leader during worship, in reading and exhortation, and in financial support and administration.[115] Brooten concludes, "Seen in the larger context of women's participation in the life of the ancient synagogue, we have strong reasons to interpret the titles as functional and to assume that female heads or elders of the synagogues had functions parallel to male heads or elders of synagogues."[116] As

113. Brooten, "Female Leadership," 216.

114. Levine, *The Ancient Synagogue*, 512–15, 517. Levine also points to statistical observations that minimize women's participation in comparison to men's.

115. A third- or fourth-century inscription from Aphrodisias depicts an association of Jews and God-fearers meeting for meals. *SEG* 6.970. Women and men patrons would also be expected to show leadership on these occasions. Jael is named as the president. If a man, use of Jael as a male name would be unprecedented. So this is another possibility for a woman's patronage and leadership.

116. Brooten, "Female Leadership," 223.

was the case for other wealthy widows, such as Atalante and Pontia Apelliane, it seems that Rufina's religious status depended on her socioeconomic status rather than on constructions of women's subordination.

PATRONAGE AND LEADERSHIP

Leadership, wealth, and patronage were inextricably intertwined in Asia Minor of the early imperial period. This is the context for understanding the status of wealthy widows as patrons.

Wealth was the sine qua non of patronage. The possession of wealth itself created the expectation of leadership.[117] Veyne has discussed benefaction in terms of socioeconomic status and politics. Benefaction divided cities into two camps—givers and receivers—with authority entrusted to the first. Different sets of legal rights and penalties prescribed for the elite and the masses (*honestiores* and *humiliores*) enshrined the division.[118] The distinction of honors erected a symbolic ideological barrier: they ratified a person's membership in the elite and the superiority of the elite. Van Nijf explains: "Honorific epigraphy was instrumental in the gradual process whereby the wealthy classes of the later Greek cities established their social superiority, and re-invented themselves as a ruling order."[119] Wealthy non-elites shared in this social order as well. Economically successful members of the urban population drew on patronage and the epigraphic habit to achieve social integration through participation and leadership in associations. On any scale of wealth, patronage functioned to establish the wealthy in leadership roles by providing a rationale and a stage for their patronal status.

Atalante was a city's patron while Pontia Apelliane and Rufina were patrons of occupational and religious associations. Even in different contexts, however, the ideology and institution of patronage was intertwined with representations of leadership in diverse ways: visually, through inscriptions and accompanying statues in streets and plazas, and actively, in religious and civic events, such as council meetings and processions. In other portrayals, patronage was intertwined with leadership at meals and entertainments. The inhabitants of Asia Minor must have understood women's patronage to imply social, religious, and political leadership in addition to high socioeconomic status.

117. Of the second century (c.e.) in Asia Minor in particular, Paul Veyne saw ruling and giving as "one and the same." *Bread and Circuses*, 131.

118. Garnsey and Saller, *The Roman Empire*, 116, 118.

119. Van Nijf, "Collegia," 335. "Since power at the local level was in the firm grip of a small oligarchy, political participation was not a realistic source of social identity for anyone else" (334).

Epigraphic sources do not exhaust the texts about women's patronage and religious status in Asia Minor in the first two centuries of the common era. Scholars have noted that many wealthy women appear in texts about early Christian apostles and martyrs.[120] Studies have identified some widows as patrons and have discussed their activities.[121]

TRYPHAENA

Some scholarship on wealthy religious widows and patronage in second-century Asia Minor has focused on the figure of Tryphaena in the *Acts of Thecla*.[122] Tryphaena's portrayal appears in a literary source, unlike the inscriptional texts discussed above. Analysis of this text also can contribute to understanding wealthy women's religious status in relation to their socioeconomic status.

HISTORICAL CONTEXT

Scholars have dated the *Acts of Thecla* to the second century of the common era in Asia Minor. Three of the four cities mentioned, Iconium, (Pisidian) Antioch, and Seleucia, were situated in the portion of Roman Asia Minor called Galatia (also known as Phrygia), less than 150 kilometers from each other; the fourth city, Myra, was several hundred kilometers farther south, on the Lycian coast.[123] Thecla was from Iconium; she traveled west to Antioch, south to Myra, then back north to Iconium, and finally to Seleucia.[124] Among the surviving material remembrances of Thecla are fourth-century sources attesting the prominence of her shrine in Seleucia, and the fifth- or sixth-century frescoes of Thecla found in

120. Jan Bremmer, "Why Did Early Christianity Attract Upper-Class Women?" in *Fructus centesimus*, ed. A. A. R. Bastiaensen et al. (Dordrecht: Steenbrugge, 1989), 37–47.

121. Judith Perkins, "The Social World of the Acts of Peter," in *The Search for the Ancient Novel*, ed. James Tatum (Baltimore: Johns Hopkins University Press, 1994), 296–307. See discussion of Eubula in Robert Stoops, "Patronage in the Acts of Peter," *Semeia* 38 (1986): 93–94.

122. M. Misset-van de Weg, "A Wealthy Woman Named Tryphaena: Patroness of Thecla of Iconium," in *The Apocryphal Acts of Paul and Thecla*, ed. Jan N. Bremmer (Kampen: Kok Pharos, 1996), 16–35.

123. Richard Talbert, ed., *Atlas of Classical History* (London and New York: Routledge, 1985), 160.

124. Seleucia was a primary site for the cult of Thecla. Stephen J. Davis has gathered the evidence for pilgrimages associated with a shrine commemorating Thecla at Seleucia in Asia Minor. Davis, *The Cult of Saint Thecla: A Tradition of Women's Piety in Late Antiquity* (Oxford: Oxford University Press, 2001), 1–80.

a cave at Ephesus.[125] Just northwest of Seleucia, the region of Phrygia contained towns with names rich in the history of religious groups: Eumeneia, Apameia, Akmonia, and Hierapolis. The area was notable for Jewish settlements,[126] the oldest inscriptions to mention Christians,[127] and the New Prophecy movement that began in the second century.[128] The geography and date of the *Acts of Thecla* position the text in an area central to the development of Jewish and Christian religious tradition.

The *Acts of Thecla* appears to have been inserted into the *Acts of Paul* at some point in the development of the known text.[129] In support of this interpretation, Sheila McGinn has argued that the *ATh* portrays Paul in an unflattering light, and that this tendency is inconsistent with other episodes in the *Acts of Paul*.[130] Thecla's trials in the arena occur twice, in different cities, with a different cast of characters. Paul is minimally present in the first narrative (he leaves at the time of Thecla's execution) and he disappears completely at the start of the second narrative, when Thecla encounters Alexander and Tryphaena in Antioch. Elements of the romance genre connect Thecla and Paul, and frame the insertion of the *ATh* within the *Acts of Paul*; these romance elements are less pronounced in the Antioch narrative in which Tryphaena appears.

125. Ruth Ohm Wright, "Rendezvous with Thecla and Paul in Ephesus: Excavating the Evidence," in *Distant Voices Drawing Near*, ed. Holly Hearon (Collegeville, MN: Liturgical, 2004), 230–31.

126. Leonard L. Thompson, *The Book of Revelation: Apocalypse and Empire* (New York: Oxford University Press, 1990), 139–40.

127. These are funerary inscriptions dated to the mid-third century that reference the epithet, "Christian." Elsa Gibson, *The "Christians for Christians" Inscriptions of Phrygia: Greek Texts, Translations and Commentary* (Missoula, MT: Scholars, 1978), 4, 98, 118.

128. Christine Trevett places the origin of the New Prophecy movement c. 160–170 C.E., east of Philadelphia. Trevett, *Montanism: Gender, Authority and the New Prophecy* (Cambridge: Cambridge University Press, 1996). William Tabbernee locates it in Phrygia around 165 C.E. Tabbernee, *Montanist Inscriptions and Testimonia: Epigraphic Sources Illustrating the History of Montanism* (Macon, GA: Mercer University Press, 1997), 53. On Prisca and Maximilla as the leading prophets and the movement formerly known as Montanism, see Anne Jensen, *God's Self-Confident Daughters: Early Christianity and the Liberation of Women* (Louisville: Westminster John Knox, 1996),133–67.

129. Willy Rordorf, "Tradition and Composition in the Acts of Thecla: the State of the Question," in *The Apocryphal Acts of the Apostles*, ed. Dennis Ronald MacDonald (Semeia 38; Decatur, GA: Scholars, 1986), 52.

130. Sheila McGinn, "The Acts of Thecla," in *Searching the Scriptures*, vol. 2, *A Feminist Commentary*, ed. Schüssler Fiorenza (New York: Crossroad, 1994), 800–828. Since Paul abandons Thecla to Alexander's sexual advances, there is some difficulty in claiming this text for a "Pauline" tradition.

RELIGIOUS STATUS

In the Antioch narrative, Thecla and Tryphaena develop distinctive religious roles. Both women have marriage-free lifestyles.[131] The text presents the women as a complementary pair, each modeling a different set of contributions. Called "slave of God" four times in this section, the apostolic Thecla baptizes and teaches, and evangelizes the widow Tryphaena (καὶ τὴν Τρύφαιναν εὐαγγελισθεῖσαν, 39). The narrative reiterates that the "foreigner" Thecla is celibate ("pure"), and refers to her as "solitary one." Virginity symbolized purity necessary to approach deities; chastity was a virtue of the elite, similar to religious roles like priesthoods. Repeated threat of assault by Alexander and his soldiers implies the vulnerability of a woman who was temporarily without family, friends, or resources.[132] Thus Thecla requires Tryphaena's patronal provisions of protection, hospitality, inheritance, clothing, gold, and companionship. Tryphaena's influence with the Romans allows her to intervene at critical moments on Thecla's behalf.

For both Tryphaena and Thecla, the narrative associates access to wealth, marital status, and religious roles. The narrative emphasizes Tryphaena's widowhood, status as head of her household, and financial ability to direct her resources to Thecla and the poor. Thecla's religious association accompanies her refusal to marry and subsequent loss of a wealthy family's resources. Tryphaena's patronage allows Thecla to avoid marriage and pursue her apostolic calling.

In its portrayal of patronage *Acts of Thecla* provides a representation of the benefits that might accrue from benefaction. Tryphaena's declaration, "Now I believe that the dead are raised up!" is followed immediately by her offer of financial support, "Come inside and I will assign to you all that is mine" (39). Tryphaena next appears giving a benefaction described as service for the poor (41). In return, Tryphaena twice receives prayers from Thecla immediately after an act of protection (29, 31) and therein regains a daughter; she also receives catechesis in the word of God for herself and her household, and she gains in both reputation and prayers from the people who hear Thecla's account (41). Through these incidents in the narrative, *Acts of Thecla* portrays clients displaying the usual reverence and prominence due their patrons. And just as for

---

131. In uplifting a lifestyle without marriage, the social organization challenges the traditional male-headed household. Kate Cooper, *The Virgin and The Bride: Idealized Womanhood in Late Antiquity* (Cambridge, MA: Harvard University Press, 1996), 9.

132. According to Jennifer Glancy, Alexander mistakes Thecla for a slave. Glancy, *Slavery in Early Christianity* (Oxford: Oxford University Press, 2002), 14. Slaves in *Acts of Thecla* symbolize sexual vulnerability and wealth.

patrons who supported an artisan or physician, Tryphaena and her household benefit from Thecla's apostolic skill in instruction and ritual.[133]

The narrative constructs an opposition between the religious women and two men depicted as wealthy and politically influential. Thamyris and Alexander both instigate significant public events through their followers and their connections with civic leadership. Thamyris seduces Demas and Hermogenes with a banquet and wine so that they betray Paul (13–14). Thamyris is able to muster a crowd that includes "rulers and officers" to take Paul to the governor (15). Alexander, who belongs to the elite of the Antiochenes, is "powerful," wears a crown, arranges games, and frequently advises the governor (27, 30, 33, 35, 36). Both Thamyris and Alexander try to dissuade or force Thecla away from her decision to remain free of sexual relationships; each attempts to use his wealth and sociopolitical leadership to attempt to bring about his wish. While their actions provoke the conflict propelling the plot, the text codes these elite men's activities as treacherous to Thecla's religious status.

Set in contrast to these men are Thecla herself and Tryphaena. When the story opens, Thecla is one of the elite of the Iconians, with the leisure to simply sit and learn for three days (26, 8). Her household includes slaves, and she owns bracelets and a silver mirror (10, 18). Tryphaena is rich, connected imperially, and owns slaves and gold (27, 36, 39, 41). In actions of which the text clearly approves, Thecla uses her wealth to free Paul from prison; Tryphaena uses hers to host Thecla and to provide relief to the poor (39, 41). The text contrasts wealthy men and women, and associates women's wealth with promotion of the gospel.

The narrator of *Acts of Thecla* also explores associations of wealth and imperial power in the construction of socioeconomic prominence. Thamyris and Alexander both appeal to Roman authorities to arrest and sentence Thecla. Thecla receives a typical Roman death sentence in the arenas at Iconium and Antioch.[134] Both cities were Roman colonies, situated on the main Roman road that ran east and west through south central Asia Minor. The narrative line emphasizes the Roman Empire's control over life and death.[135] A plot twist near

133. Paul breaks bread in 5, with Thecla in 25. Thecla baptizes in 34.

134. The popularity of Roman spectacles involving beasts led to modifications of theaters throughout Asia Minor: the first rows of seats were removed and a retaining wall erected around the stage.

135. "The *Acts of Paul* is consistent with many apocryphal Acts of the apostles in that it portrays numerous instances in which the primary characters and their followers come into conflict with figures holding political power, such as governors, emperors, and other officials." Ann Graham Brock, "Political Authority and Cultural Accommodation," in *The Apocryphal Acts of the Apostles*, ed. François Bovon,

the end results from the sudden revelation of "Queen" Tryphaena's imperial connections. This character's name seems to draw significance from an allusion to Queen Antonia Tryphaena, who appears on coins and in three inscriptions from Kyzikos (in northwest Asia Minor) that date to 37 to 54 C.E.[136] In the narrative of *Acts of Thecla*, Alexander fears imperial retribution for Tryphaena's (apparent) death from shock; this fear prompts him to end his torture of Thecla (36). Tryphaena's Roman rank enhances her influence as a wealthy woman.

The text of *Acts of Thecla* treats conditions that affected socioeconomic status for women: wealth, gender, marital status, and access to Roman power. The portrayal of women is quite favorable in contrast to the depiction of their male persecutors.[137] Men abuse their political influence with Romans whereas wealthy single women promote the gospel.[138] In this text, Tryphaena's socioeconomic status as a wealthy widow with Roman influence is integral to her religious status.[139] As a woman without access to wealth, Thecla requires Tryphaena's patronage to fulfill her religious aspirations.

TRYPHAENA'S PATRONAGE

While the *Acts of Thecla* depicts Thecla and Tryphaena quite favorably in comparison to their male persecutors, the text also qualifies the portrayals of Thecla's and Tryphaena's status to subordinate them to Paul's status. This is not

Ann Graham Brock, and Christopher R. Matthews (Cambridge, MA: Harvard University Press, 1999), 147.

136. Scott Fitzgerald Johnson, *The* Life and Miracles of Thekla: *A Literary Study* (Cambridge, MA: Harvard University Press, 2006), 48 n. 47. IMT Kyz Kapu Dag 1540, 1430, 1431. Antonia Tryphaena was herself a queen, daughter of King Polemon, wife of King Kotys, and mother of kings. She rebuilt the city's harbors and served in many patronal offices. Ramsay argued the historical possibility for Queen Tryphaena's appearance in Iconium at the time of Paul's travels in southern Galatia. William Mitchell Ramsay, *The Church in the Roman Empire before A.D. 170* (1904; repr., Boston: Longwood, 1978), 382–89.

137. As if to accentuate its high esteem for women, the text features a female lion that defends Thecla against a male lion, and the audience is invited to join a chorus of women who vocalize reactions to movements of the plot (27, 28, 33, 38).

138. This depiction of Tryphaena and Thecla is similar to that developed by Misset-Van de Weg, "Tryphaena," 27–30. Misset-Van de Weg's main concern is to show that the portrayal of Tryphaena does resemble that of a patron more closely than that of the mother (as other scholars argued).

139. The formation of a "Christian" group in opposition to Romans could be seen as part of Christian ethnic identification. Denise Buell has argued persuasively that religious groups used ethnoracial reasoning to accomplish a variety of objectives: "By the first century C.E., religion was well established as a public discourse that was especially useful for asserting, contesting, and transforming ethnoracial as well as civic identities across the Mediterranean basin." Denise Buell, *Why This New Race: Ethnic Reasoning in Early Christianity* (New York: Columbia University Press, 2005), 49.

surprising since the text of the *Acts of Thecla* was edited to situate it within the *Acts of Paul* (discussed above).

In contrast to Paul's teaching authority, Thecla first appears in the narrative as Paul's disciple. Thecla pursues her mission by assuming the appearance of a man, cutting her hair (25), and adopting masculine clothing (40). From the perspective of the text's author or editor, Thecla's religious status as apostle and missionary depends on access to male gender privilege. This interpretation can be debated.[140] Certainly, the attention to gender indicates that women's leadership was a point of contention. Further, the text presents Thecla's marriage-free lifestyle as a matter of sexual status. In the preceding chapter I argued that marriage for wealthy women was also a matter of socioeconomic status and leadership. The elements of romance that harness the narrative of Thecla to the *Acts of Paul and Thecla* have been explored by Virginia Burrus. Her observation of "a conflict of interest between eros and *gamos*" in the *Acts of Paul and Thecla* affirms the distinction between sexual love and marriage in traditional Greek culture.[141] The depiction of Thecla's celibacy in the *Acts of Thecla* remains silent on the socioeconomic aspect of marriage, thereby obscuring an important avenue for Thecla's leadership.

As for Tryphaena, the text's presentation of her patronage in Antioch differs somewhat from the patronage of Onesiphorus in Iconium. The narrative includes an "*ekklesia* in the house of Onesiphorus" in Iconium that includes Paul as well as men and women who were not servants or slaves (2–7). In comparison, Tryphaena's religious gathering is limited to the group in her household (39).[142] Hermeios also hosts a group gathered at his house that includes Paul and nonhousehold members (41). There are other aspects of the

---

140. Thecla "becomes like a man, with male privileges and without any questioning of her rights of these privileges." Gunhild Vidén, "The Twofold View of Women—Gender Construction in Early Christianity," in *Aspects of Women in Antiquity: Proceedings of the First Nordic Symposium on Women's Lives in Antiquity*, ed. Lena Larsson Lovén and Agneta Strömberg (Jonsered, Sweden: P. Åströms, 1998), 146. As Elizabeth Castelli writes, "gender serves as a shorthand and a code for signifying certain social and power relations and their transgression." *Martydom and Memory: Early Christian Culture Making* (New York: Columbia University Press, 2004), 141. In the apocryphal *Acts*, the female convert's "equality with the male apostle is implied by assumption of his apostolic roles (teaching, miracle-working, baptizing), rather than being explicitly stated." Gail Corrington, "'The Divine Woman'? Propaganda and the Power of Chastity in the New Testament Apocrypha," in *Rescuing Creusa*, ed. Marilyn B. Skinner, *Helios* 13, no. 2 (1986): 155.

141. Virginia Burrus, "Mimicking Virgins: Colonial Ambivalence and the Ancient Roman," in *Arethusa* 38, no. 1 (2005): 49–88, quotation on 56–57.

142. There are significant differences between the narratives at Iconium and Antioch in the *Acts of Thecla*. For instance, "Christian" is used only in the former, not the latter. So the use of *ekklesia* may

portrayal of Tryphaena's patronage that are unexpected considering the model of patronage developed from inscriptions.

Tryphaena's leadership status is correlated almost exclusively with women in the *Acts of Thecla*. In Antioch, the narrative treats Tryphaena as a leader among the women of the city since they all share the same reactions to the events, but Tryphaena is the only one singled out by name and with specific identifiers: wealthy, widow, host to Thecla, and patron who protects and receives benefits. However, those women of the city leave the story after their remarkable acclamation at the news of Thecla's release. One might expect them at Tryphaena's house to receive catechesis along with Tryphaena and her household, but the text is silent on any such gathering in Tryphaena's house. The leader's expected followers fail to materialize.

This surprising silence occurs with respect to Tryphaena's financial leadership as well. In the account of her patronage, the usual connection between patron and clients is interrupted. She provides service (the verbal form of "minister," *diakonos*) to the poor in another city who know her only by reputation. In some manuscripts, she sends this material help by way of Paul.[143] The existence of manuscript variations at this point suggests that the question of who had the authority to distribute a patron's resources was a point of contention in some religious groups. Certainly, the overall effect is a depiction of Tryphaena's patronage as bereft of crucial aspects of the usual construction of leadership, particularly clients.

Overall, the portrait of Tryphaena that remains is a weak shadow of portrayals of patrons presented in inscriptions. The narrative accomplishes this effect by severing the connection between a patron and her clients. On the civic stage, she plays the role of a famous wealthy lady rather than a public benefactor. The text also presents Tryphaena primarily in the household setting, as mistress of a large staff, rather than as a leader of an association. The whole household converts when Tryphaena does; their low status (and lack of individuality) helps to construct the impression of Tryphaena's wealth, influence, and social prominence. The repetitive allusions to motherhood also contribute to the image of Tryphaena as a matron in a household. The portrayal of Tryphaena's patronage admits her social and economic leadership, but keeps her in the background of the religious mission. The text associates this diminishment of

accompany the use of "Christian." In that case, its absence in the description of Tryphaena's gathering would seem less unusual.

143. ἡ μὲν οὖν Τρύφαινα πολὺν ἱματισμὸν καὶ χρυσὸν ἔπεμψεν αὐτῇ, ὥστε καταλιπεῖν τῷ Παύλῳ εἰς διακονίαν τῶν πτωχῶν (41). Richard Adelbert Lipsius, ed., *Apocryphal Acts of the Apostles* (Lipsiae: Apud Hermannum Mendelssohn, 1891–1903), 267–68.

the patron's roles (compared to those expected from the analysis of inscriptions) with ideals of women's passivity and subordinate household status (discussed in the previous chapter).

WOMEN'S LEADERSHIP IN ACTS OF THECLA

The *Acts of Thecla* qualifies the portrayals of Thecla's and Tryphaena's status when these portrayals are compared to the figure of Paul and to other representations of patronage. The attention to gender indicates the presence of struggle with regard to the status of missionary apostolic leaders in religious groups. The construction of gender in Tryphaena's civic leadership and Thecla's arena trials offers a powerful portrayal of "female solidarity."[144] In the world of the text, privilege is linked to men, so Thecla and Tryphaena both require the benefit of this mutually "supportive community of women."[145] Overall, the text associates single wealthy women with leadership, but it subordinates women's religious status to men's.

It seems that members of religious associations in Asia Minor held differing views on the issues of patronal authority and gender privilege. Struggles centered on women's roles as traveling apostolic missionaries and the relationship between patrons and clients. The portrayal in the *Acts of Thecla* tempers women's leadership roles. The subdued depiction of Tryphaena's patronage indicates the presence of controversy in religious groups in regard to the religious status of wealthy widow patrons. My evaluation that Tryphaena's patronage is truncated emerges from comparing the portrayal of Tryphaena with the presentations of widows' patronal leadership in inscriptional texts. Severed from clients, Tryphaena's leadership lacks followers.

CONCLUSION

PHOEBE

Representations of wealthy women's patronage and leadership from a similar era and geographic locale inform my argument about Phoebe's religious leadership. Analysis of inscriptional representations of wealthy women indicates that members of religious associations would understand Phoebe to be literate and accustomed to public speaking. As a wealthy widow, she expected to

---

144. Castelli, *Martrydom and Memory*, 140.
145. Schüssler Fiorenza, *In Memory of Her*, 174.

engage in patronage and demonstrate leadership. Phoebe, like Rufina, served as more than host and financial supporter. Audiences who heard or saw these women identified as patrons would expect their activities to extend to the religious, intellectual, and political realms. In addition to their identification with wealth, these women carry titles of religious leadership. Phoebe is called *diakonos*, the word Paul uses for himself and Apollos. Rufina is known as an *archisynagogos*, as are Jairus and the teacher or preacher in Luke 13:14. Wealthy widows' patronal religious leadership could have included reading and preaching in assemblies, evangelizing, occupying a prominent seat, wearing distinctive clothing, hosting travelers, reading and writing letters of recommendation, and making organizational decisions.[146]

PATRONAL WOMEN'S RELIGIOUS LEADERSHIP

In this chapter I have analyzed representations of wealthy widows as patrons in order to explore the possibilities for writing the history of wealthy women in religious groups. Scholars have debated the religious leadership status of wealthy women. In the preceding chapter I established that wealthy women's religious status depended on their socioeconomic status in households. In this chapter I have sought to understand wealthy widows' status with respect to their patronage of religious associations. I focused first on patronage, and then turned to the texts about women's status.

With the model of kyriarchy, we can analyze patronage as a political economic institution integral to the Roman Empire. Patronage flourished in part because of the vast gulf between the wealthy and the masses living at or below subsistence level; this is clear in the inscription dedicated to Atalante discussed above. The institution of patronage contributed to reproducing and maintaining kyriarchal structures, reinscribing inequities in wealth through its institution and ideology of leadership. Wealthier members of society occupied positions in which they influenced socioeconomic and political policies to maintain their own wealth and their roles as patrons and leaders. While the highest levels of political leadership were closed to women, wealthy women did serve as patronal leaders for cities, cults, and associations.

I have shown how the inscriptions represent wealthy freeborn women as leaders through their patronage. The ancient texts present wealthy women as literate and educated in both rhetoric and public performance. Inscriptions and

---

146. In our last glimpse of her, Phoebe is traveling with a missionary message. Unfortunately, none of her correspondence with the assembly in Cenchreae has survived.

statues honor them as patronal leaders within civic and religious organizations. Economically successful members of cities drew on patronage to achieve social integration through participation and leadership in associations. Inhabitants of Asia Minor would have expected wealthy women to provide patronage, and they would have understood patronage to imply leadership in social, political, religious, and economic realms. That is, the gender ideal of women's secondary social status is a moot point for these wealthy widows.

The inscription that presents Rufina as a Jewish widow also depicts her wealth and her religious leadership. Similarly, the best interpretation of Phoebe's status sees her as a leader in terms of religious status (as *diakonos*) as well as socioeconomic status (as *prostatis*).

In comparison to the texts about Rufina and Phoebe, the *Acts of Thecla* presents the wealthy widow Tryphaena as a patron with only weak ties to a religious group. This literary portrayal of Tryphaena conforms more closely to the figure of the matron than to the figure of the religious, political, and social leader of the wealthy widow patrons presented in the inscriptions of Asia Minor. A comparison of epigraphic sources with *Acts of Paul and Thecla* confirms the finding of historians of Roman women who have established that genre plays a large role in determining representations of women. The literary portrayal of Thecla subordinates her religious leadership to that of Paul. The Christians Thecla and Tryphaena are compared favorably with their Roman male opponents, but the portrayal circumscribes these women's status in comparison to Christian men's religious and patronal leadership.

In the preceding chapter, I argued that wealthy widows exercised socioeconomic leadership as heads of households and that this status was associated with a distinct religious status. Analysis of the activities of wealthy widows in patronage has concluded that the socioeconomic status of such wealthy women enabled their status as leaders of religious groups. Nonetheless, in some texts we can see a display of tension between the wealthy widow's religious leadership and the ideal matron's subordination to a male leader.

Traditions about women refusing marriage need not be understood as relevant to erotic love at all.[147] However, the *Acts of Paul and Thecla* presents Thecla's marriage-free lifestyle as a matter of sexual status, thus obscuring the implications of marriage for women's socioeconomic status. The intertwining of a wealthy widow's socioeconomic status with the ideology of celibacy requires further investigation.[148] Since Tryphaena's interventions enabled

---

147. The funerary monuments cited in the preceding section do not seem to reference the women's purity or sexual status.

Thecla's marital, sexual, and religious status, a complete treatment would attend to gender, marriage, household, empire, wealth, patronage, and religious leadership.

A question that remains concerns the status of wealthy women who were not freeborn: Did wealthy freed women or slave women have access to patronage and leadership in a way similar to wealthy freeborn women? I turn next to investigate how legal and occupational status affected religious status.

148. Literary and postcolonial analysis of the text could fruitfully contribute to feminist materialist analysis. As Joseph Marchal has argued, "[A] feminist project that focuses its efforts on recognizing, critiquing, and resisting kyriarchal structures (and their multiple effects) should find common cause with postcolonial efforts that grapple with gender, sexuality, and status alongside and within racial, ethnic, imperial, and colonial formations" (*The Politics of Heaven: Women, Gender, and Empire in the Study of Paul* [Minneapolis: Fortress Press, 2008], 6). See Elisabeth Schüssler Fiorenza, *The Power of the Word: Scripture and the Rhetoric of Empire* (Minneapolis: Fortress Press, 2007), 111–29, 157–62; and Rosemary Hennessy, *Materialist Feminism and the Politics of Discourse* (New York: Routledge, 1993).

4

Slave Women

I argue that determination of women's religious status depends on analysis of their socioeconomic status in the institutions of household, patronage, and slavery. In preceding chapters, I show how access to wealth and widowhood accompanied women's status as socioeconomic heads of households and patronal leaders of political and religious groups. Analysis of sources on women from inscriptional and literary texts and iconography have formed the basis for these conclusions. I have used the framework of historical feminist materialism and the analytic model of kyriarchy to investigate the economic status of freeborn wealthy women in households and women patrons in religious groups. Many women in religious groups were slaves or freed slaves rather than freeborn. How did legal status affect women's access to religious leadership?

In this chapter, I examine the status of slave women in religious groups in Asia Minor.[1] Differences in interpretations of slaves' religious status emerge most distinctly in discussions of texts that allude to changes in slaves' status. Hence I select texts about slaves in religious groups that focus most specifically on changes in slaves' status. Scholars have identified several key texts for such discussion in Asia Minor in the first two centuries of the common era: the letter of Ignatius to Polycarp, and the Bosporan synagogue manumission inscriptions. These texts are especially rich for elaborating the socioeconomic status of slaves. (I argued in the second chapter that understanding women's religious status depends on study of women's socioeconomic status in institutions such as

1. This study builds on research featuring early Christian and Jewish slaves that has already been produced, particularly the studies of J. Albert Harrill, *Slaves in the New Testament: Literary, Social and Moral Dimensions* (Minneapolis: Fortress Press, 2006); Jennifer Glancy, *Slavery in Early Christianity* (Oxford: Oxford University Press, 2002); Allen Dwight Callahan, Richard A. Horsley, and Abraham Smith, eds., *Slavery in Text and Interpretation* (Semeia 83/84; Atlanta: SBL, 1998); J. Albert Harrill, *The Manumission of Slaves in Early Christianity* (Tübingen: J. C. B. Mohr, 1995); and Dale Martin, "Slavery and the Ancient Jewish Family," in *The Jewish Family in Antiquity*, ed. Shaye Cohen (Atlanta: Scholars, 1993), 113–29.

slavery.) I will not discuss two other texts that have often featured in scholarship about attitudes toward slavery in religious groups: Paul's First Letter to the Corinthians and Paul's Letter to Philemon.[2] While the Pauline texts have lent themselves to studies of attitudes toward slavery, the texts I focus on allow me to examine slave women's actual status in religious groups, rather than attitudes toward them.

Before moving to those texts on slave women's religious status, I investigate the socioeconomic status of women slaves, since slavery was an essential institution of the socioeconomic system. This step is particularly important because slave women in Asia Minor have received relatively meager scholarly attention. Sources that explicitly identify women slaves include iconographic sources as well as epigraphic and literary. As in the preceding chapters, I analyze these sources with the model of kyriarchy in which slaves occupy the bottom stratum as the most oppressed social group (see Figure 2 in Introduction). I compare the portrayals of slave women with those of free women and slave men. These comparisons allow me to discuss constructions of slaves' status and gender. Then I focus on slave women's occupations depicted in inscriptions in the historical context of Asia Minor. I show how representations of women slaves in the sources reproduce control and exploitation by slaveholders.

With this understanding of representations of slave women, I turn to the texts on slave women's status among religious groups in the second part of the chapter. The synagogue inscriptions present manumission of slaves, including women, by religious groups in the Bosporus. Ignatius' *Letter to Polycarp* suggests that religious groups in Smyrna manumitted slaves by using the group's common funds. Scholars have debated manumission by religious groups and the religious status of manumitted slaves. I contribute to this discussion by interpreting the texts in light of representations of slaves' socioeconomic status analyzed in the first part of the chapter.

PORTRAYALS OF SLAVE WOMEN

Some of the discussion in this chapter draws on funerary monuments because these are the sources that depict women workers. Many of the women represented in the sources by way of their occupations seem to have been slaves or freed persons.[3] Greek sources rarely make legal status explicit, and women's names are not certain indicators of their status as free or slave. Furthermore, the

---

2. For recent studies that incorporate earlier scholarship, see Glancy, *Slavery*, and Harrill, *Slaves*.

vocabulary for legal status is not stable across different sources.[4] This situation reflects the complexity of ancient labor systems: many workers did not fit neatly into the free/slave divide. Some terms represent persons who enjoyed status and privileges somewhere in between free and slave.[5] "Among workers there were numerous groups or categories of those whose positions, defined not in purely juridical terms, but in terms of obligations, privileges and degree of subjection to another's power, fell somewhere between the chattel slaves of the ranches and mines and free peasant proprietors and self-employed artisans."[6] Ancient sources agree that in most occupations, free, freed, and slave women worked side by side.

Women workers are underrepresented in historical sources. For example, many surviving sources depict urban settings although the Roman economy depended primarily on agriculture, and as much as 90 percent of the population engaged in farm work. Cross-cultural studies of agricultural labor show that women have been vital to food production. In Western Hemisphere slave societies, women and men often assumed the same tasks, "including heavy agricultural work such as hauling logs, ploughing with teams of mules and oxen, hoeing, digging ditches, spreading manure, picking cotton, and reaping corn."[7] Passing references in literary texts to women in the Roman era depict women who hoed and weeded. They participated in the harvest as reapers, gleaning and cutting stubble, and some were hired laborers. Women treaded barley under their feet and labored in wine and olive cultivation.[8] Although women were vital to the economy in ancient Asia Minor, many remain invisible in the archaeological sources.

3. That is, women's names appear frequently without a patronymic; the presence of a husband's name adds to the supposition of a freeborn or freed person, but is not definitive.

4. In particular, for Asia Minor, θρετη might be a freeborn woman, a houseborn slave, or just a woman's personal name. E. S. Golubcova, "Sklaverei und Abhängigkeit in den Städten," in *Die Sklaverei in den östlichen Provinzen des römischen Reiches im 1.-3. Jahrhundert* (Moscow, 1977; translated and reprinted, Stuttgart: Franz Steiner, 1992), 90–93.

5. For example, registered citizens were distinguished from those who occupied rural territory. David B. Magie, *Roman Rule in Asia Minor* (Princeton: Princeton University Press, 1950), 640. Legal sources represent freed persons—a woman freed to be married to her former owner, for example--with considerably less access to legal protections than freeborn persons.

6. Peter Garnsey, "Non-Slave Labour in the Roman World," in *Non-Slave Labour in the Greco-Roman World*, ed. Peter Garnsey (Cambridge: Cambridge University Press, 1980), 34.

7. Walter Scheidel, "The Most Silent Women of Greece and Rome: Rural Labour and Women's Life in the Ancient World I and II," pt. 1, *Greece and Rome* 42, no. 2 (1995): 202–17, and pt. 2, *Greece and Rome* 43, no. 1 (1996): 1–10.

8. Scheidel, "The Most Silent Women," pt. 2, 2–3.

TRENDS IN REPRESENTATION

Analysis of representations shows that portrayals of slave women vary with the rhetorical strategies and goals of the sources. For instance, sources may choose to depict slaves' low status, distinguish free women from slave women, discriminate between slave men and slave women, or, indicate a slave's status in relation to the slave's owner.

Representations of slaves in ancient Asia Minor commonly attribute to them characteristics of low rank, marginality, smallness, and reduced visibility. This is true of written portrayals as well as visual imagery. The succession of names in the funerary inscriptions of Asia Minor (as well as all other inscriptions in which persons or offices are named in order of their rank in imperial society) follows the ideal kyriarchal order: man followed by wife, followed by children, freed people, and slaves.[9] Extended groups might include siblings, parents, grandchildren, partners and family of freed and slaves, and fellow slaves or former slaves, for example:

τὸν πλάτην κατ<ε>σκεύασεν Γενέθλειος
Ἑρμᾶ τοῦ Ἀδρά<σ>του? αὐτῷ καὶ γυναικὶ
καὶ τέκνοις καὶ ἐγγόνοις καὶ θρεπτοῖς καὶ γυ-
ναιξὶν αὐτῶν· ἄλλῳ δὲ οὐκ ἐξέσται κτλ.

Genethleios Erma son of Adrastos prepared the tomb for himself and his wife and his children and his grandchildren and his slaves and their wives, but no one else, etc.[10]

This inscription, which dates to the imperial era in southwest Asia Minor, demarcates a household order: a freeborn man, wife, children, parents, slaves, and their wives. Only the first man's name is given; other people are collected within categories of kinship or status rather than named individually. Slaves and their wives are the fifth and sixth named entities. The wording implies that the slaves are all male, at least those who are permitted burial. Their wives' status is unclear.[11]

9. Dale B. Martin, "Constructions of Ancient Family: Methodological Considerations," *Journal of Roman Studies* 86 (1996): 42.

10. *CIG* 2825.

Funerary reliefs from Asia Minor also depict most slaves at the bottom of the household hierarchy. Meal scenes, or funerary banquets, are common on tombstones, and slaves constitute a characteristic element. They are located on the margins of the scene, almost part of the frame, below the protagonists, and in miniature. Numbers 1134 and 1141 in the catalog of Pfuhl and Möbius are good examples.[12] Neither of these stones has an (intact) inscription. Both date to the first century B.C.E. and both depict rural objects.

Figure 8. Pfuhl and Möbius.[13]

In Pfuhl and Möbius 1134, findspot unknown, the objects depicted in the lower panel are a hunter, dog, tree, and deer (Figure 8). In 1141, which is from northwest Turkey, a figure drives a plow behind a pair of oxen.[14] Two female slaves and one male slave appear in the wings. In these examples, the slaves

11. While slave marriages were not valid in Roman law, inscriptions such as this one indicate that social practices recognized such marriages.

12. Ernst Pfuhl and Hans Möbius, *Die ostgriechischen Grabreliefs*, 2 vols. (Mainz am Rhein: Von Zabern, 1977–79).

13. No. 1134. Permission granted courtesy of Bursa Müzesi Müdürlüğü

14. Ibid., no. 1141, plate 286.

belong to the interior scene: the slaves are serving a meal rather than farming or hunting. Iconographically, this depiction highlights slaves' subordinate status in the household.

Commonly, slaves appear as much smaller figures than other individuals that are present in the same scenes. Johanna Fabricius has found slaves shown in miniature in funerary meal scenes in Byzantium and Kyzikos.[15] In Pfuhl-Möbius 443, a slave woman appears to be the same size as a baby in another panel.[16] Slaves are distinguished from children by their clothing, and sometimes by their aged appearance or the activities in which they are engaged.[17] George Hanfmann and Kemal Polatkan identify a small figure as a daughter and question Pfuhl's assertion that all such figures are "servants."[18] In examples with parallel compositions, however, small figures are identified as servers. Nancy Ramage identifies a diminutive figure as a servant or attendant rather than as a child, because she has breasts.[19] A short *chiton* is typical of slaves, as is a standing (or leaning) posture or the action of handing an object to a seated woman or man.[20] The motif of miniaturized slave figures also appears on mass-produced goods of the late Hellenistic and imperial periods.[21] The physical size of the slaves in these instances renders them less prominent than the other figures, especially when viewed at a distance from the funerary monuments.

In addition to visual diminishment, the texts of many inscriptions omit slave presence. Scholars have presumed that slaves who appear in inscriptions as members of a household must also have been workers in that house. Engraved reliefs that depict slaves at the sides of meal scenes and in work scenes omit their names. For example, a relief accompanies the tombstone of a blacksmith and Ammia from Laodikeia in the later imperial period.[22] One male figure, perhaps dressed in a chiton, hammers a metal object while another in a chiton stokes the fire. If the scene represents two men in a blacksmith's workshop, as

15. Johanna Fabricius, *Die hellenistischen Totenmahlreliefs* (München: Pfeil, 1999), 93, 286.

16. Pfuhl and Möbius, *Die ostgriechischen Grabreliefs*, no. 443, plate 74. Findspot unknown but in the style of the Greek East. Dated to 150–100 B.C.E.

17. Ibid., 67–68.

18. George M. A. Hanfmann and Kemal Ziya Polatkan, "A Sepulchral Stele from Sardis," *American Journal of Archaeology* 64, no. 1 (January 1960): 50–51. The stele dates to the third century B.C.E.

19. Nancy Hirschland Ramage, "A Lydian Funerary Banquet," *Anatolian Studies* 29 (1979): 92. The monument dates to the fourth century B.C.E.

20. The inactivity of a slave figure portrays the wealth of a huge household with specialized laborers. Johanna Fabricius, *Die hellenistischen Totenmahlreliefs: Grabrepräsentation und Wertvorstellungen in ostgriechischen Städten* (München: Verlag Dr. Friedrich Pfeil, 1999), 93.

21. Pfuhl and Möbius, *Die ostgriechischen Grabreliefs*, 68.

22. Ibid., no. 1171, plate 178.

the editors suggest, the helper may have been a slave. In this case, however, the second man appears close to normal size. His name is not recorded, nor is he mentioned in the burial permissions for the tomb. In another example, a tomb dedicated to Soteride mentions her husband, his employer (or owner), and her three children (Figure 9).[23] The accompanying sculpture depicts two slaves: a relatively large female figure stands behind a woman holding several implements, while a typically small male figure leans in a mourning pose at the side. Even though slaves are present visually and in relationship to the deceased, the written memorial recognizes none of them.

Figure 9. Tombstone of Soteride[24]

23. Ibid., no. 1142, plate 172, Bursa Museum. First or second century c.e., findspot unknown but executed in the style of the Greek East. Soteride died at the age of twenty after seven years of marriage and bearing three children. Ἕσπερος Ἑσπέρου υἱός, Τιβερίου δὲ Κλαυδίου Πωλίωνος Φαίτρου οἰκονόμος, Σωτηρίδι τῇ ἑαυτοῦ συνβίῳ συνζησάσῃ αὐτῷ ἔτη ἑπτὰ καὶ ἀπολιπούσῃ αὐτῷ τέκνα τρία μνή[μ]ης χάριν· τελευτήσασα ἐτῶν εἴκοσι· χαῖρε. IK Prusa ad Olympum 165.

To summarize the iconography and inscriptional sources investigated thus far, we have seen that representations in ancient Asia Minor mark slaves with the characteristics of marginality, smallness, low rank, and reduced visibility.

Slave women are also distinguished from free women and from men with the use of motifs of clothing and posture. The way figures pose, their activities, and the setting all communicate status. In their study of grave reliefs, Pfuhl and Möbius attribute with certainty only one monument to a female "servant." She is identified as such by her clothing, a short chiton; no inscription survives. The figure faces forward and holds a box with both hands. The small slave women discussed above also hold various objects or are in the process of passing them to others.

These acts of handling objects distinguish slave from free women. As discussed in a preceding chapter, passivity marks the portrayal of free women. The tomb of Alexandros, which dates to 100–150 c.e., consists of a relief and a funerary inscription from the northern shore of the Propontis in Thrace, opposite Bithynia (Figure 10).

χαῖρε παροδεῖτα
Ἀλέξανδρος Διοτείμου
κατεσκεύασεν ἐκ τῶν
ἰδίων τὴν στήλην καὶ τὸ
λατόμιον ἐαυτῷ καὶ
τῇ γυναικί μου Ἀθηνα-
ίδι, ὡς μηδένα ἕτερον κτλ.

Greetings, passerby. Alexandros son of Dioteimos constructed the plaque and tomb from his own funds for myself and my wife, Athenaidis, but no one else, etc.[25]

---

24. Findspot unknown. Stele in marble 118 x 67 x 9 cm. Inv. No. 2575. Photo I. Luckert reproduced by permission of Bursa Museum.

25. Pfuhl and Möbius, Die ostgriechischen Grabreliefs, no. 1166, figure 75.

Figure 10. Stele of Alexandros and Athenaidis[26]

A man in a chiton, presumably Alexandros, stands on the right side of the relief with his right hand grasping a hatchet and his left hand pinning down a lamb on a chopping block. To his right and slightly behind him, a much smaller woman, Athenaidis, sits with her right hand holding fast her head covering and outer garment. Behind her in the left side of the scene are more pieces of meat on a table, a rack, a balance, and a tie rack. Athenaidis's passivity is remarkable next to her husband, caught in the middle of chopping and surrounded by the accoutrements of a butcher's shop. The contrast heightens their distinct representations. Her presence is obvious, as she is located in the middle of the scene, but her activities and working role are unclear. The portrayal obscures

26. Seen in Silivri, Slg. Stamulis. G. Seure, b.c.H 36, 1912, 599, Fig. 37. Funerary stele, marble, 90 x 41 cm. From Herakleia-Perinth.

her contributions to the work of the household. The inscription identifies her as a wife; her quiet pose and restrictive clothing characterize this wife as unoccupied and unable to move without disrupting her costume. This depiction distinguishes a free woman from a slave even though the figure appears in a workshop.

Inscriptions also show the ways in which slave women are distinguished from their husbands. Gladiators, for example, were typically slave or freed men, and their wives likely also came from the same socioeconomic status. This may explain why these women do not appear in images, and, in inscriptions, their names lack patronymics. However, they did dedicate inscriptions and reliefs to gladiators.[27]

> Νεικηφόρῳ πα(λῳ) α′
> Μαρκελλεῖνα ἡ γυνὴ τὸ
> μνημεῖον ἐκ τῶν ἰδίων
> κατεσκεύασεν.

Markelleina, his wife, prepared the memorial from her own funds for Neikephoros, gladiator.[28]

---

27. Both couples appear in marital relationships that were invalid under Roman law, but this practice seems common among Roman Empire slaves nonetheless.

28. Pfuhl and Möbius, *Die ostgriechischen Grabreliefs*, no. 1231.

Figure 11. A Stele Erected by Markelleina for Neikephoros[29]

As with the farmer and blacksmith above, gladiators appear with their occupational implements. However, in these cases, women are absent from the picture. A dynamic scene of sailing accompanies the inscription dedicated by Tyche to her own master and husband, Demetrios, who appears in chiton and at work.

Τύχη Δημητρίῳ Χρήσστου, ὃ κατεσ-
κεύβασεν [κατεσκεύασεν] μνείας χάριν τῷ ἰ-
δίῳ κυρέῳ καὶ ἀνδρί.

Tyche prepared the memorial for Demetrios son of Chresstos, her own master [or 'lord'] and husband. (See Figure 12.)[30]

29. Ibid., no. 1231, plate 184. Marble stele from Herakleia Salbake in Caria, 150–200 c.e.
30. Ibid., no. 1181. 150–200 c.e., Mysia. Istanbul, Arch. Mus. Inv. Nr. 4251.

Figure 12. A Memorial for Tyche's Husband[31]

Perhaps Tyche was a concubine or freed wife. Such women, probably slaves or freed, have a much lower monumental profile than do their slave or freed husbands. For the illiterate majority of the population, these women are literally invisible.

Nonetheless, these slave or freed women did erect gravestones, and this suggests that they had access to more than subsistence-level resources. Since the inscriptions name no one else, it seems this property belonged to these widows themselves. The free or slave persons who left such inscriptions and images belonged to a narrow socioeconomic stratum who had access to some economic resources above subsistence level; it included prosperous vendors and artisans, medics, innkeepers, and some skilled house slaves.[32]

---

31. Ibid., no. 1181, plate 178. A. Müfid, AA 1933, 133 no. 44, Fig. 14. Stele from Lampsakos, in marble, 63 x 47 x 12 cm.

Access to economic resources varied widely among slaves; some slaves enjoyed higher economic status than did many free people. A first-century (c.e.) stone displays the bust of a girl that two slaves, Kale and Satorninos, a *notarius*, identified as their daughter.[33] An elegant epigram also appears on the stele. A monument erected for slave horseman Agathopodos, his wife Domna, and their children depicts a small bearded rider on horseback.[34] The rider is dressed in chiton and chlamys and seems to represent Agathopodos (rather than Karikos, who dedicated it). In these two cases, a daughter of high-ranking slaves and a slave horseman, the pictorial representations leave the slave tombs undistinguished from the memorials of freeborn persons. We would not know their legal status as slaves if the inscriptions had not noted this.

Other high-ranking slaves are less obvious, but the format of the inscription allows us to infer a relatively high socioeconomic status. The kyriarchal household hierarchy is visible in the order of names in this later inscription by a slave woman who established a tomb for her husband, children, parents, nephew, son-in-law, and a female slave with her own husband and children.[35]

Ἑλενούς, δούλη Αὐρ(ηλίας) Ἀρτεμεισίας,
κατεσκεύασα τὸν τύνβον ἑαυτῇ καὶ
ἀνδρὶ καὶ τέκνοις καὶ ἐνγόνοις καὶ
γανβρῷ Φιλοσεράπι καὶ δούλῃ μου Μελίννῃ
καὶ ἀνδρὶ αὐτῆς Ἁρποκρᾷ καὶ τέκνῳ αὐτῶν· ἑτέ-
ρῳ δὲ μηδενὶ

Helenous, slave of Aurelia Artemeisia, constructed the tomb for herself and husband and children and grandchildren and son-in-law Philoserapis, and for her slave Melinne and her husband Harpokras and their children, but for no other, etc.

32. Natalie Boymel Kampen, "Social Status and Gender in Roman Art: The Case of the Saleswoman," in *Roman Art in Context: An Anthology*, ed. Eve D'Ambria (Englewoods Cliffs, NJ: Prentice Hall, 1993), 130.

33. Pfuhl and Möbius, *Die ostgriechischen Grabreliefs*, no. 2191, plate 312. From Madytos, in southernmost Thrace.

34. Ibid., no. 1285, Bursa Museum Inv. Nr. 56, no photo. From Synnada in Phrygia. This entry is very similar to 1284, which is from 100 c.e., Miletopolis.

35. *TAM* 2.967. Olympos in Lycia, Roman era, after 212 c.e.

Exceptions to the typical household order are present in that Helenous herself prepared the monument rather than her master or her husband.[36] Helenous, a slave, claims a slave as her own.[37] Both Helenous and Melinne are named at the head of their household hierarchies, contrary to expectations for married women in households with their husbands present.[38] This depiction suggests that the women's occupations (and economic value) outweighed the usual assumption of male precedence. Although the wording adheres generally to the form of the ideal order in a household, it shows that for some slave women other factors of status affected representations of household rank.

To review and summarize this investigation of iconography and epigraphy, we have seen that marginality and pseudo-invisibility characterized representations of lower-strata free women and slave women and men in comparison to elites in the western and northern provinces of Roman Asia Minor during the early imperial period. In certain memorials discussed above, slave women are distinguished from both free women and from slave men through different strategies. The slave woman's handling of household items reinforced her mistress's leisure, and thus, the family's wealth. Yet relative to slave or freed men, we see a slave or freed wife only in words, while her working or gladiator husband appears in images, in action or ready to act. However, the representations also indicate that the ideology and iconography of slave and lower-strata women were not homogenous. Many women dedicated the stones described above even though depictions of this act do not appear in the images themselves. And some slave women's names precede those of their husbands despite the dominant ideology of household order.

Portrayals of slave women vary with their relationship to others. When slave women are contrasted with free women, they are shown standing and involved in their work. When slave women are contrasted with their gladiator husbands, they dedicate memorials but are not depicted in them. When their importance to the slaveowner is highlighted, they precede their husbands (while still following relatives and free persons). Further, the status of slaves' occupations affected their funerary representations. The variety of depictions point to tensions inherent in slave women's status relative to others. The

---

36. Curiously, husband, children, and parents are not listed by name, while the son-in-law and slave woman and her husband are. Perhaps there is no doubt of the identity of the former, whereas the latter designations might have multiple referents.

37. Several other surprises appear here: the slave Melinne is said to be married, her name precedes her husband's, and this slave couple is accompanied by "their children." Again, the presence of Melinne's marriage and children raises the question of the relevance of Roman slave law to practices in Asia Minor.

38. See chapter 2.

kyriarchal system that depicted slave marginality also relied extensively on exploitation of the work of slaves throughout the economic system.

I turn now to focus on representations of slave women in occupational inscriptions.

OCCUPATIONS

Scholars have disputed the number of slaves engaged in industrial production or in managerial or professional roles in Asia Minor. T. R. S. Broughton has estimated that most of the slaves reported in Pergamon by Galen were women domestics, but this estimate is based on contemporary gender presuppositions.[39] Stamps on tableware excavated at Pergamon date from the middle of the second century B.C.E. to the middle of the second century C.E.[40] Possible women's names on pieces from the first century B.C.E. are Neike and Charis; Methe comes from the next century. Kyras (Kyra) appears on stamps imported to Pergamon. Production flourished there in the early imperial period and pottery manufactured in Pergamon has been found in other cities in the western region of Asia Minor. Women's names have been found stamped onto amphoras recovered from around the Aegean in the Hellenistic era.[41] Diokleia, Hagneia, Nikagis, Kallio, Timo, and Doso are all feminine names found on stamps at Rhodes. Kallio and Timo occur with particular frequency.[42] Amphora stamps also indicate that some workers were immigrants to Rhodes from nearby Asia Minor, Selge in Pisidia, and Kabalie in Lycia. One woman's name appears with the title "head of the workshop" (ἐργαστηριάρχας); Martin Nilsson interprets these as the head workers, supervisors, or managers.[43]

Slave agents known as stewards (οἰκονόμοι) exemplify the slaves' managerial status. Anthousa, steward/manager in Bithynia during the imperial era, for example, was almost certainly a slave.[44]

---

39. T. R. S. Broughton, "Roman Asia," in *An Economic Survey of Ancient Rome*, ed. Tenney Frank (Paterson, NJ: Pageant, 1959), 4:840.

40. Carsten Meyer-Schlichtmann, *Die Pergamenische Sigillata aus der Stadtgrabung von Pergamon* (New York: De Gruyter, 1988), 184–87.

41. *SEG* 30.706.

42. Martin P. Nilsson, *Timbres Amphoriques de Lindos*, Exploration Archéologique de Rhodes 5 (Copenhagen: Imprimerie Bianco Luno, 1909), 101–3.

43. Other possibilities are the names of individual workers or the factory owners. Nilsson, *Amphoriques*, 101–3.

44. IK Prusa ad Olympum 68. Jean-Jacques Aubert, *Business Managers in Ancient Rome: A Social and Economic Study of Institores, 200 B.C.–A.D. 250* (Leiden: Brill, 1994), 417.

Ἄνθουσα Φοί-
βου γυνή, οἰκο-
νόμισσα Τει-
μοθέου, ζήσα-
σα κοσμίως
ἐτῶν λε'·
'Ενκώμιον
θυγάτηρ
ἐτῶν ιε'.

Anthousa, wife of Phoibos, steward of Teimotheos, who lived decently for thirty-five years. Enkomion, [her] daughter, who lived fifteen years.

Similarly, Eirene was a steward manager in Pisidia.[45]

Εἰρήνη Λονγιλλιανοῦ καὶ
Σεουήρου οἰκονόμισσα Στά-
χυι τῷ ἰδίῳ ἀνδρὶ σεμνοτάτῳ
μνείας χάριν.

Eirene, steward of Longillianos and Seoueros, in memory of her own most wonderful husband, Stachus.

This memorial for the young Eupraxia is dated to the second century C.E. in Bithynia.[46]

ἔτους ηι'·
Εὐπραξία, Γ. Κ-
ατιλλίου Κλ-
αυδιανοῦ Θρ-
άσωνος οἰκ-
ονόμισα ζ-
ήσασα ἔτη κγ'.

45. *MAMA* 8, 399.
46. IK Iznik 1466.

τοῖς ἐπάνω
χαίρειν.

In the year 18, Eupraxia, steward of G. Catillius Claudianus Thrason, having lived twenty-three years. Farewell to those above.

None of these three women stewards possesses a patronymic. Two are said to be married and one claims a daughter. Each is identified by the relationship of her occupation, "steward of X." These female οἰκονόμοι in Asia Minor managed estate finances and represented slaveholders in business transactions.[47]

Jean-Jacques Aubert has investigated the status of such slave managers. "Large estates located in Asia Minor or Syria managed by a farm manager (οἰκονόμος) employing slave labor commanded by squad leaders (ἐπιστάται) under the supervision of an overseer (ἐργαστόλος) were a common feature of second-/third-century-A.D. Greek novels."[48] Such farm managers "were mostly slaves, and were in charge of operations implying fairly developed technical, organizational, and managerial skills. The villa economy soon became diversified and sophisticated enough to require from them that they enter into legal contracts with outsiders, in order to buy tools and equipment, sell surpluses or even part of the production, buy or hire additional hands and specialized workers, sell or rent out idle and unnecessary ones, etc." (415). In an urban setting, similar responsibilities would be required of workshop managers and household financial agents. Although the size of managerial unit and its associated social prestige varied, the key element that distinguished business managers from other workers and supervisors was their ability to make valid contracts (418). The skills of these slave agents represented years of training.[49]

Slave agents worked in similar roles around the Mediterranean. Although Sandra Joshel's study of occupational inscriptions in the city of Rome found no

47. G. H. R. Horsley and S. R. Llewelyn, eds., *New Documents Illustrating Early Christianity* (Grand Rapids: Eerdmans, 1981). 160. *Oikonomos* translates Latin *vilicus*, manager of an agricultural estate. Aubert, *Business Managers* 32–34. Eupraxia was only twenty-three, but there is an example of a twenty-one-year-old male engaged in the same occupation, which indicates that youth did not necessarily disqualify one from the position. I. Nikaia II.2.1336.

48. Aubert, *Business Managers*, 416.

49. Glancy notes that ostraca, wax tablets, and the parables of Jesus are also historical sources for agents who acted semi-autonomously. Glancy, *Slavery in Early Christianity*, 43. See also Christoph Schäfer, "Die Rolle der *actores* in Geldgeschäften," in *Fünfzig Jahre Forschungen zur antiken Sklaverei an der Mainzer Akademie, 1950-2000: Miscellanea zum Jubiläum*, ed. Heinz Bellen and Heinz Heinen (Stuttgart: Franz Steiner, 2001), 211–24.

women commemorated as bankers and only a few as administrators, as many as twenty women appear as business managers in brick stamps from Italy.[50] Female managers were associated with Italian villas and with hotels and restaurants.[51] Roman jurist Ulpinaus explicitly stated that business managers could be men or women.[52]

In Italy, financial agents apparently remained with the household throughout their lives, even if freed, and were able to marry and to possess their own slaves.[53] According to Moses Finley, a slave with *peculium* (allowance)

> could expect to buy his freedom with the profits, to continue the business as a freedman thereafter if he wished, and to transmit it to his heirs. In practice, furthermore, a substantial part of the urban commercial, financial and industrial activity in Rome, in Italy, and wherever else in the empire Romans were active, was being carried on in this way by slaves and freedmen from the third century B.C. on. Unlike slave bailiffs and managers, those who had a *peculium* were working independently, not only for their owners but also for themselves. And if the business were on any scale above the minimal, their *peculium* was likely to include other slaves along with cash, shops, equipment and stock-in-trade.[54]

Slave (or freed) women, such as the estate managers and the head of the workshop above, were among this group of slaves who worked independently

50. Sandra Joshel, *Work, Identity and Social Status at Rome: A Study of the Occupational Inscriptions at Rome* (Norman: University of Oklahoma Press, 1992), 69. Päivi Setälä, "Female Property and Power in Imperial Rome: Institutum Romanum Finlandiae," in *Aspects of Women in Antiquity: Proceedings of the First Nordic Symposium on Women's Lives in Antiquity*, ed. Lena Larsson Lovén and Agneta Strömberg (Jonsered, Sweden: P. Åströms, 1998). Aubert, *Business Managers*, 224. References to the economic principle of using slave agents in Italy have relevance for Asia Minor because of the widespread structural parallels in the Roman Empire. For example, see H. W. Pleket, "Urban Elites and Business in the Greek Part of the Roman Empire," in *Trade in the Ancient Economy*, ed. Peter Garnsey, Keith Hopkins, and C. R. Whittaker (Berkeley: University of California Press, 1983), 131–44. Glenn R. Storey, "Roman Economies: A Paradigm of Their Own," in *Archaeological Perspectives on Political Economies*, ed. Gary M. Feinman and Linda M. Nicholas (Salt Lake City: University of Utah Press, 2004), 105–28.

51. Aubert, *Business Managers*, 140–41, 372–73.

52. Ulpian (28 ad ed.) *Dig.* 14.3.7.1. Aubert, *Business Managers*, 141, 224, 372.

53. Marc Kleijwegt, "Freed Slaves," in *The Faces of Freedom: The Manumission and Emancipation of Slaves in Old World and New World Slavery*, ed. Marc Kleijwegt (Leiden: Brill, 2006), 98.

54. M. I. Finley, *Ancient Economy* (Berkeley: University of California Press, 1973), 64.

and managed property. The inscription of Helenous above identified her as both slave and slaveholder as well as the head of a household. Her status resembled the status of these managers who worked not only for their owners but also for themselves.

One or two inscriptions from Asia Minor also mention the *peculium* of female slaves.[55] One was Auxilia in Pisidia.[56]

[Α]ὐξιλ[ί]α δούλη Τηλεμάχου
['Αγ]αθόποδι κ[α]ὶ Γερμανῷ ὑέσ[ι]
ἐ[κ] τοῦ πεκο[υ]λίο[υ].

Auxilia, slave of Telemachos, for her sons, Agathopodos and Germanos, from [her] *peculium*.

Auxilia's occupation cannot be determined from this source. The phrase ἐ[κ] τοῦ πεκο[υ]λίο[υ] echoes a more commonly seen phrase in inscriptions, ἐκ τῶν ἰδίων, "from their own funds," which indicates that Auxilia possessed the power to dispose of her *peculium* as she wished.[57] In another inscription, Glykon pays a debt to the gods from the *peculium* of his wife Kainis.[58] Here, the term could refer to Kainis's own property as a dependent person in Glykon's *potestas* (under his authority), but her name appears without a patronymic, so the possibility that she was a slave, or earned the *peculium* as a slave, remains open.[59]

In addition to their economic value and wealth in managerial occupations, slaves also brought their owners and themselves profit through training and performance as mimes, acrobats, musicians, dancers, weavers, physicians, nurses, and sex workers. Papyri from Egypt preserve apprenticeship contracts for female weavers and nurses. The epigram of Maximinus, from Antioch in

55. There may be other sources that refer to these funds with a different Greek word; *peculium* was the Latin term.

56. *MAMA* 8.379.

57. See also Canticles Rabbah, VII.4 for a wife's use of her funds. Boaz Cohen, "Peculium in Jewish and Roman Law," *Proceedings of the American Academy for Jewish Research* 20 (1951): 152. "The Mishnah clearly supposes that women and slaves have money at their disposal with which to pay their vows" (161). Also 163–65, 181–87.

58. *SEG* 35.1267.

59. For *peculium* as the property of a wife when both names of the couple appear with patronymic, see RECAM II.218, N. Galatia, 100–150 c.e.

Pisidia, dates to the imperial era. Maximinus's father's name appears but without occupation; we learn that his mother was the actor Eutychia, who seems to have been a particularly well-known entertainer and a freed woman.[60] The epigram format of Maximinus's inscription required more expense than the usual funerary epitaph. Mimes were particularly popular entertainments in the imperial era. Based on the letters of Pliny the Younger, Ummidia Quadratilla, a wealthy Italian woman who lived in the second half of the first century c.e., acquired and trained a troupe of slave mimes.[61] She profited well from leasing the troupe for performances at public and private venues. Certainly, Eutychia received training in preparation for her profession and could earn a living from its practice.

Macedonian lyricist Antigona died in the second century c.e. and was buried by her husband Murismos.[62] Every city had a theater, and many inscriptions reserving seats for particular individuals or offices have been recovered. Temples to Dionysios stood near the theater and performers were members of Dionysiac associations. A "union" of Dionysiac artists of Ionia "greatly expanded its operations and importance under the Empire."[63] Networking improved, increasing the numbers of artists and geographical territory involved. Also, theaters were built and repaired in the imperial era, new festivals were founded, and their popularity spread. In the prizes known from inscriptions, the highest nonathletic awards were won by lyre players, followed by tragic actors and comic actors. Flute players, citharodes, trumpeters, and encomiasts also entertained audiences. Thus inscriptions depict a wide variety of possibilities for occupational training of slave entertainers. Texts and the presence of the monuments proclaim the popularity, fame, and elevated socioeconomic status for some in these occupations.[64]

Although from Egypt in 296 c.e., a petition preserved on papyrus suggests the economic significance of a slave's earning power for second-century Asia

60. *Steinepigramme aus dem griechischen Osten.* Translated by Reinhold Merkelbach and Josef Stauber. Stuttgart : B.G. Teubner, 1998-2004. No 16/61/13, p 412.

61. David H. Sick, "Ummidia Quadratilla: Cagey Businesswoman or Lazy Pantomime Watcher?" in *Classical Antiquity* 18, no. 2 (1999): 330–48.

62. *SEG* 12 (1955) 339.

63. T. Robert S. Broughton, "Roman Asia Minor," in *An Economic Survey of Ancient Rome*, vol. 4, ed. Tenney Frank (Paterson, NJ: Pageant Books, 1959), 855–56.

64. Slave women gladiators also performed in arenas: *CIG* 6855f. with relief. See Kathleen Coleman, "Missio at Halicarnassus," *Harvard Studies in Classical Philology* 100 (2000): 487–500, and Dorothea Schäfer, "Frauen in der Arena," in *Fünfzig Jahre Forschungen zur antiken Sklaverei an der Mainzer Akademie, 1950-2000: Miscellanea zum Jubiläum*, ed. Heinz Bellen and Heinz Heinen (Stuttgart: Franz Steiner, 2001), 243–68.

Minor as well.[65] According to the plaintiff, a houseborn slave named Sarmates had been providing income for herself and her sister but later stopped making payments. The income generated by the prophetic skills of a female slave supports slaveowners in Acts of the Apostles 16:16-24. An inscription from Miletus in the imperial era records a similar activity.[66]

> Εἰρηνη πρόμαντι χαῖρε.
> Eirene, prophet, farewell.

Since Eirene appears without familial affiliation, she seems to have been a slave.[67] The root word for her title, μαντι, appears also in the verb that described the activities of the female slave (παιδίσκην) in Acts 16:16, μαντεύομαι.[68] Apparently, both of these women were slaves trained in divination performance.

Like entertainers, female medical workers were able to achieve significant socioeconomic status and the money with which to buy their freedom.[69] By the fourth century B.C.E. in classical Greece, literary and epigraphical sources were attesting to the presence of women physicians.[70] A number of women worked as physicians in Asia Minor in the first couple of centuries of the common era. Physicians (and teachers) occupied a social rank between the local elite and craftspeople, although neither group was itself socially homogenous. The cities recognized a few public physicians as a group that merited such privileges as tax exemptions or immunities from public duties, and a few were members of councils and higher-status social clubs.[71]

---

65. P. Oxy. Hels. 26 (pl. 17) dated to 13 June 296 c.e. in Horsley, *New Documents 1979*, 100.

66. Peter Hermann, *Inschriften von Milet* (Berlin and New York: Walter de Gruyter, 1998), 2:546.

67. A faint engraving that may represent a staff and a snake were tentatively identified on the stone, perhaps alluding to prophetic powers of serpents. Hermann, *Milet*, 30.

68. She is also said to have the "spirit of the python (Pythos)."

69. K. R. Bradley, *Slaves and Masters in the Roman Empire: A Study in Social Control* (New York: Oxford University Press, 1987), 107.

70. Nancy Demand, "Monuments, Midwives and Gynecology," in *Ancient Medicine in Its Socio-cultural Context*, ed. Ph. J. van der Eijk, H. F. J. Horstmanshoff, and P. H. Schrijvers (Amsterdam: Rodopi, 1995), 287.

71. Pantheia practiced medicine in the second century c.e. in the city of Pergamon, where her husband Glykon was also a physician (Merkelbach 06/03/32). Like Treboulia, no patronymic marks Pantheia's monument, so she may also have been a freed slave. This stone belongs with another, although they were found in different spots near Pergamon. The other portion of the inscription praises Philadephus as another Hippocrates and Glykon's teacher. One stone was found west of the city near the

Most physicians were grouped with other occupations in which people were paid for their services.[72] Empeiria was a physician who lived in Bithynia and seems to have been slave or freed.[73] Domnina lived in Neoclaudiopolis in the second or third century c.e. The lack of patronymic indicates she may have been a slave, although the marriage and more costly epigram format suggest that she may have been freed.[74] Treboulia lived inland, closer to central Asia Minor in northern Galatia, late in the second century c.e. She made a tomb for herself and her family, mother, grandmother, grandfather, son, and husband.[75] Anonyma, the mother of Paulinus, lived in Philadelphia in the first or second century c.e. The inscription names her "savior of children, men, and women."[76] *Savior* is a multivalent epithet; it appears in political, religious, and medical contexts. Two freed *medici* are named Soter in Latin inscriptions, and Σωτήρ is a physician in a papyrus document.[77] As for entertainers, these representations in inscriptions depict the popularity of some practitioners and their access to economic resources. A number of women trained in medicine appear in sources originating outside of Asia Minor as well.

Looking at health in the larger geographic context highlights the importance of women medics. The crowded cities around the Mediterranean presented many opportunities to practice healing arts. Sanitation principles were unknown or unpracticed and disease spread rapidly.[78] In addition to women titled *iatrine/medica*, there were also medical therapists, masseurs, trainers, ointment sellers, root cutters, and practitioners acquainted with traditional dietary remedies or the use of medicinal plants and herbs, practices that had been passed along through oral traditions.[79] Four or five women

processional route from the agora in the city center to the Asklepieion. Sanctuaries of Asklepius around the Aegean were healthcare facilities where pilgrims (and their families) were patients. Hundreds of votives, casts of body parts, and inscriptions tell of cures effected there. Galen trained and worked at the treatment center at Pergamon before moving to Rome. The vast Asklepieion and its fame attracted the injured and sick as well as their healers. It seems that Pantheia, her husband, and father-in-law, practiced their skills at or near the sanctuary.

72. Onno M. van Nijf, *The Civic World of Professional Associations in the Roman East* (Amsterdam: Gieben 1997), 172–76; and H. W. Pleket "The Social Status of Physicians in the Graeco-Roman World," in *Ancient Medicine*, 27–34.

73. IK Kios 52.

74. Merkelbach 11/03/02.

75. Emin Bosch, *Quellen zur Geschichte der Stadt Ankara im Altertum* (Ankara: Türk Tarih Kurumu Basimevi, 1967), 269,205.

76. Merkelbach 04/24/13.

77. Heikki Solin, "Die sogenannten Berufsnamen antiker Ärzte," in *Ancient Medicine*, 134.

78. Alex Scobie, "Slums, Sanitation and Mortality in the Roman World," *Klio* 68 (1986): 2.

who practiced healing arts appear in the Latin inscriptions compiled by Jukka Korpela. Most of these were freed persons, as is one of two midwives (*obstetrix*) listed by Heikki Solin. Mary Lefkowitz and Maureen Fant list six female physicians in Rome in the early imperial period, three freed and one enslaved. One was buried by her husband after thirty years of marriage. Lefkowitz and Fant also list six midwives who began their careers in slavery in early imperial Rome.[80]

SLAVE WOMEN'S SOCIOECONOMIC STATUS

I have shown that funerary iconography, particularly the meal scene, places slaves in the margins and perpetuates elite portrayals of slaves' low household status through the contrast between slave women's labors and wives' leisure. In their active postures, the representations of the slave women resemble that of the husbands and other males. Occupational inscriptions portray enslaved and freed women as heading households, managing businesses, and controlling *peculium* funds. Inscriptional representations portray success, fame, and the agency of skilled women in the economic system. The investigation of representations of slave women emphasizes apparent inconsistencies in slave women's portrayals as they range from marginalized servers to independent managers.

The range of representations of slave women reflects the ambiguity of slaves' socioeconomic status. Slaves were valuable to their owners as skilled workers and an enslaved woman represented a substantial investment for the slaveowner, but slave subordination was required for slaveowners to continue to profit from enslaved laborers. Michael Rostovtzeff and G. E. M. Ste. Croix theorized that the generation of wealth for an elite few was based on the exploitation of semi-free laborers and slaves.[81] The model of kyriarchy details the ranks and relations of exploitation. Slaveowners and property owners exploited slaves and "free" laborers alike.[82] Using figures derived from imperial

79. Ralph Jackson, "The Role of Doctors in the City," in *Roman Working Lives*, ed. Ardle MacMahon (Oxford: Oxbow Press, 2005), 202.

80. Jukka Korpela, "Aromatarii, Pharmacopolae, Thurarii et Ceteri," in *Ancient Medicine*, 114–16; Solin, "Die Sogenannten," in *Ancient Medicine*, 132; and Mary R. Lefkowitz and Maureen B. Fant, *Women's Life in Greece and Rome* (London: Duckworth, 1982), 370–72, 377.

81. Michael Rostovtzeff, *The Social and Economic History of the Roman Empire*, 2 vols. (Oxford: Clarendon, 1957); and G. E. M. Ste. Croix, *The Class Struggle in the Ancient Greek World from the Archaic Age to the Arab Conquests* (Ithaca, NY: Cornell University Press, 1981).

82. Peter Garnsey and Richard Saller, *The Roman Empire: Economy, Society and Culture* (Berkeley: University of California Press, 1987), 111–12.

Italy, Glenn Storey evaluated the cost and revenues for slaveowners and concluded that a Roman male slave could bring in for his owner almost 20,000 sesterces in profit over the slave's expected forty-five-year life span. (A freeborn farm family of four needed 2,000 sesterces per annum for subsistence.[83]) Both the skills of slaves and the submission of slaves were key to slaveowners' ability to continue enjoying such economic benefits.

Different portrayals of slave women served the kyriarchal economic political system. This range of constructions of slave women, from marginalized subordinates to independent agents controlling their own funds, skilled medics and successful performers, were understandings of slave women's status that were available to authors and audiences in Asia Minor in the first two centuries of the common era. Different aspects of the representations of slave women could be deployed for a variety of rhetorical goals. In the following section, I analyze two texts about slave women in religious groups. I interpret these texts by drawing on the representations of slave women's socioeconomic status and their significance for manumission in the religious historical context.

SLAVES AND RELIGIOUS GROUPS

I turn now to texts about slave women in relation to religious groups. Scholarship on slaves' religious status has identified several sources crucial to discussions of slaves' change in status through manumission. I discuss synagogue manumission inscriptions and Ignatius' reference to manumission in his *Letter to Polycarp*. In my interpretations, I draw on the understandings of slave women's socioeconomic status that I have described in the preceding section.

BOSPORAN SYNAGOGUE INSCRIPTIONS

The religious manumission inscriptions from the Bosporus region date to the first two centuries of the common era.[84] Nine inscriptions comprise this group,

83. Glenn R. Storey, "Cui Bono? An Economic Cost-Benefit Analysis of Statuses in the Roman Empire," in *Hierarchies in Action: Cui Bono?*, ed. Michael W. Diehl (Carbondale: Southern Illinois University Press, 2000), 340–74 (359–60).

84. See Richard J. A. Talbert, ed., *Atlas of Classical History* (London and New York: Routledge, 1985), 14–15. On the north shore of the Black Sea, the Bosporus sustained connections to cities around the Aegean throughout antiquity via commercial ties, political relations, and Greek immigration. Jewish communities are well attested from the first century C.E. E. Leigh Gibson, *The Jewish Manumission Inscriptions of the Bosporus Kingdom* (Texts and Studies in Ancient Judaism 75; Tübingen: Mohr Siebeck, 1999), 17, 21.

"marked by three distinctive features: the manumissions occurred in a prayerhouse; the community (synagogue) of the Jews oversees the transaction; and the slave is bound by an ongoing obligation."[85] In four documents, slaves were freed on condition that they fulfill an ongoing obligation related to the Jewish prayerhouse.[86] This inscription dates to the first century C.E.

[— — — — — —]κα-
κου ἀφίημι ἐπὶ τῆς προσευ-
χῆς Ἐλπία[ν — —]α[.]της θρεπτῆ[ς]
ὅπως ἐστὶν ἀπαρενόχλητος
καὶ ἀνεπίληπτος ἀπὸ παντὸς
κληροόμου χωρὶς τοῦ προσ-
καρτερεῖν τῇ προσευχῇ ἐπι-
τροπευούσης τῆς συναγω-
γῆς τῶν Ἰουδαίων καὶ θεὸν
σέβων.

I free in the prayerhouse my slave Elpis, so that she is undisturbed and unassailable by any of my heirs, except that she adhere to the prayerhouse in the guardianship of the synagogue [community] of Jews and godfearers.[87]

Albert Harrill has argued that patronage from the synagogue made Elpis's manumission possible, and thus the synagogue received the usual *paramone* services owed by freed persons.[88] Harrill characterizes these actions as the redemption of enslaved Jews by other Jews as prescribed in traditional texts. Leigh Gibson, however, has noted that the slaves were not said to be Jews or to become Jews. She also contrasts these inscriptions to another manumission in which a community in Syrian Palestine initiated the action to redeem the slaves.[89] According to Gibson, Elpis's manumission was simply a donation, a

---

85. Gibson, *Jewish Manumission*, 124.

86. *CIRB* 70, 71, 73 and *SEG* 43.510. Gibson, *Jewish Manumission*, 126–27.

87. *CIRB* 71.

88. Harrill, *Manumission of Slaves*, 177, commenting on *CIRB* 70 and 71.

89. Gibson, *Jewish Manumission*, 131. In a detailed study, Harrill argues that manumission was practiced by various kinds of associations in Greek and Roman antiquity, including groups identified as Jewish and Christian. The most important evidence for Jewish practice consists of a legal document that dates to 291 C.E. in Egypt in which slaveowners declare that they are releasing their slaves Paramone and

gift to the Jewish community of the freed slave's *paramone* obligations.[90] While Harrill and Gibson disagree about Elpis's status with respect to the synagogue, they both view Elpis as a servant of the religious group after her manumission.[91]

Although the formalistic genre of legal documents limits the conclusions we can draw, freed slave women were more likely to have been managers and skilled workers than slaves of lower status. An influential model of slavery distinguishes the group of slaves who work for incentives: "care-intensive activities require rewards to motivate slaves and reduce ill-will that fosters carelessness, shirking and theft."[92] These rewards include the prospect of manumission. Care-intensive activities include "artisanal and commercial activities, domestic service, and even some forms of farming."[93] Slaves working in these activities became more valuable with experience and they worked with minimal supervision. According to this incentive model in slave systems, the slaves represented in texts about manumission were most likely to be those engaged in these "care-intensive activities" that involved high levels of skill and a minimum of supervision. These were also the slaves who had access to some

her children, "fourteen talents of silver having been paid to us for manumission and discharge by the community of the Jews through Aurelius Dioskoros" (P. Oxy 1205 = *CPJ* 3.473. Cited in Harrill, *Manumission of Slaves*, 173). Gibson's careful analysis agrees that the Jewish community redeemed Paramone and her children, yet notes that the freedpersons are not identified as Jewish, and thus concludes that the manumissions cannot be interpreted as associated with religious practice (Gibson, *Jewish Manumission*, 70–72). The genre of this document, however, a legal instrument dictated by formalized Roman custom, leaves many aspects of the transaction untold, including the reason for manumission and Paramone's occupation. Harrill's conclusions seem modest enough: "Whether or not there was religious recruitment, the function of the common chest remains socially significant: this function is unitive, joining the maid Paramone and her family to the synagogue at Oxyrhynchos"(Harrill, *Manumission of Slaves*, 174). In known sales from Egypt, it was unusual for several slaves to be included in the same transaction. According to Keith Bradley, "The overwhelming majority of attested sales concern individual slave transactions." Bradley, *Slaves and Masters*, 53. Had the synagogue been interested primarily in benefiting from the services Paramone would owe her benefactors, they need not have paid to free her children as well. This manumission represents an important aspect of the relationship of Paramone and her children with the synagogue, and it is possible that this aspect involves the participants' self-understanding as Jews.

90. That is, the conditions of the slave's manumission entailed ongoing service, even after manumission.

91. When discussing Elpis's *paramone* obligations, Gibson characterizes it as "agricultural or custodial" (151). She argues that Elpis's status with respect to the synagogue resembled that of a servant rather than a member. Gibson, *Jewish Manumission*, 134–52.

92. Walter Scheidel, "The Comparative Economics of Slavery in the Greco-Roman World," in *Slave Systems, Ancient and Modern*, ed. E. Dal Lago and C. Katsari (Cambridge: Cambridge University Press, 2008), 107–8. Bradley discussed manumission as a form of social control of slaves.

93. Scheidel, "Comparative Economics of Slavery," 107.

measure of wealth. If Elpis was one of these higher-status wealthier slaves, her obligation to "adhere to the prayerhouse" could refer to financial support rather than the work of a servant.

In the Bosporan manumissions, the slaves exchanged the slaveowner(s) for a community that served as "guardian."[94] Although this language casts slaves as dependent on their benefactors, we have seen that many slaves were highly skilled and capable of earning the funds to buy themselves free. In this case, the synagogue's manumission facilitated a slave's move to freedom by holding funds for her or allowing her to borrow the sum. However, no sums are mentioned in the inscription above, so it is possible that the slaveholder simply freed Elpis and donated her *paramone* obligation to the synagogue.[95] The support of the religious group in taking on the required legal role of guardian allowed the slave to change her legal status to become a freed client of the synagogue.

Scholars have debated the relationship between the synagogue and Elpis and the other freed slaves who owed service to the prayerhouse. In the preceding chapter, I discussed how patronage could be integral to religious associations. Relationships of religious significance were not necessarily distinct from relationships of patronage in the historical context. As a wealthy freed woman, Elpis might herself become a patron (as she paid her *paramone* obligations) and thus have access to religious leadership. Even as a wealthy slave, she could have been a patron.

Examination of another example helps to clarify the possibilities for slave women's religious status.

IGNATIUS TO POLYCARP 4.3

A number of sources indicate that religious groups cared for and ransomed prisoners in the second and third centuries.[96] A letter from Ignatius to Polycarp, for example, refers to what appears to have been a Christian manumission of slaves by the *ekklesia* in Smyrna. Ignatius specifically mentions slave women as well as men.

---

94. *CIRB* 70, 71, 73 and *SEG* 43.510. Translations by Gibson, *Jewish Manumission*, 126–27.

95. The presence of the inscription advertises the slaveholder's generosity and goodwill. Thus these manumissions were probably not instances of slaveholders ridding themselves of aged slaves.

96. C. Osiek, "Ransom of Captives: Evolution of a Tradition," *Harvard Theological Review* 74, no. 4 (October 1981): 365–86.

Δούλους καὶ δούλας μὴ ὑπερηφάνει· ἀλλὰ μηδὲ αὐτοὶ
φυσιούσθωσαν, ἀλλ᾽ εἰς δόξαν θεοῦ πλέον δουλευέτωσαν, ἵνα
κρείττονος ἐλευθερίας ἀπὸ θεοῦ τύχωσιν. Μὴ ἐράτωσαν ἀπὸ τοῦ
κοινοῦ ἐλευθεροῦσθαι, ἵνα μὴ δοῦλοι εὑρεθῶσιν ἐπιθυμίας.

Do not be arrogant towards male and female slaves, but neither let
them become haughty; rather, let them serve even more as slaves for
the glory of God, that they may receive a greater freedom from God.
And they should not long to be set free through the common fund,
lest they be found slaves of passion.[97]

Albert Harrill has argued that Ignatius was advising against the corporate
manumission of slaves only, that is, the use of the common funds, but not
against private manumissions from individuals' resources.[98] Both Jennifer
Glancy and Carolyn Osiek suggest that ekklesial manumission "would not
only rapidly consume limited funds but might offer a problematic motivation
to slaves for joining the church."[99] While these interpreters have focused on
ekklesial funds, my interpretation has focused on the socioeconomic status of
slaves themselves.

I have shown that some slave women were skilled workers who could
generate revenues above subsistence level as freed persons, and thus earn the
money to restore their purchase price to the common fund.[100] Keith Bradley
notes that the price of ransom was too high for most slaves, but some might
achieve it, including actors, doctors, and prostitutes.[101] Aubert noted that many
slave managers were able to control property of their own. Slaveowners used
manumission as an incentive to control slaves who worked in occupations
that required intensive training and skill and a minimum of supervision. Since
slave women in some occupations had access to wealth and manumission, it is
possible to interpret the texts to indicate that religious groups did facilitate their
manumission and that this practice was financially feasible.

97. Ignatius, *Pol.* 4.3, from Asia Minor early in the second century C.E. (circa 108, Ephesus).

98. J. Albert Harrill, "Ignatius, *Ad Polycarp.* 4.3 and the Corporate Manumission of Christian Slaves," in
Journal of Early Christian Studies 1, no. 2 (1993): 107–42.

99. Glancy, *Slavery*, 151. Osiek suggests the same reasons in "Ransom of Captives," 373.

100. Some will object that the price of slaves was too high for this eventuality, but Harrill has shown
that some Delphic manumissions represented a type of corporate loan that enabled the slave to purchase
freedom and then work to pay back the benefactors/investors. Harrill, "Ignatius, *Ad Polycarp* 4.3," 119.

101. Bradley, *Slaves and Masters*, 109. A female slave named Aspazatis bought her freedom in *SEG*
12.314 from Macedonia, third century B.C.E.

We can draw on analogies in other slave systems to supplement this historical information. Cross-cultural investigations of slavery prove particularly helpful for understanding slavery in the Roman world because of the greater availability of sociological data for more recent periods. Marc Kleijwegt's cross-cultural study of manumission indicates that women were freed at higher rates than men.[102] Available data contradict popular hypotheses that women were set free because they were cheaper or because of affection. Circumstances undoubtedly varied across slave societies, but it is more likely that owners rid themselves of older slaves as their productivity declined. Storey follows Keith Hopkins's suggestion that Romans freed slaves who paid for their own replacements.[103] *Paramone* contracts from Delphi and Egypt required women to replace themselves with children before their final release. Two women manumitted in late first- and late second-century Egypt after paying ransoms were aged thirty-five and forty-four.[104] Presumably, then, even such lifelong slaves still desired freedom enough to pay for it. Kleijwegt cites evidence that immediate families bought many women out of slavery. Analogously, some religious associations in antiquity also used the language of family (in terms of siblinghood) and worked to free slave members.

SLAVES' RELIGIOUS STATUS

In summary, sources from the Greek-speaking eastern regions of the Roman Empire between the first and fourth centuries present three variations of manumission: a religious synagogue membership provided funds to free three slaves,[105] a religious ekklesia provided funds to free (a) slave(s), and freed slaves adhered to the Jewish prayerhouse and joined the synagogue membership's

102. Marc Kleijwegt, *Faces of Freedom*, 30. For example, women manumitted at Delphi outnumber men three to one. L. P. Marinovic, "Die Sklaverei in der Provinz Achaia," in *Die Sklaverei in den östlichen Provinzen des Römischen Reiches im 1.–3. Jahrhundert*, übersetzung von Jaroslav Kriz unter Mitwirkung von Günter Prinzing und Elisabeth Herrmann-Otto (Übersetzungen ausländischer Arbeiten zur antiken Sklaverei 5; Stuttgart: Franz Steiner, 1992), 39. See also Ingomar Weiler, "Eine Sklavin wird frei: Zur Rolle des Geschlechts bei der Freilassung," in *Fünfzig Jahre Forschungen zur antiken Sklaverei an der Mainzer Akademie, 1950–2000: Miscellanea zum Jubiläum*, ed. Heinz Bellen and Heinz Heinen (Forschungen zur antiken Sklaverei 35; Stuttgart: Franz Steiner, 2001), 113–32.

103. Glenn R. Storey, "Cui Bono? An Economic Cost-Benefit Analysis of Statuses in the Roman Empire," in *Hierarchies in Action: Cui Bono?*, ed. Michael W. Diehl (Carbondale: Southern Illinois University Press, 2000), 359.

104. Bradley, *Slaves and Masters*, 108. Further research is needed on patterns of manumission in Asia Minor.

105. P. Oxy 1205 = *CPJ* 3.473.

network of patronage. The small number of examples might suggest that such cases were in the minority and not representative of the experience of most religious groups. This judgment, however, presupposes questionable methods. We must nuance our historical reconstructions based on ancient literary sources to account for their ideological representations and limitations. The observation that recorded instances of manumission by religious groups constitute a minority among the known manumissions does not mean that the practice was rare. As we have seen, literary sources tend to adhere more closely to dominant kyriarchal stereotypes in their representations than do inscriptions. And all sources vary with the representational interests of the inscribers, usually slaveholders. We would not expect our sources to relate narratives that would undermine elite privileges based on the slave system. Therefore, the small number of sources about manumission does not imply that these texts represent marginal groups or a rare practice. A critical historiographical method concludes that the known examples support reconstruction of a history of manumission by (some) ancient religious groups.

For some slaves, affiliation with a religious group facilitated their access to freedom through manumission. Religious affiliation accompanied an improvement in status from slave to freed. This implies that, in these cases, a slave's religious status outweighed her socioeconomic status as a controlled and exploited worker. A woman's legal standing as slave or free did not determine her religious status. Ignatius, however, sought to strengthen kyriarchal structures in the ekklesia by urging slaves to accept a religious status that spiritualized slavery while reinforcing the socioeconomic status quo ("let them serve even more as slaves for the glory of God, that they may receive a greater freedom from God"). Slaves who sought manumission did not associate their religious status with remaining in slavery, so they must have had a view different from the Ignatian proposal of religious slavery and subordination.

It seems that wealthy freed women would be able to engage in patronage and exercise leadership in religious groups in the same way that wealthy freeborn women did. And slave women who could control their own wealth may also have had the same access to patronal religious leadership as wealthy freeborn widows. However, a slave's legal standing left her vulnerable to her master's whims. Thus a further investigation of patronage by slave women remains desirable.

CONCLUSION

I have argued the necessity of determining women's religious status by studying their socioeconomic status in the institutions of household, patronage, and slavery. In this chapter I focused on texts about women's socioeconomic and religious status in the institution of slavery.

In the first part of the chapter, I analyzed sources concerning the socioeconomic status of women slaves in Asia Minor. Epigraphic and iconographic sources provide rich materials for socioeconomic analysis. Portrayals of slave women depict them differently depending on their relationship to others. Many iconographical depictions emphasize the slave woman's subordinate status in the household.

Representations of slave women also varied with their relationships to husbands and slaveowners. The slave (or freed) women themselves do not appear in the reliefs that show their gladiator husbands in action. However, the women did dedicate the memorials, an indication that they controlled property. When a memorial emphasizes the importance of a slave woman to her owner, she precedes her husband. In other words, a slave woman's marital status did not necessarily determine her household status in these representations.

In contrast to the visual depictions of slave women's marginality, the inscriptional portrayals of slave women's occupations highlight their status as managers, medics, and performers. These representations implicitly point to the slave women's training, skills, achievements, high economic value, and control of funds. A slave woman's occupational status might result in her becoming wealthy enough to buy her freedom or repay a loan that bought her freedom. Women who slaved in highly skilled and more independent "care-intensive" occupations were especially likely to receive manumission as an incentive.

The range in portrayals of slave women makes sense when analyzed with the socioeconomic political model of kyriarchy. The Roman economy depended on both the exploitation of slaves' skills and the subservient obedience of slaves. The expertise and the compliance of men and women slave managers were especially important for the continued prosperity of wealthy slaveholders. As long as a slave remained a slave, she continued to be vulnerable to the slaveholder's exploitation of her labor.

With this understanding of the complex socioeconomic status of slave women, I moved on to the texts about slave women's status in religious groups. The synagogue inscriptions present manumission of slaves, including women, by religious groups in the Bosporus region. Ignatius' *To Polycarp* indicates that religious groups in Smyrna also manumitted slaves. While allowing for the possibility of manumission, scholars have considered religious manumission impractical, given the view of slave women as unskilled and dependent. However, this view has not been based on investigation of slaves' socioeconomic status.

Religious groups facilitated the legal steps involved in slave manumission. Ignatius associates a slave's religious status with her legal status through his instruction that spiritualizes slavery. Just as the iconography of slave women as marginalized table servants reflects the interests of slaveowners, Ignatius' advice urging slaves to "slave even more" seeks to strengthen the institution of slavery through submission of slaves. Ignatius' phrasing theologizes the relationship of slavery by placing it in the context of religious practice and motivation. In contrast, the actions of some groups indicate that they distinguished religious status from legal standing since they facilitated manumission for affiliates.

My investigation of slave women's status shows that some slave women had a relatively high socioeconomic status in terms of access to wealth because of their occupations. Slave and freed women could become wealthy, control their own property, and head their households, even if married. A wealthy slave woman could finance her own manumission if a religious association assisted with the legal forms. We are left wondering whether wealthy slave or freed women served as religious leaders through patronage of the synagogue or ekklesia. Since religious status outweighed slave status in some groups, this might be possible for a slave woman who controlled her wealth.

Conclusion: Socioeconomic Religious Status

Women's religious leadership, moral agency, and political status continue to be contested widely. Writing history is political and personal: we reconstruct our past from a position engaged in struggle to envision a better future. The history of women's religious leadership early in the common era matters today because Christians and Jews read biblical texts and other literature from this era as authoritative texts. This was a historical period like many others: women participated in religious leadership and in struggles about that.

Excellent scholars have engaged the project of reconstructing the history of first-century Jewish Messianic women. A pioneer of feminist historiography, Schüssler Fiorenza, has argued that Phoebe (Rom. 16:1-2) should be seen as Paul's colleague and benefactor. Many others have expressed skepticism, reasoning that gender norms would have prevented women from achieving leadership status similar to Paul's. I have examined the question of women's status through a careful analysis of gender as a determinant. Texts about religious women distinguish free women by marital status as wives, virgins, and widows. Today, we tend to read these terms as categories of sexual status; however, since they also mark socioeconomic status, I have investigated women in the principal socioeconomic systems for Paul and his followers: marriage, patronage, and slavery.

Gender

I have found that interpretation of texts about women's religious status depends on understanding women's status in socioeconomic institutions. My analysis has shown that religious status actually depended on factors relevant to socioeconomic status because these factors inflected gender. This is significant, because prevailing views of women in antiquity have focused on women's subordination to men. Scholars have articulated this secondary status of women in terms such as family roles or honor/shame, which I reviewed in the first chapter. This scholarship has been crucial in advancing historical understandings of women in the ancient world. A common thread underlying these historical studies has been a view of gender as determined by feminine subordination. This articulation of gender, however, has not fully explained the status of some groups of women, particularly patronal women and slave women.

In order to plot all the evidence in the same historical model, I have studied texts about ancient women using kyriarchy, an analytical model in which gender overlaps with other producers of social relations such as wealth, marital status, and legal status. Behind this move is a crucial theoretical commitment elaborated by materialist feminists: an assumption that gender is constructed in and by material relations. Gender interacts with other ideologies manifest in social relations such as political and economic systems. Careful scrutiny of socioeconomic institutions reveals tensions and ambiguities in social relations.

Representations from the Roman Empire depict wealthy wives as matrons subordinate to their husbands, whereas wealthy widows who had their own households appear with a status similar to wealthy men. This was possible because ideology associated with the household also functioned to support political structures in the Roman Empire and in the colonized cities of Asia Minor. In the figure of a wealthy woman who headed her own household, the dominance that accompanied the head of a household contradicted (and overruled) the subordination exemplified in the ideal of the matron. Apparently a marriage-free state was crucial to a wealthy woman's socioeconomic status and independence. Marital status and access to wealth both affected the construction of gender for widows who headed households.

Wealthy women participated in the system of patronage. As with the household, patronage was critical to political and socioeconomic structures in the Roman Empire. Patrons served as leaders of civic organizations and associations based on occupational or religious affiliation. Displays of wealth worked with ideologies of prosperity and paternalism to establish the high status of a patron. The titles of leadership accorded wealthy widows in Asia Minor indicate that wealth and engagement in patronage significantly affected the workings of gender. Patronal leaders, women and men, engaged in the same leadership activities.

My investigation of slave women found that the inflection of gender through slavery operated differently than it did for elite women. A slave's value to the slaveholder outweighed the subordination of gender in marital status that accompanied presentations of elite women. While an ideology of household subordination accompanied the system of slavery, the prospect of manumission through prosperity controlled slaves in independent occupations. For slaves, occupation, wealth, and legal standing interacted with gender as determinants of status. It seems that slave women who controlled their own wealth would have had the same access to patronage as did wealthy freed and freeborn women; further research might clarify the possibilities. An investigation of patronage by wealthy slave and freed women might establish whether or how this patronal leadership resembled that of freeborn women.

From this analysis emerge suggestions for methodology in future research. First, we need to analyze gender in a way that makes visible its interactions with other determinants of status, such as access to wealth, race or ethnicity, colonial and legal status, age, disability, and lifestyle. I accomplished this kind of multidimensional analysis in the preceding chapters through a materialist feminist analytical model, kyriarchy. Using the model has several advantages. It allows us to move beyond dualistic analyses of rich/poor or male/female. It theorizes the interweaving of ideologies and social relations so that we can move toward robust socioeconomic analyses through disciplined investigation of a variety of sources. Adequate models include all factors that affect socioeconomics, such as marital status, inheritance, education, dependents, and occupation.

Also, a more accurate view of women's status depends on incorporating in the analysis all the diverse sources available to historians. Recourse to a range of genres, particularly nonliterary sources, can help underscore contrasts between different representations, and reveal tensions between competing ideologies. The older idea of "gender norms" follows from study of literary sources of the elite. In contrast, my investigation includes inscriptions and funerary monuments, since depictions of women vary with genre and sponsorship. While literary sources speak of male household heads, inscriptions, funerary iconography, and some legal material deploy the same set of motifs when depicting women and men heads of households. For freeborn women, this household status is linked with marital status and wealth. For slave women, it is associated with wealth and occupation. This is very important for understanding the history of religions early in the common era, since wealthy heads of households served as patrons of associations, expressing social religious leadership through hospitality, financing, and literacy.

The view from below in kyriarchal analysis highlights subordinated persons who remain invisible in other models of socioeconomic status. Many portrayals of the household depict passive slaves and freeborn wives. Such representations reproduce the prominence of the head of the household while also obscuring or devaluing the labor and contributions of subordinate persons. The construction served an important ideological function. As theorized by Joshel and Murnaghan, depictions of free women and slaves served to protect the privileged status of free men.[1] In socioeconomic terms, the invisibility (or devaluing) of the activities of slaves and wives concealed the elite free man's dependence on their labor, his inherent lack of independence (associated with masculinity). The ideology supported differential assignment of property ownership in legal and occupational systems.

Materialist feminist analysis of women's status could contribute substantially to a better understanding of how women's socioeconomic status relates to religious status today. Exclusionary economic models that omit entire categories of labor and workers cannot provide accurate analysis of global socioeconomic and political systems. The model must investigate how gender, social strata, colonial and legal status, ethnicity, and race overlap in the production of economic status and access to economic resources. Accurate analysis of religious status is not possible without thorough analysis of socioeconomic status.

RELIGIOUS WOMEN

The investigations of women's status in socioeconomic systems form the basis of interpretations of texts about women's religious status. A careful reading of the letters of Ignatius shows that he associated women's religious status with their household status as wives, widows, or slaves. Ignatius advocates male control of wealthy wives and widows through the lordship of the husband for wives, and the guardianship of the bishop for widows. Similarly, Ignatius supports slaveholders' control through his instruction that the ekklesia groups not use common funds to assist slaves in manumission.

Ignatius' advice about slaves resembles the advice he gives concerning wives. In both marriage and slavery, Ignatius associates the dominant role with divinity. He likens husbands to the Lord and implicitly associates slaveholders with God. Ignatius advises wife and slave to submit themselves to husbands and slaveowners. Both of these household relationships, marriage and slavery, are

---

1. Sandra R. Joshel and Sheila Murnaghan, "Differential Equations," in *Women and Slaves in Greco-Roman Culture: Differential Equations*, ed. Sandra R. Joshel and Sheila Murnaghan (London and New York: Routledge, 1998).

thoroughly kyriarchalized in Ignatius' advice. His advice implied economic and spiritual limitations on freeborn women and slave women; thus he sought to control women's socioeconomic and religious status. Some members of ekklesia groups had different understandings of marriage and slavery: they associated their religious status with widowhood or divorce and manumission. Ignatius' spiritualization of marriage and slavery would impose on wives and slaves a socioeconomic religious status of subservience to free married slaveholding men.

It is time to return to the question of wealthy women's religious leadership. I have shown that wealthy women could and did serve as religious leaders on the basis of their socioeconomic leadership established in households and patronage. This leadership was possible because access to wealth determined an independent woman's status. Marital status determined control of wealth in the household for freeborn women while occupation controlled access to wealth for slave and freed women. Such wealth enabled patronage that was accompanied by leadership of social groups, including religious associations. In addition, both elite and slave women received education and training that might assist their development and exercise of leadership skills.

Since a wealthy widowed or divorced woman controlled her household's resources, she could host and lead an association gathering in her house, or serve as patron and thus gain leadership status. Ignatius seeks to limit this leadership to limit competition with the bishop's leadership. Nonetheless, Rufina was a wealthy Jewish widow with religious leadership as a synagogue patron. And Phoebe was a patron of Paul and others; her religious activities involved missionary preaching as well as economic leadership.

Emphasis on the authority of the Ignatian perspective has encouraged spiritual interpretations of marriage and slavery, and it has severed the economic aspects of patronage from corresponding political understandings. These spiritualized and depoliticized interpretations have accompanied the understanding that women's secondary status in antiquity prevented their access to religious leadership. The spiritualized and depoliticized interpretations of marriage, patronage, and slavery have also accompanied the exclusion of economic analysis from religious and theological studies.

We need more research to develop the implications of the spiritualization of socioeconomic systems in other religious texts. For instance, what would a materialist analysis contribute to our understanding of discourses about poverty and wealth in the texts of early Christianity?[2] Or, how were social organization,

---

2. See analysis of such discourses by Justo L. González, *Faith and Wealth: A History of Early Christian Ideas on the Origin, Significance, and Use of Money* (San Francisco: Harper & Row, 1990).

theological imagination, and economic structures interrelated for different communities?

LEADERSHIP

Across Christian denominations, women's religious leadership remains a contentious issue. Proponents of "traditional" gender ideals have put forth a variety of arguments as grounds for limiting women's religious participation. Historically based arguments to limit women's leadership continue to be popular and are common to many church organizations. We historians tend to adopt the views of authors of elite literary texts and the dominant gender ideals of more recent eras. The foregoing chapters show that historical reconstruction of early Christian and Jewish groups certainly should proclaim the religious leadership of such women as Phoebe, Rufina, Junia, and Prisca. Inadequate analysis of gender as embedded in socioeconomic systems has allowed the portrayals of male-only leadership. These chapters have addressed certain objections put forward by the proponents of male-only historical views: that women never held positions of real leadership anywhere in ancient society, that women lacked the legal status and educational level to be leaders, and that gender ideals circumscribed a women's sphere of activity to "the home" or "private" areas. In contrast, I have argued that women were civic leaders in Asia Minor, particularly wealthy widow freeborn women; that such women held citizenship, received rhetorical education, performed in public, received honors for professional achievements; and that there is strong evidence to suggest that the same could be true for a wealthy freed woman. Thus contemporary Christian churches and leaders lack a basis in the history of early Christianity for their appeals to precedence and tradition as grounds to deny women's religious leadership.

My study has highlighted several conflicts about leadership in proto-Christian associations. Both Ignatius and the editor of the *Acts of Paul and Thecla* attempt to persuade their audiences that the distributions of a wealthy woman belong under the control of the bishop or the apostle, respectively. At least one woman in Smyrna controls enough property to house a group of widows. Ignatius would assert the bishop's religious, legal, and socioeconomic authority over this group, which would include its distributions of hospitality and food. Similarly, the author of *Paul and Thecla* depicts Tryphaena giving money to Paul, and the male apostle then redistributes her wealth to his group of dependents. The mechanism of patronage required clients to receive benefits from a wealthy person. Redirecting the flow of wealth could shift this relationship. A person who had been a wealthy patron became merely a wealthy donor with a client base controlled by others. This move would curtail the influence of the wealthy, both men and women, in proto-Christian associations.

Wealth predicated high status in all spheres of society; leadership on these grounds might conflict with other models of leadership. It seems that there were at least three groups of leaders in religious groups: local office-holders (bishops and deacons), patron-hosts (elders/presbyters), and translocal prophets and apostles. Local office-holders contested the patronal leadership of wealthy men and women. My investigation highlights at least one strategy in this contest: texts encourage the wealthy to give to the local officers so that they might carry out the charitable distribution. It seems that local officers inserted themselves as middle-level brokers operating in the system of patronage, thus disrupting the usual relationships between patron and clients. Concurrently, in depicting themselves as prophets and apostles, bishops such as Ignatius communicated their expertise as middle-level brokers of spiritual gifts as well, adjudicating between God and members of the religious group. In his role as broker of both spiritual blessings and worldly wealth, Ignatius constructed and reproduced episcopal leadership and attempted to limit other forms of leadership.

Transfer of wealth in religious systems of the Roman imperial era requires further research. Religious groups were involved in buying and ransoming slaves. This could have been a common arrangement for wealthy slaves, with the religious group functioning as a credit union would today. When slaves died, their property reverted to the slaveholders. Even for a freed slave, the former owner continued to serve as legal patron and inherited a large share of their former slave's estate. A religious group that bought and freed a slave inherited from her. Religious groups might also inherit from wealthy widows. Possible correlations and interactions between legal and theological connotations of inheritance deserve further investigation.

With this research, I attempt to contribute to understandings of relationships between socioeconomics, gender, and other discriminatory categories. I have shown that women's religious leadership in the ancient world was not prevented by ideals of femininity, matronhood, honor/shame, or dominant cultural values. Women's access to leadership depended on the socioeconomic status produced by wealth, marital status, and occupational activities. Our past matters because history of Christian and Jewish traditions relies on and constructs contemporary understandings of women, religion, and socioeconomics. In a formulation of Schüssler Fiorenza, it is important to read the kyriarchal inscriptions of power in scripture in order to bring into consciousness the workings of "sovereign power" in and through pseudo-egalitarian circulation of globalizing power today. Since kyriarchal biblical values have shaped wo/men's self-understanding and socio-cultural political discourses in Western culture, it is necessary to deploy hermeneutical strategies that can focus, in the process of reading, on inscriptions of kyriarchal power in biblical texts in order to decolonize contemporary consciousness.[3]

Historical understandings contribute to the knowledge that articulates and legitimizes socioeconomic discrimination through nationality, race, ethnicity, religion, gender, age, and sexuality. I hope that production of knowledge about agency, leadership, and socioeconomic analysis contributes to interventions for greater justice. We need to continue investigating leadership in other historical complexes and exploring the stakes involved in writing the history of socioeconomics and religion.

This work contributes to scholarship that shows that a certain degree of conflict accompanied the religious leadership of women as women. Conceptualizing movements on the model of "struggle" allows historians to explore tensions, to make sense of disparate evidence, and to find a thread of continuity in women's history and religious history more generally. Struggle has characterized the history of Christianity; the issues have included religious status and leadership as it intersects with ethnicity, sexual orientation, and legal status, as well as gender and socioeconomic status. Historical reconstructions that highlight such struggles are more accurate than those that dwell on the actions and thoughts of dominant groups. The scarcity of sources for writing history from below makes the historian's task more difficult. Nonetheless, the effort is worthwhile because writing inclusive histories allows nondominant peoples to reclaim ancestors, identities, and purpose.

3. Elisabeth Schüssler Fiorenza, *The Power of the Word: Scripture and the Rhetoric of Empire* (Minneapolis: Fortress Press, 2007), 162.

Bibliography

Achtemeier, Paul J. *A Commentary on First Peter*. Hermeneia; Minneapolis: Fortress Press, 1996.

Alföldy, Geza. *The Social History of Rome*. London: Croom Helm, 1985.

Amoore, Louise. "Invisible Subject(s): Work and Workers in the Global Political Economy." In *Poverty and the Production of World Politics: Unprotected Workers in the Global Political Economy*, edited by Matt Davies and Magnus Ryner, 14–37. New York: Palgrave Macmillan, 2006.

Ando, Clifford. *Imperial Ideology and Provincial Loyalty in the Roman Empire*. Berkeley: University of California Press, 2000.

Arlandson, James Malcolm. *Women, Class, and Society in Early Christianity: Models from Luke-Acts*. Peabody, MA: Hendrickson, 1997.

Ascough, Richard S. "The Thessalonian Christian Community as a Professional Voluntary Association," *Journal of Biblical Literature* 119, no. 2 (Summer 2000): 311–28.

Aubert, Jean-Jacques. *Business Managers in Ancient Rome: A Social and Economic Study of Institores, 200 B.C.–A.D. 250*. Leiden: Brill, 1994.

Bagnall, R. S., and Bruce W. Frier. *The Demography of Roman Egypt*. Cambridge: Cambridge University Press, 1994.

Balch, David L. *Let Wives Be Submissive: The Domestic Code in 1 Peter*. SBLMS 26. Atlanta: Scholars, 1981.

Balch, David L., and Carolyn Osiek, eds. *Early Christian Families in Context: An Interdisciplinary Dialogue*. Grand Rapids: Eerdmans, 2003.

Bang, Peter F., Mamoru Ikeguchi, and Hartmut G. Ziche, eds. *Ancient Economies, Modern Methodologies: Archaeology, Comparative History, Models and Institutions*. Bari, Italy: Edipuglia, 2006.

Baron, Ava. *Work Engendered: Toward a New History of American Labor*. Ithaca, NY: Cornell University Press, 1991.

Bellen, Heinz, and Heinz Heinen, eds. *Fünfzig Jahre Forschungen zur antiken Sklaverei an der Mainzer Akademie, 1950-2000: Miscellanea zum Jubiläum. Forschungen zur antiken Sklaverei 35*. Stuttgart: Franz Steiner, 2001.

Berg, Ria. "Wearing Wealth: *Mundus Muliebris* and *Ornatus* as Status Markers for Women in Imperial Rome." In *Women, Wealth and Power in the Roman*

Empire, edited by Päivi Setälä et al. Rome: Institutum Romanum Finlandiae, 2002.

Bernardini, Paola Angeli. "Donna e spettacolo nel mondo ellenistico." In *Vicende e Figure Femminili in Grecia e à Roma*, edited by Renato Raffaelli (Ancona, Commissione per le pari opportunità tra uomo e donna della Regione Marche, 1995).

Bieringer, Reimund. "Febe, Prisca en Junia. Vrouwen en leiderschap in de brieven van Paulus" [Women and Leadership in Romans 16: The Leading Roles of Phoebe, Prisca, and Junia in Early Christianity]. In *Paulus, Verslagboek Vliebergh-Sencie-leergang*, edited by Frans Van Segbroeck, 157–202. Bijbel 2003; Leuven-Voorburg: Vlaamse Bijbelstichting-Acco, 2004. Translated by Wolf Diedrich, http://eapi.admu.edu.ph/eapr007/bieringer.htm.

Boatwright, Mary Taliaferro. "Plancia Magna of Perge: Women's Roles and Status in Roman Asia Minor." In *Women's History and Ancient History*, edited by Sarah B. Pomeroy, 249–72. Chapel Hill: University of North Carolina Press, 1991.

Bodel, John, ed. *Epigraphic Evidence: Ancient History from Inscriptions*. London: Routledge, 2001.

Bonz, Marianne P. "Differing Approaches to Religious Benefaction: The Late Third-Century Acquisition of the Sardis Synagogue," *Harvard Theological Review* 86 (1993): 139–54.

Bosch, Emin. *Quellen zur Geschichte der Stadt Ankara im Altertum*. Ankara: Türk Tarih Kurumu Basimevi, 1967.

Bowman, Alan K. "Literacy in the Roman World: Mass and Mode." In *Literacy in the Roman World*. Archaeology Supplementary Series no. 3. Ann Arbor: University of Michigan Press, 1991.

Bradley, K. R. *Slavery and Rebellion in the Roman World*. Bloomington: Indiana University Press, 1989.

———. *Slaves and Masters in the Roman Empire: A Study in Social Control*. New York: Oxford University Press, 1987.

Bremen, Riet van. *The Limits of Participation: Women and Civic Life in the Greek East in the Hellenistic and Roman Periods*. Amsterdam: J. C. Gieben, 1996.

———. "Women and Wealth." In *Images of Women in Antiquity*, edited by Avril Cameron and Amélie Kuhrt. Detroit: Wayne State University Press, 1983.

Bremmer, Jan. "Why Did Early Christianity Attract Upper-Class Women?" In *Fructus centesimus*, edited by A. A. R. Bastiaensen et al., 37–47. Dordrecht: Steenbrugge, 1989.

Briggs, Sheila. "Slavery and Gender." In *On the Cutting Edge: The Study of Women in Biblical Worlds*, edited by Jane Schaberg, Alice Bach, and Esther Fuchs. New York: Continuum, 2004.

Brock, Ann Graham. *Mary Magdalene, The First Apostle: The Struggle for Authority*. Cambridge, MA: Harvard University Press, 2003.

———. "Political Authority and Cultural Accommodation." In *The Apocryphal Acts of the Apostles*, edited by François Bovon, Ann Graham Brock, and Christopher R. Matthews, 145–69. Cambridge, MA: Harvard University Press, 1999.

Brooten, Bernadette J. "Female Leadership in the Ancient Synagogue." In *From Dura to Sepphoris: Studies in Jewish Art and Society in Late Antiquity*, edited by Lee I. Levine and Ze'ev Weiss, 215–23. Portsmouth, RI: Journal of Roman Archaeology, 2000.

———. *Women Leaders in the Ancient Synagogue: Inscriptional Evidence and Background Issues*. Chico, CA: Scholars, 1982.

Broughton, T. Robert S. *Roman Asia Minor*. Vol. 4, *An Economic Survey of Ancient Rome*, edited by Tenney Frank. Paterson, NJ: Pageant Books, 1959.

Brown, Cheryl Anne. *No Longer Be Silent: First Century Jewish Portraits of Biblical Women: Studies in Pseudo-Philo's Biblical Antiquities and Josephus's Jewish Antiquities*. Louisville: Westminster John Knox, 1992.

Brulé, Pierre. "Enquête Démographique sur la Famille Grecque Antique," *Revues des études anciennnes* 92 (1990): 233–58.

Buell, Denise. *Why This New Race: Ethnic Reasoning in Early Christianity*. New York: Columbia University Press, 2005.

Burrus, Virginia. "Mimicking Virgins: Colonial Ambivalence and the Ancient Roman," *Arethusa* 38, no. 1 (2005): 49–88.

———. "Word and Flesh: The Bodies and Sexuality of Ascetic Women in Christian Antiquity," *Journal of Feminist Studies in Religion* 10 (1994): 27–51.

Callahan, Allen Dwight, Richard A. Horsley, and Abraham Smith, eds. *Slavery in Text and Interpretation*. Semeia 83/84; Atlanta: Society of Biblical Literature, 1998.

Callinicos, Alex. "Marx and Antiquity: Some Comments," *Helios* 26, no. 2 (Fall 1999): 174–82.

Campbell, Barth L. *Honor, Shame and the Rhetoric of 1 Peter*. Atlanta: Scholars, 1998.

Carruth, Shawn. "Praise for the Churches: The Letters of Ignatius of Antioch." In *Reimagining Christian Origins*, edited by Elizabeth A. Castelli and Hal Taussig, 295–310. Valley Forge, PA: Trinity, 1996.

Castelli, Elizabeth A. *Martyrdom and Memory: Early Christian Culture Making.* New York: Columbia University Press, 2004.

Chen, Martha, Joann Vanek, Francie Lund, James Heintz, with Renana Jhabvala, Christine Bonner. *Progress of the World's Women 2005 Overview: Women, Work & Poverty.* New York: United Nations Development Fund for Women, 2005.

Clark, Elizabeth A. "Women, Gender, and the Study of Christian History," *Church History* 70, no. 3 (September 2001): 395–426.

Chaniotis, Angelos. "Under the Watchful Eyes of the Gods: Divine Justice in Hellenistic and Roman Asia Minor." In *The Greco-Roman East: Politics, Culture, Society,* edited by Stephen Colvin. Cambridge: Cambridge University Press, 2004.

Chidester, David. "Material Terms for the Study of Religion," *Journal of the American Academy of Religion* 68, no. 2 (June 2000): 367–80.

Cohen, Boaz. "Peculium in Jewish and Roman Law," *Proceedings of the American Academy for Jewish Research* 20 (1951): 135–234.

Coleman, Kathleen. "Missio at Halicarnassus," *Harvard Studies in Classical Philology* 100 (2000): 487–500.

Collins, John N. *Diakonia: Re-interpreting the Ancient Sources.* New York: Oxford University Press, 1990.

Collins, Matthew S. "Money, Sex and Power: Women Patrons of Synagogues." In *Recovering the Role of Women,* edited by P. J. Hassa. Atlanta: Scholars, 1992.

Connelly, Joan Breton. *Portrait of a Priestess: Women and Ritual in Ancient Greece.* Princeton: Princeton University Press, 2007.

Cooper, Kate. *The Virgin and the Bride: Idealized Womanhood in Late Antiquity.* Cambridge, MA: Harvard University Press, 1996.

Corley, Kathleen. "1 Peter." In *Searching the Scriptures, Vol. 2: A Feminist Commentary,* edited by Elisabeth Schüssler Fiorenza. New York: Crossroad, 1994.

Corrington, Gail P. "'The Divine Woman'? Propaganda and the Power of Chastity in the New Testament Apocrypha." In *Rescuing Creusa,* edited by Marilyn B. Skinner. *Helios* 13 (1986): 151–62.

Cotton, Hannah. "A Cancelled Marriage Contract from the Judean Desert (XHev/Se Gr. 2)," *Journal of Roman Studies* 84 (1994): 64–86.

Countryman, L. William. *The Rich Christian in the Church of the Early Empire: Contradictions and Accommodations.* Lewiston, NY: Edwin Mellen, 1980.

Cremer, Marielouise. *Hellenistisch-römische Grabstelen im nordwestlichen Kleinasien.* Vol. 1, *Mysien.* Asia Minor Studien Band 4.1; Bonn: GMBH, 1991.

D'Arms, John H. *Commerce and Social Standing in Ancient Rome.* Cambridge, MA: Harvard University Press, 1981.

Davies, Matt, and Magnus Ryner, eds. *Poverty and the Production of World Politics: Unprotected Workers in the Global Political Economy.* New York: Palgrave Macmillan, 2006.

Davis, Stephen J. *The Cult of Saint Thecla: A Tradition of Women's Piety in Late Antiquity.* Oxford: Oxford University Press, 2001.

———. "A 'Pauline' Defense of Women's Right to Baptize? Intertextuality and Apostolic Authority in the *Acts of Paul*," *Journal of Early Christian Studies* 8, no. 3 (2000): 453–59.

———. *The Revolt of the Widows: The Social World of the Apocryphal Acts.* Carbondale: Southern Illinois University Press, 1980.

Demand, Nancy. "Monuments, Midwives and Gynecology." In *Ancient Medicine in Its Socio-cultural Context*, edited by Ph. J. van der Eijk, H. F. J. Horstmanshoff, and P. H. Schrijvers. Amsterdam: Rodopi, 1995.

Dill, Bonnie Thornton, and Ruth Enid Zambrana, eds. *Emerging Intersections: Race, Class and Gender in Theory, Policy, and Practice.* New Brunswick, NJ: Rutgers University Press, 2009.

Dixon, Suzanne. "Exemplary Housewife or Luxurious Slut? Cultural Representations of Women in the Roman Economy." In *Women's Influence on Classical Civilization*, edited by Fiona McHardy and Eirann Marshal, 56–74. London: Routledge, 2004.

———. *Reading Roman Women: Sources, Genres and Real Life.* Bath, UK: Duckworth, 2001.

———. *The Roman Family.* Baltimore: Johns Hopkins University Press, 1992.

Dmitriev, Sviatoslav. *City Government in Hellenistic and Roman Asia Minor.* Oxford: Oxford University Press, 2005.

Ecevit, Yildiz. "Shopfloor Control: The Ideological Construction of Turkish Women Factory Workers." In *Working Women: International Perspectives on Labour and Gender Ideology*, edited by Nanneke Redclift and M. Thea Sinclair, 56–78. London: Routledge, 1991.

Eijk, P. van der, H. F. J. Horstmanshoff, and P. H. Schrijvers, eds. *Ancient Medicine in Its Socio-cultural Context.* Amsterdam: Rodopi, 1995.

Eisen, Ute E. *Women Officeholders in Early Christianity: Epigraphical and Literary Studies.* Collegeville, MN: Liturgical, 2000.

Eisenstadt, S. N., and R. L. Roniger. *Patrons, Clients and Friends: Interpersonal Relations and the Structure of Trust in Society.* Cambridge: Cambridge University Press, 1984.

Elliot, J. H. *A Home for the Homeless: A Sociological Exegesis of 1 Peter, Its Situation, and Strategy.* Philadelphia: Fortress Press, 1981.

———. *1 Peter: A New Translation with Introduction and Commentary.* Anchor Bible 37B. New York: Doubleday, 2000.

Elson, Diane, Caren Grown, and Irene van Staveren, "Why a Feminist Economics of Trade?" Pages 1–10 in *The Feminist Economics of Trade.* Edited by Irene van Staveren, Diane Elson, Caren Grown, and Nilufer Çagatay. New York: Routledge, 2007.

England, Paula. "Separative and Soluble Selves: Dichotomous Thinking in Economics." Pages 33–59 in *Feminist Economics Today: Beyond Economic Man.* Edited by Marianne A. Ferber and Julie A. Nelson. Chicago: University of Chicago Press, 2003.

Fabricius, Johanna. *Die hellenistischen Totenmahlreliefs: Grabrepräsentation und Wertvorstellungen in ostgriechischen Städten.* Studien zur antiken Stadt 3. München: Dr. Friedrich Pfeil, 1999.

Fantham, Elaine, Helene Peet Foley, Natalie Boymel Kampen, Sarah B. Pomeroy, and H. A. Shapiro, *Women in the Classical World: Image and Text.* Oxford: Oxford University Press, 1994.

Ferrari, Gloria. *Figures of Speech: Men and Maidens in Ancient Greece.* Chicago: University of Chicago Press, 2002.

Finley, M. I. *The Ancient Economy.* Berkeley: University of California Press, 1973.

Friesen, Steven J. "The Cult of the Roman Emperors in Ephesus: Temple Wardens, City Titles, and the Interpretation of the Revelation of John." In *Ephesus: Metropolis of Asia*, edited by Helmut Koester, 229–50. Valley Forge, PA: Trinity, 1995.

———. "Ephesian Women and Men in Public Office During the Roman Imperial Period." In *100 Jahre Österreichische Forschungen in Ephesus. Akten des Symposions Wien 1995*, 107–13. Wien: Österreichische Akademie der Wissenschaften, 1999.

———. "High Priestesses of Asia and Emancipatory Interpretation." In *Walk in the Ways of Wisdom*, edited by Shelly Matthews, Cynthia Kittredge, and Melanie Johnson-Debaufre, 136–51. Harrisburg, PA: Trinity, 2003.

———. "Highpriests of Asia and Asiarchs: Farewell to the Identification Theory." In *Steine und Wege*, edited by Peter Scherrer, 303–7. Vienna: Austrian Archaeological Institute, 1999.

———. *Imperial Cults and the Apocalypse of John: Reading Revelation in the Ruins.* Oxford: Oxford University Press, 2001.

———. "Myth and Symbolic Resistance in Revelation 13," *Journal of Biblical Literature* 123, no. 2 (2004): 281–313.

———. "Poverty in Pauline Studies: Beyond the So-called New Consensus," *Journal for the Study of the New Testament* 26, no. 3 (2004): 323–61.

———. *Twice Neokoros: Ephesus, Asia, and the Cult of the Flavian Imperial Family.* Leiden and New York: Brill, 1993.

Gardner, Jane F. *Being a Roman Citizen.* London: Routledge, 1993.

———. *Family and Familia in Roman Law and Life.* Oxford: Clarendon, 1998.

———. *Women in Roman Law and Society.* London: Croom Helm, 1986.

Garnsey, Peter, ed. *Non-Slave Labour in the Greco-Roman World.* Cambridge: Cambridge Philological Society, 1980.

———, and Richard Saller. *The Roman Empire: Economy, Society and Culture.* Berkeley: University of California Press, 1987.

———, and C. R. Whittaker, eds. *Trade and Famine in Classical Antiquity.* Cambridge: Cambridge Philological Society, 1983.

Garrison, Roman. *Redemptive Almsgiving in Early Christianity.* Sheffield: Journal for the Study of the Old Testament Press, 1993.

Georgi, Dieter. *Remembering the Poor: The History of Paul's Collection for Jerusalem.* Nashville: Abingdon, 1992.

Gibson, E. Leigh. *The Jewish Manumission Inscriptions of the Bosporus Kingdom.* Tübingen: Mohr Siebeck, 1999.

Gibson, Elsa. *The "Christians for Christians" Inscriptions of Phrygia: Greek Texts, Translations and Commentary.* Missoula, MT: Scholars, 1978.

Glancy, Jennifer. *Slavery in Early Christianity.* Oxford: Oxford University Press, 2002.

Golden, Mark. *Sport and Society in Ancient Greece.* Cambridge: Cambridge University Press, 1998.

———. "The Uses of Cross-Cultural Comparison in Ancient Social History," *Echos du Monde Classique* 36, no. 11 (1992): 309–31.

Golubcova, E. S. "Sklaverei und Abhängigkeit in den Städten." In *Die Sklaverei in den östlichen Provinzen des römischen Reiches im 1.-3. Jahrhundert.* Translated by Jaroslav Kriz with Günter Prinzing and Elisabeth Hermann-Otto. Stuttgart: Franz Steiner, 1992.

González, Justo L. *Faith and Wealth: A History of Early Christian Ideas on the Origin, Significance, and Use of Money.* San Francisco: Harper & Row, 1990.

Gordon, Richard. "The Veil of Power." In *Pagan Priests: Religion and Power in the Ancient World*, edited by Mary Beard and John North, 199–231. Ithaca, NY: Cornell University Press, 1990.

Günther, Linda-Marie. "Zur Familien- und Haushaltsstruktur im Hellenistischen Kleinasien," *Studien zum antiken Kleinasien* 2, no. 1–2 (1991–92): 23–42.

Grant, Frederick C. *Hellenistic Religions: The Age of Syncretism.* New York: Liberal Arts Press, 1953.

Hanfmann, George M. A., and Kemal Ziya Polatkan. "A Sepulchral Stele from Sardis," *American Journal of Archaeology* 64, no. 1 (January 1960): 49–52.

Hanson, Ann Ellis. "Widows Too Young in Their Widowhood." In *I, Claudia II: Women in Roman Art and Society*, edited by Diana E. E. Kleiner and Susan B. Matheson, 149–65. Austin: University of Texas Press, 2000.

Harland, Philip. *Associations, Synagogues and Congregations: Claiming a Place in Ancient Mediterranean Society.* Minneapolis: Augsburg Fortress Press, 2003.

Harrill, J. Albert. "Ignatius, *Ad Polycarp.* 4.3 and the Corporate Manumission of Christian Slaves. *Journal of Early Christian Studies* 1, no. 2 (1993): 107–42.

———. *The Manumission of Slaves in Early Christianity.* Tübingen: J. C. B. Mohr, 1995.

———. *Slaves in the New Testament: Literary, Social and Moral Dimensions.* Minneapolis: Fortress Press, 2006.

Hatzopoulos, Miltiade B. *Revue des Études Grecs* 115 (2002): 672, no. 254.

———. *Revue des Études Grecs* 112 (1999): 639–40, no. 349.

Hemelrijk, Emily A. "City Patronesses in the Roman Empire," *Historia* 53, no. 2 (2004): 209–45.

———. *Matrona Docta: Educated Women in the Roman Elite from Cornelia to Julia Domna.* London: Routledge, 1999.

Hennessy, Rosemary. *Materialist Feminism and the Politics of Discourse.* New York: Routledge, 1993.

———, and Chrys Ingraham, eds. *Materialist Feminism: A Reader in Class, Difference, and Women's Lives.* New York: Routledge, 1997.

Henten, Jan Willen Van, and Pieter Willem Van der Horst, eds. *Studies in Early Jewish Epigraphy.* Leiden: Brill, 1994.

Hermann, Peter. *Inschriften von Milet.* Berlin and New York: Walter de Gruyter, 1998.

Higginbotham, Elizabeth, and Mary Romero, eds. *Women and Work: Exploring Race, Ethnicity, and Class.* London: Sage, 1997.

Hodge, Caroline E. Johnson. *If Sons, Then Heirs: A Study of Kinship and Ethnicity in the Letters of Paul.* Oxford: Oxford University Press, 2007.

Hopkins, Keith. *Conquerors and Slaves: Sociological Studies in Roman History.* Cambridge: Cambridge University Press, 1978.

———. "Rome, Taxes, Rents and Trade." In *The Ancient Economy*, ed. W. Scheidel and S. Reden.

Horsley, G. H. R. *New Documents Illustrating Early Christianity: A Review of the Greek Inscriptions and Papyri Published in 1979.* North Ryde, Australia: The Ancient History Documentary Research Centre, Macquarie University, 1987.

Horsley, G. H. R., and S. R. Llewelyn, eds. *New Documents Illustrating Early Christianity.* Grand Rapids: Eerdmans, 1981–2002.

Horsley, Richard A., ed. *Paul and Empire: Religion and Power in Roman Imperial Society.* Harrisburg, PA: Trinity, 1997.

———, ed. *Paul and Politics: Ekklesia, Israel, Imperium, Interpretation.* Harrisburg, PA: Trinity, 2000.

———. "The Slave Systems of Classical Antiquity and Their Reluctant Recognition by Modern Scholars," *Semeia* 83/84 (1998): 19–66.

Hunter, David G. *Marriage, Celibacy, and Heresy in Ancient Christianity: The Jovinianist Controversy.* Oxford: Oxford University Press, 2007.

Ignatius, Bishop of Antioch (Syria). Bart Ehrman's recent English translation of the Ignatian correspondence appears in the Loeb series, *Apostolic Fathers*, Vol. 1 (Cambridge, MA: Harvard University Press, 2003).

Ilan, Tal. *Integrating Women into Second Temple History.* Tübingen: Mohr, 1999.

———. *Jewish Women in Greco-Roman Palestine: An Inquiry into Image and Status.* Peabody, MA: Hendrickson, 1996.

———. "Premarital Cohabitation in Ancient Judea: The Evidence of the Babatha Archive and the Mishnah (Ketubbot 1.4)," *Harvard Theological Review* 86, no. 3 (1993): 247–64.

Jackson, Ralph. "The Role of Doctors in the City." In *Roman Working Lives*, ed. Ardle MacMahon (Oxford: Oxbow, 2005),

Jacobs, Andrew S. "A Family Affair: Marriage, Class, and Ethics in the Apocryphal Acts of the Apostles," *Journal of Early Christian Studies* 7, no. 1 (1999): 105–38.

Jensen, Anne. *God's Self-Confident Daughters: Early Christianity and the Liberation of Women.* Louisville: Westminster John Knox, 1996.

Jewett, Robert, assisted by Roy D. Kotansky. *Romans: A Commentary.* Hermeneia; Minneapolis: Fortress Press, 2007.

Johnson, Scott Fitzgerald. *The* Life and Miracles *of Thekla: A Literary Study.* Cambridge, MA: Harvard University Press, 2006.

Johnson, Terry, and Christopher Dandeker. "Patronage: Relation and System." In *Patronage in Ancient Society*, edited by Andrew Wallace-Hadrill, 219–42. London: Routledge, 1989.

Jones, A. H. M. *The Roman Economy: Studies in Ancient Economic and Administrative History.* Oxford: Blackwell, 1974.

Jongman, Willem, and Marc Kleijwegt, eds. *After the Past.* Mnemosyne 233; Leiden: Brill, 2002.

———. "H. W. Pleket, Epigraphist and Comparative Historian." In *After the Past*, edited by Jongman and Kleijwegt, ix–xxiii.

Joshel, Sandra R. *Work, Identity and Social Status at Rome: A Study of the Occupational Inscriptions at Rome.* Norman: University of Oklahoma Press, 1992.

———, and Sheila Murnaghan, eds. *Women and Slaves in Greco-Roman Culture: Differential Equations.* New York: Routledge, 1998.

Joubert, Stephan. *Paul as Benefactor: Reciprocity, Strategy and Theological Reflection in Paul's Collection.* Tübingen: Mohr Siebeck, 2000.

Kalinowski, Angela. "The Vedii Antonini: Aspects of Patronage and Benefaction in Second-Century Ephesus," *Phoenix* 56 (2002): 109–49.

Kampen, Natalie. *Image and Status: Roman Working Women in Ostia.* Berlin: Mann, 1981.

———. "Social Status and Gender in Roman Art: The Case of the Saleswoman." In *Roman Art in Context: An Anthology*, edited by Eve D'Ambria. Englewood Cliffs, NJ: Prentice Hall, 1993.

Kant, Laurence H. "Jewish Inscriptions in Greek and Latin," *Aufstieg und Niedergang der Römischen Welt* II.20.2 (1987): 672–708.

Kearsley, Rosalinde A. "Asiarchs, Archiereis, and Archiereiai of Asia," *Greek, Roman, and Byzantine Studies* 27 (1986): 183–92.

———, ed. *Greeks and Romans in Imperial Asia: Mixed Language Inscriptions and Linguistic Evidence for Cultural Interaction Until the End of the A.D. III.* IGSK Vol. 59; Bonn: Habelt, 2001.

———. "Women in Public Life in the Roman East: Iunia Theodora, Claudia Metrodora and Phoebe, Benefactress of Paul," *Tyndale Bulletin* 50, no. 2 (1999): 189–211.

Kent, J. H. *The Inscriptions, 1926-1950. Corinth: Results,* Vol. 8, pt. 3. Princeton: American School of Classical Studies at Athens, 1966.

Kidd, Reginald. *Wealth and Beneficence in the Pastoral Epistles: A "Bourgeois" Form of Early Christianity?* SBL Dissertation Series 122; Atlanta: Scholars, 1990.

Kittel, G., and G. Friedrich, eds. *Theological Dictionary of the New Testament.* Translated by G. W. Bromiley. 10 vols. Grand Rapids, Eerdmans, 1964–76.

Kittredge, Cynthia Briggs. *Community and Authority: The Rhetoric of Obedience in the Pauline Tradition.* Harrisburg, PA: Trinity, 1998.

Marc Kleijwegt, "Freed Slaves." In *The Faces of Freedom: The Manumission and Emancipation of Slaves in Old World and New World Slavery,* ed. Marc Kleijwegt (Leiden: Brill, 2006),

Kloppenborg, John S., and Stephen G. Wilson, eds. *Voluntary Associations in the Graeco-Roman World.* London: Routledge 1996.

Korpela, Jukka. "Aromatarii, Pharmacopolae, Thurarii et Ceteri." In *Ancient Medicine in Its Socio-cultural Context,* edited by Ph. J. van der Eijk, H. F. J. Horstmanshoff, and P. H. Schrijvers. Amsterdam: Rodopi, 1995.

Kraemer, Ross S., ed. *Her Share of the Blessings: Women's Religions Among Pagans, Jews, and Christians in the Greco-Roman World.* New York: Oxford University Press, 1992a.

———. *Maenads, Martyrs, Matrons, Monastics: A Sourcebook on Women's Religions in the Greco-Roman World.* Philadelphia: Fortress Press, 1988.

———, and Mary Rose D'Angelo. *Women and Christian Origins.* New York: Oxford University Press, 1999.

Kummel, Werner Georg. *The New Testament: The History of the Investigation of Its Problems.* New York: Abingdon, 1972.

Lampe, Peter. *From Paul to Valentinus: Christians at Rome in the First Two Centuries.* Minneapolis: Fortress Press, 2003.

Lefkowitz, M. R., and M. B. Fant. *Women's Lives in Greece and Rome.* Baltimore: Johns Hopkins University Press, 1992.

Levine, Lee I. *The Ancient Synagogue: The First Thousand Years.* 2nd ed. New Haven: Yale University Press, 2006.

Ligt, Luuk de. "Restraining the Rich, Protecting the Poor: Symbolic Aspects of Roman Legislation." In *After the Past,* ed. Jongman and Kleijwegt, 1–45.

Lipsius, Richard Adelbert, ed. *Apocryphal Acts of the Apostles.* Lipsiae: Apud Hermannum Mendelssohn, 1891–1903.

Longenecker, Bruce. *Remember the Poor: Paul, Poverty, and the Greco-Roman World.* Grand Rapids: Eerdmans, 2010.

Lovén, Lena Larsson. "LANAM FECIT—Woolworking and Female Virtue." In *Aspects of Women in Anitquity*, edited by Lovén and Agneta Strömberg. Jonsered, Sweden: Paul Åströms, 1998.

MacDonald, Margaret Y. *Early Christian Women and Pagan Opinion: The Power of the Hysterical Woman.* Cambridge: Cambridge University Press, 1996.

———. "Rereading Paul: Early Interpreters of Paul on Women and Gender." In *Women & Christian Origins*, edited by Ross Kraemer and Mary Rose D'Angelo, 236–53. New York: Oxford University Press, 1999.

MacMullen, Ramsey, "Women in Public in the Roman Empire," *Historia* 29 (1980): 208–18.

———. *Roman Social Relations: 50 B.C. to A.D. 284.* New Haven: Yale University Press, 1974.

Madden, John. "Slavery in the Roman Empire: Numbers and Origins," *Classics Ireland* 3 (1996). http://www.ucd.ie/~classics/ClassicsIreland.html.

Magie, David. *Roman Rule in Asia Minor to the End of the Third Century After Christ.* 2 vols. Salem, NH: Ayer, 1988 (reprint of Princeton: Princeton University Press, 1950).

Maier, Harry O. "Heresy, Households, and the Disciplining of Diversity." In *A People's History of Christianity.* Vol. 2, *Late Ancient Christianity*, edited by Virginia Burrus, 213–33. Minneapolis: Fortress Press, 2005.

———. *The Social Setting of the Ministry as Reflected in the Writings of Hermas, Clement and Ignatius.* Waterloo, ON: Wilfrid Laurier University Press, 2002.

Manning, J. G., and Ian Morris. *The Ancient Economy: Evidence and Models.* Stanford: Stanford University Press, 2005.

Mantas, Konstantinos. "Women and Athletics in the Roman East," *Nikephoros* 8 (1995): 125–44.

Marchado, Daisy L. "Response to 'Solidarity and the Accountability of Academic Feminists and Church Activists to Typical (World Majority) Women,'" *Journal of Feminist Studies in Religion* 20, no. 2 (2004): 152.

Marchal, Joseph. *The Politics of Heaven: Women, Gender, and Empire in the Study of Paul.* Minneapolis: Fortress Press, 2008.

Marinovic, L. P. "Die Sklaverei in der Provinz Achaia." In *Die Sklaverei in den östlichen Provinzen des Römischen Reiches im 1.-3. Jahrhundert.* Übersetzung von Jaroslav Kriz unter Mitwirkung von Günter Prinzing und Elisabeth Herrmann-Otto. Übersetzungen ausländischer Arbeiten zur antiken Sklaverei 5:7–76. Stuttgart: Franz Steiner, 1992.

Martin, Clarice J. "Womanist Interpretations of the New Testament: The Quest for Holistic and Inclusive Translation and Interpretation," *Journal of Feminist Studies in Religion* 6 (1990): 41–61.

Martin, Dale B. "The Construction of the Ancient Family: Methodological Considerations," *Journal of Roman Studies* 86 (1996): 40–60.

———. "Slave Families and Slaves in Families." In *Early Christian Families in Context: An Interdisciplinary Dialogue*, edited by David L. Balch and Carolyn Osiek, 207–30. Grand Rapids: Eerdmans, 2003.

———. "Slavery and the Ancient Jewish Family." In *The Jewish Family in Antiquity*, edited by Shaye Cohen, 113–29. Atlanta: Scholars, 1993.

———. *Slavery as Salvation: The Metaphor of Slavery in Pauline Christianity*. New Haven: Yale University Press, 1990.

Masson, Olivier. *Onomastica Graeca Selecta*, 2 vols. Paris: Université de Paris, 1990.

Matthews, Shelly. *First Converts: Rich Pagan Women and the Rhetoric of Mission in Early Judaism and Christianity*. Stanford: Stanford University Press, 2001.

———. "Thinking of Thecla: Issues in Feminist Historiography," *JFSR* 17, no. 2 (2001): 39–55.

McGinn, Sheila. "The Acts of Thecla." In *Searching the Scriptures*, vol. 2, *A Feminist Commentary*, edited by Elisabeth Schüssler Fiorenza, 800–828. New York: Crossroad, 1994.

McLean, B. H. *An Introduction to Greek Epigraphy of the Hellenistic and Roman Periods from Alexander the Great Down to the Reign of Constantine (323 B.C.-A.D. 337)*. Ann Arbor: University of Michigan Press, 2002.

Meeks, Wayne A. *The First Urban Christians: The Social World of the Apostle Paul*. New Haven: Yale University Press, 1983.

Meggitt, Justin J. *Paul, Poverty and Survival*. Edinburgh: T. & T. Clark, 1998.

Merkelbach, Reinhold, and Josef Stauber, eds. *Steinepigramme aus dem griechischen Östen*. Stuttgart: B. G. Teubner, 1998–2002.

Methuen, Charlotte. "The 'Virgin Widow': A Problematic Social Role for the Early Church?" *Harvard Theological Review* 90, no. 3 (1997): 285–98.

Meyer, Elizabeth A. "Explaining the Epigraphic Habit in the Roman Empire: The Evidence of Epitaphs," *Journal of Roman Studies* 80 (1990): 74–96

Meyer-Schlichtmann, Carsten. *Die Pergamenische Sigillata aus der Stadtgrabung von Pergamon*. New York: De Gruyter, 1988.

Mies, Maria. *Patriarchy and Accumulation on a World Scale: Women in the International Division of Labour* (London: Zed Books, 1986).

———. "Colonization and Housewifization." In *Materialist Feminism: A Reader in Class, Difference, and Women's Lives*, edited by Rosemary Hennessy and Chrys Ingraham, 175–85. New York: Routledge, 1997.

Migeotte, Léopold. *Les Souscriptions Publiques dans les Cités Grecques*. Hautes Études du Monde Gréco-Romain 17. St. Jean Chrysostome, Québec: Les Éditions du Sphinx, 1992.

Milgram, B. Lynne. "Women, Modernity, and the Global Economy: Negotiating Gender and Economic Difference in Ifuago, Upland Philipines." In *Gender at Work in Economic Life*, edited by Gracia Clark. Walnut Creek, CA: AltaMira, 2003.

Millar, Fergus. "Epigraphy." In *Sources for Ancient History*, edited by Michael Crawford. Cambridge: Cambridge University Press, 1983.

Misset-van de Weg, M. "A Wealthy Woman Named Tryphaena: Patroness of Thecla of Iconium." In *The Apocryphal Acts of Paul and Thecla*, edited by Jan N. Bremmer. Kampen: Kok Pharos, 1996.

Mitchell, Margaret M. "New Testament Envoys," *Journal of Biblical Literature* 111, no. 4 (1992): 641–62.

Mitchell, Stephen. *Anatolia: Land, Men, and Gods in Asia Minor*. Oxford: Clarendon, 1993.

Mitchell, Stephen, and Constantina Katsari, "Introduction: The Economy of Asia Minor." In *Patterns in the Economy of Asia Minor*, edited by Mitchell and Ktasari, xiii–xxxii. Swansea: Classical Press of Wales, 2005.

Morley, Neville. "Marx and the Failure of Antiquity," *Helios* 26, no. 2 (Fall 1999): 151–64.

———. "Narrative Economy." In *Ancient Economies, Modern Methodologies: Archaeology, Comparative History, Models and Institutions*, edited by Peter F. Bang, Mamoru Ikeguchi, and Hartmut G. Ziche. Bari, Italy: Edipuglia, 2006.

Moxnes, Halvor. *The Economy of the Kingdom: Social Conflict and Economic Relations in Luke's Gospel*. Philadelphia: Fortress Press, 1988.

———. "Patron-Client Relations and the New Community in Luke-Acts." In *The Social World of Luke-Acts*, edited by Jerome H. Neyrey, 241–68. Peabody, MA: Hendrickson, 1991.

———. *Constructing Early Christian Families: Family as Social Reality and Metaphor*. London: Routledge, 1997.

Nijf, Onno van. *The Civic World of Professional Associations in the Roman East*. Amsterdam: Gieben, 1997.

———. "Local Heroes, Festivals and Elite Self-Fashioning in the Roman East." In *Being Greek Under Rome: Cultural Identity, the Second Sophistic and the Development of Empire*, edited by Simon Goldhill, 306–34. Cambridge: Cambridge University Press, 2001.

———. "*Collegia* and Civic Guards: Two Chapters in the History of Sociability." In *After the Past*, edited by Willem Jongman and Marc Kleijwegt, 305–39. Leiden: Brill, 2002.

Nilsson, Martin P. *Timbres Amphoriques de Lindos*, Exploration Archéologique de Rhodes 5. Copenhagen: Imprimerie Bianco Luno, 1909.

Økland, Jorunn. "'In publicum procurrendi': Women in the Public Space of Roman Greece." In *Aspects of Women in Antiquity: Proceedings of the First Nordic Symposium on Women's Lives in Antiquity*. Edited by Lena Larsson Lovén and Agneta Strömberg. Jonsered, Sweden: P. Åströms, 1998.

Osiek, Carolyn. "Ransom of Captives: Evolution of a Tradition," *Harvard Theological Review* 74, no. 4 (October 1981): 365–86.

———. *Families in the New Testament World: Households and House Churches.* Louisville: Westminster John Knox, 1997.

———. "Women in House Churches," In *Common Life in the Early Church*. Edited by Julian V. Hills, 300–315. Harrisburg, PA: Trinity, 1998.

———. "Diakonos and Prostatis: Women's Patronage in Early Christianity," *Hervormde Teologiese Studies* 61, no. 1–2 (2005): 347–70.

Osiek, Carolyn, and Margaret MacDonald with Janet Tulloch. *A Woman's Place: House Churches in Earliest Christianity*. Minneapolis: Fortress Press, 2006.

Pandermalis, D. "Dion 2000," Το αρχαιολογικο εργο στη Μακεδονια και Θρακη 14 (2000): 377–82.

Paterson, Jeremy. "Trade and Traders in the Roman World: Scale, Structure, and Organisation." In *Trade, Traders and the Ancient City*, edited by Helen Parkins and Christopher Smith, 149–67. London: Routledge, 1998.

Patterson, Cynthia B. "'Hai Attikai': The Other Athenians." In *Rescuing Creusa: New Methodological Approaches to Women in Antiquity*, edited by Marilyn B. Skinner, 49–67. Lubbock: Texas Tech University Press, 1987.

Perkins, Judith. "The Social World of the Acts of Peter." In *The Search for the Ancient Novel*, edited by James Tatum, 296–307. Baltimore: Johns Hopkins University Press, 1994.

Peskowitz, Miriam. "'Family/ies' in Antiquity: Evidence from Tannaitic Literature and Roman Galilean Architecture." In *The Jewish Family in Antiquity*, edited by Shaye J. D. Cohen, 9–36. Atlanta: Scholars, 1993.

Petzl, G. *Die Beichtinschriften Westkleinasiens.* Epigraphica Anatolica 22; Bonn: Habelt, 1994.

Pfuhl, Ernst, and Hans Möbius, *Die ostgriechischen Grabreliefs.* 2 volumes. Mainz am Rhein: Von Zabern, 1977–79.

Pleket, H. W. *Epigraphica.* Vol. 2. *Texts on the Social History of the Greek World.* Leiden: Brill, 1969.

———. "The Social Status of Physicians in the Graeco-Roman World." In *Ancient Medicine in Its Socio-cultural Context,* edited by Ph. J. van der Eijk, H. F. J. Horstmanshoff, and P. H. Schrijvers. Amsterdam: Rodopi, 1995.

———. "Urban Elites and Business in the Greek Part of the Roman Empire." In *Trade in the Ancient Economy,* edited by Peter Garnsey, Keith Hopkins, and C. R. Whittaker, 131–44. Berkeley: University of California Press, 1983.

Pölönen, Janne. "The Division of Wealth Between Men and Women in Roman Succession (ca. 50 B.C.–A.D. 250)." In *Women, Wealth and Power in the Roman Empire,* edited by Päivi Setälä et al., 147–79. Acta Instituti Romani Finlandiae Vol. 25. Rome: Institutum Romanum Finlandiae, 2002.

Pomeroy, Sarah, ed. *Plutarch's* Advice to the Bride and Groom *and* A Consolation to His Wife: *English Translations, Commentary, Interpretive Essays, and Bibliography.* New York: Oxford University Press, 1999.

Price, S. R. F. *Rituals and Power: The Roman Imperial Cult in Asia Minor.* Cambridge: Cambridge University Press, 1984.

Pui-lan, Kwok. "Mercy Amba Oduyoye and African Women's Theology." *Journal of Feminist Studies in Religion* 20, no. 1 (2004): 7–22.

Quinn, Jerome D. *The Letter to Titus.* Anchor Bible; New York: Doubleday, 1990.

Rabinowitz, Nancy Sorkin, and Amy Richlin, eds. *Feminist Theory and the Classics.* New York: Routledge, 1993.

Rajak, Tessa. "Benefactors in the Greco-Jewish Diaspora." In *Geschichte—Tradition—Reflexion.* Vol. 1, *Judentum,* edited by Peter Schafer. Tübingen: J. C. B. Mohr, 1996.

———, and David Noy. "*Archisynagogoi*: Office, Title and Social Status in the Greco-Jewish Synagogue," *Journal of Roman Studies* 83 (1993): 75–93.

Ramage, Nancy Hirschland. "A Lydian Funerary Banquet," *Anatolian Studies* 29 (1979): 91–95.

Ramsay, William Mitchell. *The Church in the Roman Empire before A.D. 170.* London: Hodder & Stoughton, 1904. Reprint, Boston: Longwood, 1978.

Rathbone, Dominic. "Poverty and Population in Roman Egypt." In *Poverty in the Roman World*, edited by Margaret Atkins and Robin Osborne. Cambridge: Cambridge University Press, 2006.

Reimer, Ivoni Richter. *Women in the Acts of the Apostles: A Feminist Liberation Perspective*. Translated by Linda M. Maloney. Minneapolis: Fortress Press, 1995.

Rogers, Guy MacLean. "The Constructions of Women at Ephesus," *Zeitschrift für Papyrologie und Epigraphik* 90 (1992): 215–23.

———. *The Sacred Identity of Ephesus: Foundation Myths of a Roman City*. London: Routledge, 1991.

Rordorf, Willy. "Tradition and Composition in the Acts of Thecla: The State of the Question." In *The Apocryphal Acts of the Apostles*, edited by Dennis Ronald MacDonald, 41–52. Semeia 38; Decatur, GA: Scholars, 1986

Rostovtzeff, Michael. *The Social and Economic History of the Roman Empire*. 2nd ed. 2 vols. Oxford: Clarendon, 1957.

Royalty, Robert M. *The Streets of Heaven: The Ideology of Wealth in the Apocalypse of John*. Macon, GA: Mercer University Press, 1998.

Schwertheim, E. "Ein postumer Ehrenbeschluss für Apollonis in Kyzikos." *Zeitschrift für Papyrologie und Epigraphik* 29 (1978): 213–28 (plates 11, 12) lines 42–47. Translated by G. H. R. Horsley in *New Documents Illustrating Early Christianity: A Review of the Greek Inscriptions and Papyri Published in 1979*. North Ryde, Australia: The Ancient History Documentary Research Centre, Macquarie University, 1987), 12.

Saller, Richard P. "Framing the Debate over the Growth in the Ancient Economy." In *The Ancient Economy: Evidence and Models*, edited by J. G Manning and Ian Morris, 223–38. Stanford: Stanford University Press, 2005.

———. "The Hierarchical Household in Roman Society: A Study of Domestic Slavery." In *Serfdom and Slavery: Studies in Legal Bondage*, edited by M. L. Bush, 112–29. London: Longman, 1996.

———. *Patriarchy, Property and Death in the Roman Family*. Cambridge: Cambridge University Press, 1994.

———. "Patronage and Friendship in Early Imperial Rome: Drawing the Distinction." In *Patronage in Ancient Society*, edited by Andrew Wallace-Hadrill, 49–62. London: Routledge, 1989.

———. *Personal Patronage under the Early Empire*. Cambridge: Cambridge University Press, 1982.

Scheidel, Walter. *Debating Roman Demography*. Leiden: Brill, 2001.

———. "Finances, Figures and Fiction," *The Classical Quarterly* 46, no. 1 (1996): 222–38.

———. "The Most Silent Women of Greece and Rome: Rural Labour and Women's Life in the Ancient World (I)," *Greece & Rome* 42, no. 2 (1995): 202–17.

———. "The Most Silent Women of Greece and Rome: Rural Labour and Women's Life in the Ancient World (II)," *Greece & Rome* 43, no. 1 (1996): 1–10.

———. "Quantifying the Sources of Slaves in the Early Roman Empire," *Journal of Roman Studies* 87 (1997): 156–69.

———. "The Comparative Economics of Slavery in the Greco-Roman World." In *Slave Systems, Ancient and Modern*, edited by E. Dal Lago and C. Katsari, 105–26. Cambridge: Cambridge University Press, 2008.

———, and Sitta von Reden, eds. *The Ancient Economy*. Edinburgh: Edinburgh University Press, 2002.

Schnabel, Eckhard J. "Divine Tyranny and Public Humiliation: A Suggestion for the Interpretation of the Lydian and Phrygian Confession Inscriptions." *NT* 45, no. 2 (2003): 160–88.

Schoedel, William R. *Ignatius of Antioch: A Commentary on the Letters of Ignatius of Antioch*. Hermeneia; Philadelphia: Fortress Press, 1985.

Schotroff, Luise. *Lydia's Impatient Sisters: A Feminist Social History of Early Christianity*. Translated by Barbara and Martin Rumscheidt. Louisville: Westminster John Knox, 1995.

Schröder, Hannelore, "The Economic Impoverishment of Mothers Is the Enrichment of Fathers." In *Women, Work and Poverty*, edited by E. Schüssler Fiorenza and Anne Carr, 10–18. Concilium; Edinburgh: T. & T. Clark, 1987.

Schultz, Celia E. *Women's Religious Activity in the Roman Republic*. Chapel Hill: University of North Carolina Press, 2006.

Schüssler Fiorenza, Elisabeth. *Bread Not Stone: The Challenge of Feminist Biblical Interpretation*. 1984. 10th anniversary edition; Boston: Beacon, 1995.

———. *But She Said: Feminist Practices of Biblical Interpretation*. Boston: Beacon, 1992.

———. *In Memory of Her: A Feminist Theological Reconstruction of Christian Origins*. New York: Crossroad, 1982.

———. *Jesus: Miriam's Child, Sophia's Prophet*. New York: Continuum, 1994.

———. *Jesus and the Politics of Interpretation*. New York: Continuum, 2000.

———. "Missionaries, Apostles, Coworkers: Romans 16 and the Reconstruction of Women in Early Christian History," *Word & World* 6, no. 4 (1986): 420–33.

———. *The Power of the Word: Scripture and the Rhetoric of Empire*. Minneapolis: Fortress Press, 2007.

———. *Rhetoric and Ethic: The Politics of Biblical Studies*. Minneapolis: Fortress Press, 1999.

———, ed., with the assistance of Ann Brock and Shelly Matthews. *Searching the Scriptures*. 2 vols. New York: Crossroad, 1994.

Schwarz, H. *Soll oder Haben? Die Finanzwirtschaft Kleinasiatischer Städte in der Römischen Kaiserzeit am Beispiel von Bithynien, Lykien und Ephesus (29 v. Chr.–284 n. Chr.)*. Bonn: Habelt, 2001.

Scobie, Alex. "Slums, Sanitation and Mortality in the Roman World," *Klio* 68 (1986): 399–433.

Setälä, Päivi. "Female Property and Power in Imperial Rome: Institutum Romanum Finlandiae." In *Aspects of Women in Antiquity: Proceedings of the First Nordic Symposium on Women's Lives in Antiquity*, edited by Lena Larsson Lovén and Agneta Strömberg. Jonsered, Sweden: P. Åströms, 1998.

———, ed. *Women, Wealth and Power in the Roman Empire*. Rome: Institutum Romanum Finlandiae, 2002.

Severy, Beth. *Augustus and the Family at the Birth of the Roman Empire*. New York: Routledge, 2003.

Sherk, Robert K., ed. and trans. *The Roman Empire: Augustus to Hadrian*. Cambridge: Cambridge University Press, 1988.

Sick, David H. "Ummidia Quadratilla: Cagey Businesswoman or Lazy Pantomime Watcher?," *Classical Antiquity* 18, no. 2 (1999): 330–48.

Sidebotham, Steven E. *Roman Economic Policy in the Erythra Thalassa, 30 B.C.–A.D. 217*. Leiden: Brill, 1986.

Sinclair, M. Thea. "Women, Work and Skill: Economic Theories and Feminist Perspectives." In *Working Women: International Perspectives on Labour and Gender Ideology*, edited by Nanneke Redclift and M. Thea Sinclair, 1–24. London: Routledge, 1991.

Skinner, Marilyn B, ed. *Rescuing Creusa: New Methodological Approaches to Women in Antiquity*. Special issue, *Helios* 13, no. 2 (1986).

Smith, R. R. R. "The Imperial Reliefs from the Sebasteion at Aphrodisias. "*Journal of Roman Studies* 77 (1987): 88–138.

———. "*Simulcra Gentium*: The *Ethne* from the Sebasteion at Aphrodisias," *Journal of Roman Studies* 78 (1988): 50–77.

Solin, Heikki. *Die griechische Personennamen in Rom: Ein Namenbuch*, CIL, Auctarium, 3 vols. Berlin: W. de Gruyter, 1982.

———. "Die sogenannten Berufsnamen antiker Ärzte." In *Ancient Medicine in Its Socio-cultural Context*, edited by Ph. J. van der Eijk, H. F. J. Horstmanshoff, and P. H. Schrijvers. Amsterdam: Rodopi, 1995.

———. *Die stadtrömischen Sklavennamen: Ein Namenbuch*. Stuttgart: Franz Steiner, 1996.

Ste. Croix, G. E. M. Ithaca, NY: Cornell University Press, 1981.

Stegemann, Ekkehard W., and Wolfgang Stegemann. *The Jesus Movement: A Social History of Its First Century*. Translated by O. C. Dean. Minneapolis: Fortress Press, 1999.

Stichele, Caroline Vander, and Todd Penner. *Contextualizing Gender in Early Christian Discourse: Thinking beyond Thecla*. London: T. & T. Clark International, 2009.

Stoops, Robert. "Patronage in the Acts of Peter," *Semeia* 38 (1986): 91–100.

Storey, Glenn R. "Archaeology and Roman Society: Integrating Textual and Archaeological Data," *Journal of Archaeological Research* 7, no. 3 (1999): 203–48.

———. "Cui Bono? An Economic Cost-Benefit Analysis of Statuses in the Roman Empire." In *Hierarchies in Action: Cui Bono?*, edited by Michael W. Diehl. Carbondale: Southern Illinois University Press, 2000.

———. "Roman Economies: A Paradigm of Their Own." In *Archaeological Perspectives on Political Economies*, edited by Gary M. Feinman and Linda M. Nicholas, 105–28. Salt Lake City: University of Utah Press, 2004.

Sugirtharajah, R. S. *Postcolonial Criticism and Biblical Interpretation*. Oxford: Oxford University Press, 2002.

Tabbernee, William. *Montanist Inscriptions and Testimonia: Epigraphic Sources Illustrating the History of Montanism*. Macon, GA: Mercer University Press, 1997.

Talbert, Richard J. A., ed. *Atlas of Classical History*. London and New York: Routledge, 1985.

Taniguchi, Yuko. *To Lead Quiet and Peaceable Lives: Rhetorical Analysis of the First Letter of Timothy*. Harvard University Th.D. Dissertation, 2002.

Temin, Peter. "The Labor Market of the Early Roman Empire," *Journal of Interdisciplinary History* 34, no. 4 (2004): 513–38.

Theissen, Gerd. *The Social Setting of Pauline Christianity: Essays on Corinth*. Translated by John H. Schütz. Philadelphia: Fortress Press, 1982.

Thompson, Leonard L. *The Book of Revelation: Apocalypse and Empire*. New York: Oxford University Press, 1990.

Thonemann, Peter. "The Women of Akmoneia," *Journal of Roman Studies* 100 (2010): 163–78.

Tolbert, Mary Ann. "Social, Sociological, and Anthropological Methods." In *Searching the Scriptures*. Vol. 1, *A Feminist Introduction*, edited by Elisabeth Schüssler Fiorenza, 255–71. New York: Crossroad, 1993.

Treggiari, Susan. "Lower Class Women in the Roman Economy," *Florilegium* 1 (1979): 65–86.

Trevett, Christine. *Christian Women and the Time of the Apostolic Fathers (A.D. c 80-160): Corinth, Rome and Asia Minor*. Cardiff: University of Wales Press, 2006.

———. *Montanism: Gender, Authority and the New Prophecy*. Cambridge: Cambridge University Press, 1996.

Trümper, Monika. "Material and Social Environment of Greco-Roman Households in the East: The Case of Hellenistic Delos." In *Early Christian Families in Context*, edited by David L. Balch and Carolyn Osiek, 19–43. Grand Rapids: Eerdmans, 2003.

UNICEF. *Women and Children: The Double Dividend of Gender Equality*. The State of the World's Children 2007. New York: United Nations Children's Fund, 2006.

Verner, David. *The Household of God: The Social World of the Pastoral Epistles*. SBL Dissertation Series 71. Chico, CA: Scholars, 1983.

Veyne, Paul, and Oswyn Murray. *Bread and Circuses: Historical Sociology and Political Pluralism*. London: Penguin, 1992. Reprint and translation of *Le pain et le cirque*. Paris: Seuil, 1976.

Vidén, Gunhild. "The Twofold View of Women—Gender Construction in Early Christianity." In *Aspects of Women in Antiquity: Proceedings of the First Nordic Symposium on Women's Lives in Antiquity*, edited by Lena Larsson Lovén and Agneta Strömberg, 142–53. Jonsered, Sweden: P. Åströms, 1998.

Vuolanto, Ville. "Women and the Property of Fatherless Children in the Roman Empire." In *Women, Wealth and Power in the Roman Empire*, edited by Päivi Setälä et al., 245–302. Rome: Institutum Romanum Finlandiae, 2002.

Waelkens, Marc. *Die kleinasiatischen Türsteine: Typologische und epigraphische Untersuchungen der kleinasiatischen Grabreliefs mit Scheintür*. Mainz am Rhein: P. von Zabern, 1986.

Wallace-Hadrill, Andrew, "*Domus* and *Insulae* in Rome: Families and Housefuls." In *Early Christian Families in Context*, edited by David L. Balch and Carolyn Osiek, 3–18. Grand Rapids: Eerdmans, 2003.

———, ed. *Patronage in Ancient Society*. London: Routledge, 1989.

Waltzing, J. P. *Étude historique sur les corporations professionelles chez les Romains depuis les origines jusqu'à la chute de l'Empire d'Occident*. 4 volumes. Louvain: C. Peeters, 1895–1900. Reprint Bologna: Forni, 1968.

Wan, Sze-kar. "Collection for the Saints as Anticolonial Act: Implications of Paul's Ethnic Reconstruction." In *Paul and Politics: Ekklesia, Israel, Imperium, Interpretation*, edited by Richard A. Horsley, 191–215. Harrisburg, PA: Trinity, 2000.

Whelan, Caroline F. "Amici Pauli: The Role of Phoebe in the Early Church," *Journal for the Study of the New Testament* 49 (1993): 67–85.

Winter, Bruce W. "The Public Honoring of Christian Benefactors," *Journal for the Study of the New Testament* 34 (1988): 87–103.

———. *Roman Wives, Roman Widows: The Appearance of "New" Women and the Pauline Communities*. Grand Rapids: Eerdmans, 2003.

———. *Seek the Welfare of the City: Christians as Benefactors and Citizens: First-Century Christians in the Graeco-Roman World*. Grand Rapids: Eerdmans, 1994.

Wire, Antoinette Clark. *Corinthian Women Prophets: A Reconstruction through Paul's Rhetoric*. Minneapolis: Fortress Press, 1990.

Woodhead, A. Geoffrey. *The Study of Greek Inscriptions*. London and Norman: University of Oklahoma Press, 1992.

Woolf, Greg. "Monumental Writing and the Expansion of Roman Society in the Early Empire," *Journal of Roman Studies* 86 (1996): 22–39.

———. "Roman Urbanization of the East." In *The Early Roman Empire in the East*, edited by Susan Alcock. Oxford: Oxbow, 1997.

———. "World Systems Analysis," *JRA* 3 (1990): 44–58.

Wörrle, M. *Stadt und Fest im kaiserzeitlichen Kleinasien*. Munich: C. H. Beck, 1988.

Wycherley, R. E. *How the Greeks Built Cities*. New York: Norton, 1962.

Wright, Ruth Ohm. "Rendezvous with Thekla and Paul in Ephesus: Excavating the Evidence." In *Distant Voices Drawing Near*, edited by Holly E. Hearon. Collegeville, MN: Liturgical, 2004.

Yoon, Sojung. "Phoebe, a Minister in the Early Christian Church." In *Distant Voices Drawing Near*, edited by Holly E. Hearon, 19–31. Collegeville, MN: Liturgical, 2004.

Xenophon, *Oeconomicus*. Translated by Sarah Pomeroy. Oxford: Clarendon, 1994.

Zanker, Paul. "Bürgerliche Selbstdarstellung am Grab im römischen Kaiserreich." In *Die Römische Stadt im 2. Jahrhundert nach Christ: Der Funktionswandel des öffentlichen Raumes*, edited by Hans-Joachim Schalles, Henner von Hesberg, and Paul Zanker. Köln: Rheinland, 1992.

———. "The Hellenistic Grave Stelai from Smyrna: Identity and Self-image in the Polis." In *Images and Ideologies: Self-definition in the Hellenistic World*, edited by Anthony Bulloch et al., 212–30. Berkeley: University of California Press, 1993.

———. "In Search of the Roman Viewer." In *The Interpretation of Architectural Sculpture in Greece and Rome*, edited by Diana Buitron-Oliver. Washington, DC: National Gallery of Art; Hanover, NH: University Press of New England, 1997.

———. *The Power of Images in the Age of Augustus*. Translated by Alan Shapiro. Ann Arbor: University of Michigan Press, 1988.

Zgusta, Ladislav. *Kleinasiatische Personennamen*. Prague: Tschechoslowakischen Akademie der Wissenschaften, 1964.

Zuiderhoek, Arjan. "The Ambiguity of Munificence." *Historia* 56, no. 2 (2007): 196–213.

———. "The Icing on the Cake: Benefactors, Economics, and Public Building in Roman Asia Minor." In *Patterns in the Economy of Roman Asia Minor*, edited by Stephen Mitchell and Constantina Katsari. Swansea: Classical Press of Wales, 2005.

Index of Names

Index of Ancient Sources

INSCRIPTIONS AND PAPYRI

CPSIA information can be obtained at www.ICGtesting.com
Printed in the USA
LVOW05s1306150414

381724LV00006B/6/P